LEARN MAGIC

BY

HENRY HAY

Illustrations by Hans Jelinek

Second edition

DOVER PUBLICATIONS, INC., NEW YORK

Published in Canada by General Publishing Company, Ltd., 30 Lesmill Road, Don Mills, Toronto,
Ontario.
Published in the United Kingdom by Constable
and Company, Ltd.

This Dover edition, first published in 1975, is
an unabridged republication of the work originally
published by Perma Giants, Garden City Publishing Co., Inc., New York, in 1947. The author has
prepared a new Introduction and Index and has
revised material in Chapter 2 especially for the
Dover edition.

International Standard Book Number: 0-486-21238-6
Library of Congress Catalog Card Number: 74-80337

Manufactured in the United States of America
Dover Publications, Inc.
180 Varick Street
New York, N.Y. 10014

Foreword

A book on magic, if it be a good one, needs no excuse: eight out of ten people who have ever seen a magician want to know how he does it, and probably five wish they could do it themselves.

This little volume is intended for the five people who wish they could do it, with just an occasional nod to those who merely want to know how it's done. I think Mr. Jelinek's excellent drawings (perhaps the best ever printed in a magic book) make good any failures of mine to explain clearly or teach correctly.

On one point I differ with other men who have written about magic. They say either that you can do their tricks with no practice at all (which is never quite true of any trick good enough for you to show), or that you must practice incessantly to be a magician (as if this were a chore and something against magic).

All conjuring worth the name needs some kind of practice; in these pages you will find practice broken down into its elements, with a warning against too much as well as too little.

But remember that practicing magic is great fun in itself: to the beginning wizard, there is literally never a dull moment.

I trust you will find that statement almost as true of *Learn Magic* as of the art it teaches.

HENRY HAY

Introduction to the Dover Edition

A curtain call for a book almost a generation old naturally flatters the author. It may also lead the children and grandchildren of the original audience to wonder: Does he still stick to his story, or has he learned something since 1947?

Happily the answer can be a double yes. I don't think anyone who tries to follow the injunction of my title will find the art today transformed beyond recognition. As I once remarked elsewhere, the surprising thing, really, is that in the electronic age conjuring should have changed so little. The decline of the waistcoat has affected magic more than the invention of communications satellites.

I have, however, learned some things that make better sense of the whole subject—not new tricks, but new insights into all tricks. The following points abstract and sum up this additional information, which I hope will enable you to begin with a good understanding of the quintessence of each trick, something you might otherwise gain only by long experience. (In this connection I would like to recommend a particularly valuable recent book entitled *Magic and Showmanship* by Henning Nelms [Dover original, 1969] which concentrates much of the stagecraft that I had to accumulate by trial and error over a forty-year period; more about this interesting volume in a moment.)

Point No. 1: What *is* conjuring?
I call it *the game of entertaining by tempting a particular*

audience to accept, temporarily, infractions of natural law.

If you ask people to accept permanently—to believe—you are a charlatan, an Uri Geller, a D. D. Home, not a prestidigitator.

"Primitive," "real" magic and occultism (especially fortune-telling) try to soften the impartiality of natural law—to make it rain today, not next week; to see the future in detail. The object is not entertainment but results.

POINT NO. 2: How, in general, do we go about tempting our audience?

Conjuring, like most human endeavor, is built on interest —but more precisely on a *manipulation of interest.*

And here is the key to the whole affair: *interest is not identical with attention.* INTEREST can be defined as a *sense of being involved in some process, actual or potential;* whereas ATTENTION is a *simple response to a stimulus*—either a loud bang or (far more powerful) a feeling of interest. A potential process creates curiosity (will it or won't it?); and curiosity is the mainspring of conjuring and all other drama.

A practical corollary to this definition of interest is that processes too big, too small, too fast, too slow, or too confused to be taken in are not interesting, because they do not provide an apparent process in which you can feel involved. On this, see also point 6, below.

Next key thought, one apparently new to almost everybody: *Interest is selective, and therefore demands an expenditure of energy by the interested party.* You as a performer can never command it; you can only invite it.

You may grab a moment's attention with a sudden noise or a bright light, but it can be sustained only by interest on the spectator's part. Enforced attention without interest is a fine definition of boredom. Just try memorizing a string of random figures; you can hardly do it at all without some mnemonic device—a superimposed process.

What you as a magician *can* do is to encourage interest: offer the onlooker a process to involve himself in. That is, you can demand his attention, and if you don't let him down he may well respond with interest.

Also, cheer up: merely because interest involves an effort on his part, you needn't fear your spectator will automatically shun it. He will probably volunteer the work so long as you lead him instead of trying to drive him. Nobody is lazy about anything he's truly interested in. In fact, unless he keeps giving off his energy somehow, he'll go crazy. Shut a man up in a bare cell and he'll hunt for patterns in the plaster.

To sum up, every normal person projects interest in something every waking moment, and many sleeping moments (you can dream, can't you?). Luck and good management will help you win him for what you're interested in—your performance.

Just remember, it's always *his* choice.

POINT No. 3: *Perception,* like interest, *originates with the perceiver, not with the object perceived.* No two people see or hear a given event or even a given object exactly the same.

You couldn't do magic at all if this were not so: people would take in everything with complete objectivity, attaching the appropriate meaning to every gesture, and nothing would seem surprising—or even very interesting, since there would be little uncertainty, few potential processes.

In other words, *the magic show takes place in the spectator's head.* Any single performance has as many versions as it has viewers.

Nevertheless you can exert a certain degree of control: you can determine what the audience shall *not* pay attention to, what shall *not* be interesting (a process known in conjuring as misdirection), thereby restricting the ways in which each onlooker shapes his own private performance.

What you must realize is that your game is fishing, not shooting. You can't propel, you must try to lure. Even the effective "fly" is in the trout's appetite, not on the hook.

You can encourage the audience to perform their own magic, with coaching from you.

POINT No. 4: *The audience's performance is not complete until it has become a memory.* And here we're back at interest: *Memory is an internally edited record of interest (not of attention, much less of "events").*

Memory creates surprise at magic, because the outcome seems to contradict what the spectator remembers has gone before.

Memory also helps (not to say makes) the conjurer by selecting only what's interesting, and then magnifying that choice. Just as people sketching from memory tend to make the colors brighter and the design bolder than in the original, so in describing a magic trick people transform it for the better. If you catch half a dozen small oranges from empty air, your spectators are likely to remember quite honestly that you caught half a bushel of grapefruit, and piled them on the stage.

Their memory, of course, is not the same as yours. You have a different recollection of what went before, but you must try to forget this.

Cagliostro and other medicine men have set us an example here: to be really convincing, a wizard must at least half believe his own story.

At last I come back to Henning Nelms and his marvelous *Magic and Showmanship,* mentioned above. He provides:

POINT No. 5: How to be surprised at your own wonders. He calls it the *"silent script."*

"Every performer needs lines to think whenever he is silent." (I may add that this applies quite as much to acting, dancing, and pantomime as to magic.) "The technique consists of writing out on paper enough lines to fill all the gaps in your speech. Then recite these lines mentally while you perform. Do not attempt to memorize them exactly, just get the basic ideas in mind. . . . Note that although both the spoken and silent scripts fit your assumed character, the silent lines do not fit your real situation at all. . . . On points like these . . . you must forget the facts as they are and think as you would if the facts were what you pretend them to be."

POINT No. 6 (again emphasized by Nelms): *Your trick, your suggested process, must hang together; it must be self-consistent.* In Nelms' surprising but irrefutable words, "Audiences hate surprises."

Now obviously your whole art consists of promising to provide surprises; each trick concludes with one. But it isn't really a surprise, it's just an impossibility—one you have carefully led up to. Nelms gives the example of finding a chosen card by "mind-reading." From the very start you sketch a process of thought-transference. It's surprising that you have such powers, but once under way it would be almost more surprising if you proved not to.

Next, says Nelms, you might paint the lily by turning the back of the chosen card from red to blue. This is a bad surprise: it destroys the whole mind-reading illusion for the sake of an insignificant card trick.

You can very well do an act consisting wholly of incongruities—every enterprise miscarrying, surprising you more than the audience. In that case your suggested process consists of your own incompetence or uncertain control; the audience wouldn't sit still for earnest mind-reading.

In either case they *know* that what you are doing is not real. But they must *feel* it is real, just as if they were reading a novel whose author insists that all the persons depicted in it are purely imaginary.

The same person can enjoy P. G. Wodehouse and *War and Peace* successively; he can hardly enjoy them scrambled.

So much for the theory of magic I've formulated since the original edition of the work was published. Of course the past fifteen or so years have brought us some losses as well as gains.

The performers I held up as examples—Al Baker, Blackstone, John Mulholland—are gone from us, though present in spirit to those of us who knew them.

The opportunities for making a full-time living from magic have shrunk, which means more and more fine magicians are amateurs whom you can see only by chance, or by attending conjurers' conventions.

Many of the classic books on the art have passed from print, some without finding worthy successors. (I should mention here that the "Where to Learn More" sections at the start of each lesson remain unchanged from the first edition, and that some titles listed there are now to be found only in out-of-print bookshops.)

I trust you of the new generation will have as much fun as I did learning magic.

HENRY HAY

Düsseldorf
May, 1974

Contents

PART III

Part 1

CHAPTER 1. How to Watch a Magician

I'm going to show you how to watch a magician.

Oh. You mean how to find out his secrets?

No, not that at all. In a way, the different secrets all melt into one big secret, and I shall try to give you an idea of that in the next chapter.

To find out a magician's secrets, I might tell you never to take your eyes off his right hand. That wouldn't do you any good, though, because a professional magician can force your eyes away from his right hand whenever he likes.

Besides, if you only watched his right hand you couldn't enjoy the show.

I'm going to tell you how to watch a magician so as to get the most fun out of it. A good magic show is one of the most enchanting things in the world (no pun intended) ; whether you enjoy it because you are mystified, or because you take delight in seeing a familiar trick done perfectly, is not important.

When you are through with this book you will know how most of the common tricks work. You will also know, I hope, that how a trick works is a mere detail in the magician's whole process of acting it out.

Robert-Houdin, the most famous of all French magicians, once said (or some writer said for him) : "A conjurer is an actor playing the part of a magician." You can take this in several ways, because there are several kinds of magician; but any good performer gets close to that definition somehow.

The Greatest Magician?

Perhaps you are surprised to hear that there are several kinds of magician; when you too have become a wizard people will always be asking you, "Who's the world's greatest magician?" Why they never seem to think it may be you, I can't say. Anyway, there is no answer.

A hundred years ago there might have been an answer, even if not a convincing one; most magicians tried to give a varied performance, including samples of all the different styles then known. Since their shows lasted two hours or more, they had plenty of time.

Nowadays there are only a handful of magicians left who put on a long show; the rest pack into twenty minutes fully as much real entertainment as the old boys did into their two hours.

Take the magician whom I would rather watch than any other: Cardini. Not the greatest magician in the world, you understand. Probably the greatest card and cigarette manipulator, yes. But if you demanded that he saw his pretty wife in two, he might find trouble getting the halves together again; if you buckled him into a strait jacket, he might have to rely on a stagehand to undo him after the performance.

Put him in his top hat and tails on a bare night-club dance floor, though, and you will learn a new meaning to the word *magic* that you never dreamed of.

It is evident that he has stopped too long at the bar on his way in; his hands don't obey him quite as they should. Faster than he can throw away cigarettes, great fans of playing cards, or ivory billiard balls, new ones keep appearing.

Furthermore, Cardini is none too sure how well he likes having an audience out there. He is polite about it, but seems as if he might be happier wrestling with the cards by himself. Every so often something goes right, however, and then he is so pleased with himself that every man is his friend.

In short, Cardini is an actor playing with unbelievable perfection the part of a tipsy man about town, whose hands won't behave—not with a pack of cards, anyway.

You can see that there is plenty of comedy about Cardini; in fact, the closer you watch, the funnier he becomes. He depends for his laughs partly on surprise—his own and yours—and partly on pantomime. I doubt if two people in five realize that he never speaks a word while he is on stage.

It happens that his tricks are pure sleight-of-hand, and very difficult to do, although he could be just as mystifying with no sleight-of-hand at all. You would have to practise almost incessantly for a couple of years before you could even imitate the tricks. Cardini's show is odd that way: after you know how the tricks are done, it surprises you more than when you were just puzzled.

In a sense he has no secrets. I could tell you how he does each trick in the act; but it would take me longer to explain than it does for him to do it. More important, although I have seen his show probably twenty times and know just what to look for, I have never yet *seen* him do anything that he chose to keep hidden. I know where the cigarettes come from, I could tell you when they are about to appear, and that's all.

Besides, unless you are a magician, you ought not to care greatly how Cardini's tricks *work*. You might as well poke around in the jewels of your watch. The hands are what you care about, not the wheels; and with Cardini it is the little drama, not the palming.

If you are going to watch him as one magician watches another, you will have the added pleasure of seeing something very difficult done easily and perfectly. In return for this pleasure you give up the simple puzzlement of the onlooker who is not a magician.

That is something to be very careful of in becoming a magician: people say, and usually also believe, that magic fascinates them simply because they can't guess how it's done; your tricks are like the wire-link puzzle that they sit up all night trying to unhook.

But don't you be fooled. I know several very ingenious men who call themselves magicians, and spend all their time devising tricks that other magicians can't explain. (It is a breach of magical etiquette ever to ask a fellow magician how he does a trick. You should admit he has fooled you, and then let him tell you if he likes.) But none of these men has any public reputation as a magician. They have no gift for acting; they can't play the part. A trick in their hands is just a trick; there is no magic about it.

Let me tell you about another magician whom you should see if you ever get the chance, who stands at the other end of the scale from Cardini. Harry Blackstone is probably the liveliest stage illusionist of our time in this country.

The Different Kinds of Magic

Before I talk any more about "illusionists" and "manipulators," I had better explain how magicians refer to the different kinds of magic shows.

A manipulator in ordinary life is most likely to be someone who tries to drive the stock market up and down. A magician who calls himself a manipulator means that he does tricks, largely by pure skill, with small objects that he can hold in his hand, such as cards and cigarettes. The small size of the things he uses means that he probably won't appear on a big stage; he is more likely to be in a night club or at a private party. In the days of vaudeville, card and coin manipulators were so common that people got tired of them. Besides, most of them gave quite tiresome shows, because—unlike Cardini—they were not actors.

If you look up "illusion" in the dictionary, you find simply, "deception, delusion." When a magician says "illusion," or more particularly "stage illusion," he means a big trick that can be seen from the back row of a big theater; he may even limit the word to tricks that do things with people or large animals—sawing a woman in two, or Houdini's vanishing elephant.

An illusionist has to perform on a big stage; he needs space, and he may need trap doors and other things that you don't find in the living room. Howard Thurston used to travel with two freight-car loads of apparatus.

Harry Blackstone has not quite so much, probably. Most of his best tricks are what you might call small big illusions. In fact, he *could* do a good deal of his show in the living room. His hobby is card manipulation; you hardly ever see him at his hotel without a pack of cards in his hand. But his real business is a big stage show, and everyone in the theater loves it.

Perhaps the ordinary layman in the audience will be most impressed by his vanishing bird cage. Magicians are more likely to remember the dancing handkerchief. This is a perfect example of a great conjurer at work. The trick itself is not particularly novel or mysterious; in fact, it has been explained in nearly every magic book for at least two hundred and fifty years. It isn't even a complicated or ingenious looking affair. Blackstone ties a knot in a handkerchief—whereupon the handkerchief starts wandering around, paying very little attention to Blackstone. That's all. But Blackstone the actor makes you see that roving handkerchief by turns as a snake, a puppy, and a ghost. I have sometimes wondered whether the trick wouldn't be just as fascinating even if the handkerchief didn't move at all.

Possibly there has been some awful night in Blackstone's career when the handkerchief refused to move. Things go wrong at every performance of every magician who ever lived. One of the pleasures of being a magician watching another magician is that you can admire the way he pulls out of scrapes.

The best way is usually by sheer gall. Nate Leipzig, the great card manipulator, was once causing cards to float up from the pack to his right hand, two feet above. The trick is done with a black thread, and after the second card the thread broke. Leipzig had no way of making the third card really rise. So he swooped gracefully down upon the pack, nipped the card with his right hand, and simply carried it aloft—to great applause.

If you are a real actor, and give people magic, not just tricks, their imagination will help you out. Blackstone on the stage is a wizard, a wonder-worker. After the glass of milk has floated, and the bird cage has disappeared for the second time, you give up and take what he gives you. He used to surprise people very much by producing a live goat from under a shawl. If you can become as fine an actor as he, you may get away with his method of doing the trick, which consisted of picking up the goat under his arm and rushing on stage waving the shawl in front of him. When he stopped waving, the goat appeared.

Secrets don't amount to very much in good magic.

Manipulation and stage illusions are two important kinds of magic, but not the only ones, by a long shot. Comedy magic is another branch—one that ought to be much better than it usually is. Of course there is a lot of comedy in a show like Cardini's, or in one like Blackstone's; but with them the comedy is not the main thing. Their personalities are not chiefly comic.

Al Baker is a real comedy magician. Everything he does combines to give you a laugh. Most "comedy" magicians depend on jokes for their laughs; there is no good reason why they should do tricks at all. Another variety, imitating the late Frank Van Hoven, have all their efforts come to grief—nothing ever works. Al Baker builds up each trick into a funny situation, which can be saved only by magic. His side remarks along the way are funny, too (though I have learned by trying to repeat them that they are funnier in the setting of the trick), but each trick is a little comedy in itself, even if Baker did not speak a word.

Al's best trick for my money is the cake baked in a hat—one more proof that the secret doesn't matter. If my great grandfather ever saw a magician, he probably saw a cake baked in a hat; and if I live to have great grandchildren, I shan't forget the farce that Al Baker makes out of the trick.

He borrows a hat; in looking for his cake recipe he makes a false start with one that turns out to be for home brew; as he breaks raw eggs into some perfect stranger's hat, he tosses away the shells, remarking, "Just throw them in the sink—you know, the place where you scrape the toast." He hunts for a red-headed girl over whose hair he can warm his felt saucepan; finally, when the gooey mess in the victim's fedora proves instead to be a fluffy sponge cake, he passes out pieces as magicians always do, but first he helps himself with relish, like you or me.

In private, Al Baker is among the most ingenious living inventors of puzzling tricks. As I hinted before, great magicians often make a hobby of magic; they make a profession of acting. Orson Welles has tried to do it the other way around—an actor making a profession of magic. But he has made a fortune out of acting, and he has to do his magic for charity, which I think proves my point.

The three magicians I have mentioned all give shows that need a certain amount of elbow room. There is another kind of magic that may be even more fun for you or me—tricks done in the midst of a few friends, say at lunch or in a corner at a party. For want of a better name, I shall simply call this type intimate magic.

The late Nate Leipzig was a master at intimate magic. John Mulholland, one of the great living authorities on every aspect of magic, has a trick with two half dollars, a trick in which he asks someone—preferably a good-looking girl—to sit on his knees and hold his wrists. Although nothing can then go up his sleeves (and nothing does) the half dollars, not more than two feet from the amateur assistant's face, turn into quarters and back, just as the whim takes them. There is no equipment, no nothing; the coins just keep sliding one over the other, and one moment they're half dollars, the next they're quarters; again, one may be a half and the other a quarter.

This is where the ingenious and thoroughly puzzling trick comes into its own. An intimate magician can use any acting talents he has, but all he necessarily must do is play the part of a private citizen toying with a pencil or a pack of cards.

For a person like you or me, who does magic mainly to amuse himself, intimate performances are ideal. You can choose your own audience, both as to size and as to gullibility. You can pick the moment when they are most likely to enjoy it. You can stop when they have had enough.

So long as you are particularly careful about the last point, people will always eagerly look forward to seeing you.

There are difficulties, too. With people so close, and on such a personal footing, either the tricks must be very clever or you must be very skilful to keep from being detected. You may have to do the same trick twice for the same people; this is always hard. And, performing often for the same friends, you have to add new tricks to the show occasionally, which a professional magician seldom does.

All in all, intimate magic is the kind that a person who reads this book is most likely to make a big hit with, anyway at first. The part he has to act is harder than it sounds, but is still the most natural—himself as a magician.

Then there are other, more limited, specialties, each with its particular fascination for the people who like it.

Mind-reading acts allow a man and his wife to work together on the stage.

Escapes are for muscular people who like to be sensational.

Children's shows are perhaps the most noisily popular, but not with magicians! Don't tackle children unless you always get on well with them, and even then not unless you know your act so perfectly that nothing can shake you. As a parting word on how to watch a magician, let me tell you that when you see some beaming, sweet-natured performer wowing the toddlers, you'll know he's bombproof.

CHAPTER 2.   How to Be a Magician

If you found out anything from the last chapter, you found out that secrets don't make the magician. Unfortunately for me, it's a great deal easier to teach tricks than to teach magic. At the same time, you can't teach a great deal of magic without teaching some tricks.

Let me put your mind at rest about one thing. You may wonder whether just anybody can learn magic. Doesn't it take specially long fingers or big hands or a giant brain or something?

Not at all. Big hands are sometimes a convenience, never a necessity. I know one magician who has lost his right little finger. The aptest pupil I ever had was a fourteen-year-old girl with hands so small that she had to use toy-size cards.

There is a magician who performs from a wheel chair. I know magicians who are truck drivers, shipping clerks, jewelers, florists. Lots of quite good magicians are still in high school; others are in their nineties. A few women have been professional magicians, and I never could see why there weren't more among amateurs.

So—come one, come all. If you can read simple English you can make yourself into a magician.

First, I have a few words to say so that you can get the best out of the tricks (and, I hope, the magic) that follow.

In the last chapter I mentioned the one big secret of magic. I should have added, of successful magic. When you get through with this book I want you to be a good magician. A bad magician is almost as awful as a bad soprano.

But don't be scared by my plans for you; they aren't so impractical as you think. Some of the best magicians succeed without half the work that has been wasted by other performers whom you would run a mile to avoid.

Rehearsal Before Practice

Though you can't become a high-powered conjurer without preparation and a certain amount of practice, you can make your head save your hands more than anyone would believe. Some sleight-of-hand takes hard practice—but what law says you must use sleight-of-hand?

You can make a playing card disappear with the back palm, which takes skill of hand, or with a small spring clip, which takes none. Personally, I think the back palm is more fun for you because it gives you a sense of success when you master it; but those in the audience don't know how you did it anyway. The spring clip may be more fun for them because it is quite as puzzling and not so fussy.

If you do magic for your own satisfaction—a perfectly sound reason—then enjoy using the hard way.

To entertain other people, fool them the easy way and save your energy for acting.

Just now, I shall assume you are performing to amuse others. Three-quarters of this book would be quite unnecessary if you had only yourself to please.

Every magic trick that is to please anyone but its performer must be cast in the form of a little drama.

It must have a beginning, a middle, and an end. The end must be surprising, and it may be amusing.

You remember what the stage director said about writing a

play: "In the first act you chase your hero up a tree. In the second act you throw rocks at him. In the third you get him out of the tree."

Sometimes the middle of a magic trick is so short that you can't tell it from the beginning or the end; but it's there, all the same.

How to Get Applause

This brings me to something that magicians are always forgetting. There are things about every trick that the audience must not know. But even more important, there are things the audience *must* know. If you don't tell them those things, the trick will be worse than detected: it will be tiresome.

First, they must know what you are working with—the hero of your drama. If you just flash a card at them they don't know whether your hero is "playing card" or "ace of hearts." When "ace of hearts" miraculously changes into "ace of clubs," they may be disappointed that it didn't change to "American flag."

Next, they must know you are doing something. You may or may not find it convenient to tell them what; you certainly must warn them to expect something.

It needn't be in words, either; a look or a gesture will do; only there must be some kind of signal. You can't stand holding the ace of hearts and simply gape at the ceiling. You must wave the card, or point to it, or look at it.

You must warn people that they are about to be surprised.

Finally, hardest of all, you must tell them that they *have been* surprised; that the miracle is over; they may now applaud. People want to be pleased, but *you* have to say when. You might as well not do the trick as not tell them when it's done.

If you change the ace of hearts into the ace of clubs and just stand there looking vague, people will expect you to turn it next into the ace of spades.

How can they know? They didn't plan the trick.

Which brings us a little closer to what you might call the big secret of magic.

I believe the mystic formula comes down to two elements: your personality, and careful planning. Once those two are taken care of, the rest will follow.

Your Personality and Your Patter

Personality comes first, because you can suit the planning to the kind of person you are. Unluckily, it's much harder to change yourself to suit the plan.

This difficulty would more or less take care of itself except for the well-meant help of writers on magic. They tell you how to do a trick, and then give the exact words you must say.

As a result, the drama won't fit the personality of any magical actor except the man who first wrote the part.

Magicians call their own talk "patter"; they put a lot of work on it, partly to help themselves as actors and partly for technical reasons that will appear later in the book.

In fact, they put too much work into it.

One of my prime rules is: *never* memorize another man's patter. Better, indeed, never to memorize any at all. Just because you are doing a trick is no reason to talk like a high school elocution teacher. You must be understood, but it is better to maul a few words than to crop out suddenly with a Back Bay accent in south Texas.

You should talk like yourself. If you're a poor talker, then, as a magician, probably you should still talk haltingly and let your hands speak for you. Cardini found he couldn't develop a ready flow of chatter, which is why he does his "silent act," a masterpiece of pantomime.

You must know exactly *what* you want your audience to know, and *when* you want them to know it. With that fixed in your mind, tell the story in your own words. In order to sketch out the plot of certain tricks that I'm going to teach you, I may have to give a few words of patter. I say again: don't memorize mine. Make up your own.

When you really know a trick and have done it many times, you'll find you have formed the habit of saying the same thing at the same time in the trick—your own patter. If you don't form the habit, so much the better for offhand performances.

The same thing that goes for patter goes for the choice of tricks. With all the time, all the patience, and all the money in the world you couldn't learn a fraction of the good tricks there are to be learned. And lots of the good ones aren't good for you. If you are a burly garage mechanic (some excellent magicians are), you'll look pretty foolish stepping into the front office in your dungarees to do a trick with a powder puff, a pink ribbon, and a bottle of perfume.

The lessons in this book are meant to give you a wide choice. If you have scruples against card playing, you can pass up all the card tricks and still have plenty. If you are a five-days-a-week bridge player, the card tricks alone will carry you far toward earning the distrust of your fellow contract fiends.

In any event, you will be able to go on from here. You will know how tricks are planned and something about how they are presented. A hint or two will enable you to learn a new trick easily from a book or a magician friend. That is, you will have some idea how to turn tricks into magic.

To turn tricks into magic, furthermore, you should concentrate on a small repertory. David Devant, a great English conjurer, used to boast that he knew only eight tricks. Many street vendors have just one, which they do all day, every day. I would rather have you *learn* a third of the material in this book than *try* to learn it all. Indeed, I have purposely given you too much. Try everything, but learn only what you really like.

Planning

I have kept on talking about planning; now I had better explain. You need not do the original planning yourself. In fact, the inventor of the trick generally does it for you. That is what you have to memorize—the plan, not the patter.

Your own planning can be of three different kinds.

First, you may simply learn the steps of a trick. There are a few good card tricks like that, which you can work if you merely know how.

Second, you may practise a sleight. Usually, one sleight will help you accomplish several different tricks.

Third, you may buy or make apparatus. Some apparatus (like the thumb tip and the pull) will also do for several tricks; most pieces are made for one particular feat.

Practice sounds like the most frightening part of magic. You have probably thought often enough, "Gosh, I could never be a magician! Think of all those years of practice!"

Actually, it's nothing to be afraid of. Between the tricks that work by just knowing how and the tricks where the apparatus does it, you can give quite a magic show without any hand practice at all.

Skull practice you must have, but you're willing to do that or you wouldn't be reading this book.

The next thing about hand practice is that it's fun.

No single magical sleight is as hard as learning to write. Perhaps each one is as hard as mastering two letters of the alphabet. Some are only as hard as a punctuation mark.

And when you've learned the alphabet, you can write whole sentences. When you've learned, say, ten sleights, you can show a whole line of tricks that need no apparatus, no careful secret preparation—tricks that can't be found out, because you never do them twice the same way.

To practise the piano, you have to set aside a special place and time. You can practise magic anywhere; with most magicians practice becomes a nervous habit. I have practised coin tricks (which always involves dropping the coins) in college lectures and in Quaker meeting. A little offhand practice in a day coach will always collect an audience if you get tired of looking out the window.

In fact, there is such a thing as too much practice. If you don't fully understand a trick, and try to beat it by main strength and persistence, you only make trouble for yourself.

An hour's practice the wrong way is much worse than fifteen minutes spent just reading the description and getting it clear in your mind.

This book will teach you magic step by step, and I shall begin with teaching you to practise step by step.

Learning a Trick

The first step, as I say, is to read the description.

Read it again.

Look at the pictures.

Understand what you have to accomplish. Is it to put the top half of the pack of cards underneath, or to turn the bottom half face up, or to turn the whole pack end for end? If you just have a general idea that it's one of the three, you aren't ready to start practising.

Know *exactly* what you are to do.

Perhaps the next step is the most important of all: memorize *how* to do what you have to do. Memorizing any process is at least half of learning to do it. Do you hold the coin between your first and second fingers, or between your second and third? Do you reach through the loop of the handkerchief from in front or from behind?

Stick with the book until you don't have to ask, "Now how did that go, again?"

All this is true of any trick—a mathematical puzzle, a stage illusion where you only pull the string and the assistants do the rest, a mystery out of a chemical magic set.

If you like, you can call it rehearsal instead of practice. Not only a magic trick, but anything in life that you want to have go smoothly needs rehearsal. Anyway, it's also the biggest part of practice.

The last part is just going through the motions—making your hands do over and over what they have to do. That's where the nervous habit comes in. You won't be able to pick up your check in a cafeteria without back-palming it, or put on your silk muffler without tying a few vanishing knots.

You probably can't spare an hour a day for practising magic, but once you get the habit I bet you'll find that, bit by bit, the time adds up to more than that.

While I'm talking about practice, let me dispose of an untruth that magicians rather like to hear repeated for their own protection.

If you hear someone say, "The hand is quicker than the eye," don't contradict him. It makes your job as a magician easier. But it isn't so. I don't think I know more than three tricks that happen so fast the eye can't follow. To outrun the eye you have less than a sixteenth of a second, and that's not long. Furthermore, only one of those three swift tricks is done by the hand at all.

When you practise a sleight, don't even try for speed. Try for neatness and silence. After a while, you will automatically get to make the motions quite as fast as there is any need for. Neat and quiet is the one way to do sleight-of-hand.

While you are on the second step of your practice, before you come to simple repetition, a mirror can help you a lot. It will show you whether you look unusually awkward, and it will warn you about the angles from which people can see what they shouldn't.

When a magician says, "Watch your angles," he doesn't mean you should develop more business connections. He means you are giving the audience a flash of a palmed card or a (you hoped) hidden "load."

Once the mirror has straightened you out on the more obvious difficulties, though, the only way you can really learn to show a trick is to show it.

Of course you'll be afraid they may catch you, and sometimes they will catch you. No matter; each time will teach you something new about fooling them, until at last almost every possible disaster has happened, and you know from experience how to deal with each one.

Besides, the fear of detection is just something that goes with being a magician. Houdini and Herrmann were afraid of detection every moment they were on the stage; one famous and successful magician is so keyed up that he can't go on without half a glass of spirits three times during the show. The fear of detection and the dropping of anything you practise with will go on as long as you do magic. Don't think they prove that you're stupid; they just prove that you're a magician.

When I was thirteen years old, and had only been doing magic for three years, I had the Arabian Nights dream experience of spending two days with the late Nelson Downs, the all-time king of coin manipulators. He palmed a stack of sixty half-dollars with less fuss than I made over one; he could back-palm eight without a sound. I felt very sheepish because I dropped the coins every time I tried to do what he showed me.

"Son," he said, "I've been doing magic for forty years, and I still drop the coins, so what can *you* expect?"

Enlarging Your Repertory

One of the standard questions that people ask is, "Where do you learn those tricks?"

Of course this book and my own rather larger one, *The Amateur Magician's Handbook* (T. Y. Crowell, New York), will give you a good start, but you will probably want to go further in some special branch of magic. To help you do that, there are scores of books. They run from pamphlets, with a few puzzles and parlor stunts, all the way to $65 sets describing the most advanced and difficult professional illusions. At the end of the chapter I shall give a list of some good titles, and there are many more.

The leading American magic magazines are *Genii, The Conjurer's Magazine,* edited by William Larsen, Jr. (P.O. Box 36068, Los Angeles 90036, and *The Linking Ring,* the organ of the International Brotherhood of Magicians (28 North Main St., Kenton, Ohio 43326).

The most active British publisher of books and magazines is the Supreme Magic Co. (64 High Street, Bideford, Devon). Goodliffe (Arden Forest Industrial Estate, Alcester, Warwickshire) issues a weekly called *Abracadabra.* The Magic Circle of London publishes *Magic Circular.*

American book publishers are Lou Tannen's Magic Shop (1540 Broadway, New York, New York 10036) and Abbott's Magic Mfg. Co. (Colon, Michigan 49040).

You can also learn tricks from fellow conjurers. Magicians are a clannish lot, and most of them belong to some magic club. There are many local groups and two national organizations, the above-mentioned International Brotherhood of Magicians and the Society of American Magicians (20 Sutton Place South, New York 10022).

Another thing you may not have thought about: most big towns have one or more dealers in magical supplies. Look in the classified telephone book, and write to Tannen, Abbott, or Supreme Magic. Tannen's catalog, which is worth its nominal cost, is a sort of reference book in itself, though like all dealers' catalogs it does not explain the-miracles it offers. The magic magazines are full of mail-order dealers' ads.

The whole question of magic apparatus is one you will have to settle for yourself. Personally, I like sleight-of-hand, and am too lazy to lug stuff around; so I own very little apparatus. Many people take the same kind of pleasure in collecting and using apparatus that they might in cameras. It costs nearly as much. Natural-born home mechanics will have a great deal of fun building, and perhaps inventing, their own apparatus.

The one sure thing about apparatus is that it takes just as much care and rehearsal to use properly as sleight-of-hand does. It may not need the hand practice, but you can't skip the skull practice without having a flop.

BOOK LIST

Many of the titles on this list are out of print, but they can often be found secondhand in book and magic shops.

FUNDAMENTAL

Hay, Henry, *Amateur Magician's Handbook,* third revised edition.

————, editor, *Cyclopedia of Magic.*

Hoffmann, Professor, (pen name of Angelo John Lewis), *Modern Magic; More Magic; Later Magic.* (All out of print, but the last-named in particular is still invaluable.)

Neil, C. Lang, *The Modern Conjurer and Drawing-Room Entertainer.*

Nelms, Henning, *Magic and Showmanship.* (Dover Publications, 1969.)

GENERAL

Hugard, Jean, *Modern Magic Manual.* (Now available in England only.)

Sachs, Edwin T., *Sleight-of-Hand.*

Tarbell, Dr. Harlan, *The Tarbell Course in Magic.* (6 vols.)

SPECIALTIES

Annemann, Theodore, *Practical Mental Effects.* (The great classic.)

Blackstone, Harry, *Blackstone's Modern Card Tricks and Secrets of Magic.* (2 vols. in one.)

Bobo, J. B., *Modern Coin Magic.*

Christopher, Milbourne, *Fifty Tricks with a Thumb Tip.*

————, *The Illustrated History of Magic.*

————, *Panorama of Magic.* (Illustrated history; no tricks; Dover Publications, 1962).

Erdnase, S. W., *The Expert at the Card Table.* (Another classic.)

Ganson, Lewis, *The Art of Close-Up Magic,* Vols. I and II.

Hugard, Jean, *Silken Sorcery.* (Reprinted by Dover under the title *Handkerchief Magic.*)

————, and Braue, Frederick. *Expert Card Technique.* (Reprinted by Dover.)

————. *The Royal Road to Card Magic.*

Hull, Burling, *Thirty-Three Rope Ties and Chain Releases.*

Rice, Harold, *Rice's Encyclopedia of Silk Magic.* (3 vols.)

Thurston, Howard, *Four Hundred Tricks You Can Do.*

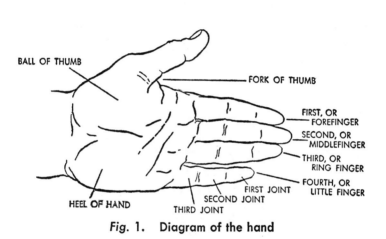

Part 2

BALL OF THUMB

FORK OF THUMB

FIRST, OR
FOREFINGER

SECOND, OR
MIDDLEFINGER

THIRD, OR
RING FINGER

FOURTH, OR
LITTLE FINGER

FIRST JOINT

SECOND JOINT

THIRD JOINT

HEEL OF HAND

Fig. 1. **Diagram of the hand**

LESSON 1. The Flying Coin

What Seems to Happen: You hold a half dollar in each hand. Suddenly they are both in your right hand.

What You Need: Two half dollars

Where to Learn More: Professor Hoffmann, *Modern Magic;* Edwin Sachs, *Sleight-of-Hand*

Most of this lesson has nothing to do with the "secret" of the trick, which is perfectly simple. Your gestures and acting can make this a surprising, rather amusing trick. But if you just rattle it off, one two three, nobody will know you have done a trick at all.

The first step is that you must give the appearance of being natural without being natural.

Now, just for practice—stand up.

Take a half dollar from your right hand into your left.

How did you do it?

More than likely, you held it between the thumb and finger of your right hand, and took it with your left hand the same way. Your elbows were held close to your sides. (*Fig. 2*).

That's the natural way. But you can't do magic like that.

Your movements have to be cruder, more obvious, you might say.

Fig. 2.   **The wrong way to pass a coin from hand to hand**

Hold your elbows away from your sides, and your hands at least six inches from your chest. You want everyone to see what you're doing—or at least most of it.

Don't turn your back on the audience (or on the mirror, if you are practising before one). Lots of magicians are so afraid the crowd will see what it shouldn't that, half unconsciously, they turn away and hide the whole trick. Don't be like that.

Hold the half dollar very near the edge between the tips of your thumb and second finger. Hold it up and forward so that people can see it.

By the way, in my book you have four fingers and a thumb, not five fingers. Your forefinger is your first finger; your middle finger is your second finger; your ring finger is your third finger; and your little finger is your fourth finger.

Now put the half dollar flat against your left palm.

Close your left fist over it. Don't clench your fingers, just flap them shut. (*Fig. 3*).

Let go with your right hand, and move your *left* hand away. Your *left* hand, *not* your *right*.

Stretch your left arm out almost full length.

Keep your eyes on your left hand, where the coin is.

That is not the natural way to take a coin from one hand into the other. But it's the magic way. If you want to make a coin disappear, you have to do it that way.

And *that* means you must always make these motions in handling a coin, whether it's going to disappear or not. If you are natural all the rest of the time, you will look conspicuous and silly when you do want to do something tricky.

Try passing the coin from one hand to the other the new way ten or a dozen times, until you can make a habit of it.

You needn't be quite so slow as you were the first time, but don't speed up much. *Everyone* must have time to see the half dollar in your right hand, and then to realize that it has gone to your left fist. I say everyone, and you must remember that any

Fig. 3.   The right way to pass a coin from hand to hand

crowd is as slow as the slowest person in it. Some people are very slow indeed.

John Mulholland's rule for showing anything—a coin, or your empty hand, or whatever—is to take three times as long as you naturally would. He says to himself (not out loud!), "Nothing in my hand—once. Nothing in my hand—twice. Nothing in my hand—three times, and now maybe Slow Joe in the back row knows that my hand is empty."

Keep your arms out and up. You mustn't look like a henpecked husband threading a needle; it makes people uncomfortable, and besides, they can't see the miracle if your hands are practically buried in your vest.

And "keep your eye on the ball." I said before, and I will say again and again: *follow the coin from one hand to the other with your eyes.* If you remember to follow with your eyes, any trick like this is practically self-working.

You know you can gather a crowd on the street by just standing and staring up. When you look hard at something, everyone else looks there too. I said in the first chapter that a good magician could force your eyes away from his right hand (or his left) whenever he liked. He does it—you do it—by keeping both eyes "on the ball."

And by moving the left hand away while the right stays still. Anything that moves catches the eye; anything that stands still becomes part of the background.

All right. Once more. Stand up straight, elbows out, arms up; half dollar out front where everyone can see it. Put it slowly in your left hand, close your fist, move your left hand away, and follow through with your eyes.

Now we're going to go through the motions of the trick with the two half dollars.

Hold one in each hand, sticking up from thumb and second finger, just the same as you have been doing. Hold them up shoulder high where everyone can see.

Now put the left one between your teeth.

Hold out your left hand, and put the right coin in your left fist, exactly as you have been practising. (*Fig.* 4).

Follow through with your eyes.

Wait. Give Slow Joe in the back time to realize that you have one half dollar in your left hand and one between your teeth.

Now take the coin from your teeth between your right thumb and forefinger. Hold your left hand out and up, and your right hand down and out to the right.

Look at your left hand. Then turn your head around and down to look at your right hand. You should almost crane your neck. Again, remember Slow Joe in the back. You must get it through *his* skull that you have a half dollar in your left hand, up high, and a half dollar in your right hand, down low.

Let's try it over again. Coin in each hand, up where everyone can see. Left coin between your teeth. Hold out your left hand.

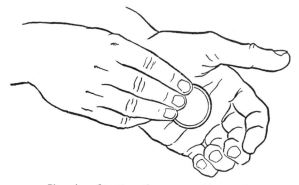

Fig. 4. **Starting the pass with a coin**

Right coin to left hand. Follow through with your eyes. Pause. Coin from teeth to right hand. Pause. Look at left hand, look at right hand.

The reason I keep making you do this over is so that you'll get the habit of following through with your eyes, and of waiting for Slow Joe in the back.

If you were to do as some magic books tell you, and act perfectly natural, you would simply show two coins put one in your teeth change one from one hand to the other take the other in your other hand and then where would you be? You have to have punctuation in a sentence, and you have to punctuate any trick, even one as simple as this, with waits for the slow people to catch up.

Now you have learned to do the whole performance gracefully and plainly—everything but the trick.

The trick comes last, and it's so simple that you'll almost be ashamed. But as long as you remember what you've learned so far, it will work without fail.

Hold the half dollar by one edge between your right thumb and second finger tips, just as you have been doing. (*Fig.* 5a).

Now try pushing the far edge of the coin against a table top. Don't clamp the coin too tight.

As you push, the coin will slide back between your thumb and finger until it hardly shows. You will now be holding it by the far edge instead of the near edge, and from the back of your hand your fingers will hide the coin. (*Fig.* 5b).

That's all there is to the trick. Try sliding the half dollar back four or five times; and then try pushing against your left palm instead of the table.

You know the motions of passing the coin from your right hand to your left—I've made you go through them often enough. This time, there's just one little difference: when you put the coin against your left palm, you slide it back between your right thumb and finger.

Don't stop. Go right on with the act. Close your left fist, move your left arm out, and follow your *left* hand with your eyes.

Never mind about the coin still slid back between your right thumb and finger. The nearer you can come to forgetting about that, the surer you may be that everyone else also has his mind on your left hand.

Make your pause. Your left fist is held out, with your eyes on it. It is closed loosely, as if there were something fair sized inside, so why should anyone think the half dollar wasn't there?

Your right hand has been quite still—nothing to catch the eye about that.

Now you can venture to curl your right fingers in and hide the coin entirely. But keep your forefinger and thumb stretched out.

That's to grab the other coin from between your teeth.

Remember how matters are supposed to stand: one half dollar in your left hand, one between your right thumb and forefinger.

When you move your right hand up to take the coin from

your teeth, it's safe to look at your right hand for a moment.
Anything that moves you can look at. If you don't dare move it,
you don't dare look at it either.

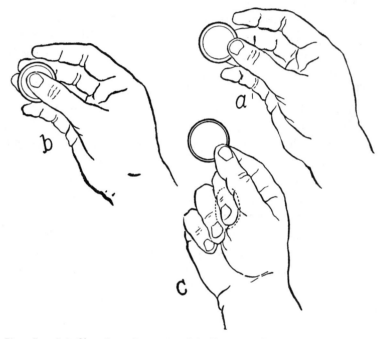

Fig. 5. (a) Showing the coin; (b) The coin hidden; (c) One coin
hidden, one showing

Back to your routine. Left hand up and out; look at it. Right
hand down and out; crane around and look at that.

Actually, of course, both half dollars are in your **right hand**,
one hidden, one showing. (*Fig.* 5c).

All ready for the big climax. Look back and forth from one
hand to the other a couple of times.

You want people to remember that there's a coin in each hand,
and **you want them** to know that you're about to spring your
trick.

(In this trick, as in many, many others, they mustn't know that the trick is about to begin until it's really all accomplished.)

Zip! Snap your left fingers and fling open your left hand.

The next moment, shake the two coins together in your right hand with a loud jingle.

Your eyes keep pace with the noise: watch the snapping fingers, then turn quick to look at the jingle.

Hold your right hand out flat with the two half dollars.

Applause!

This trick is simple enough, and the pantomime is plain enough, so that you can do it with no patter at all. Personally, I usually say something foolish about how you have to know your right hand from your left—clink! But that doesn't mean that *you* should use the same remarks. You can say anything or nothing, whatever you find holds people's attention best.

Now that you've learned how to do it, and won't be too impressed with yourself, I may as well tell you that you have mastered a coin sleight called the pass, and are in a position to make a coin disappear whenever you feel like it.

There are several ways of making the pass with a coin, some of them more difficult but none more deceptive than this. I bet you thought there was more to sleight-of-hand than that!

Come now, didn't you?

LESSON 2.   Handling a Deck of Cards

What Seems to Happen: Your handling of cards is neat but not gaudy. You find a chosen card at a chosen place in the pack, and also outguess someone from the audience.

What You Need: A pack of cards. For most simple tricks you can use any cards that come handy. Use the joker or not, as you like. Whether you use poker cards or the longer, narrower bridge cards is also a matter of choice. For most tricks that demand smooth manipulation, a thin, elastic card with a high finish and a symmetrical scroll-back design, such as the Aristocrat brand, is best. For fancy flourishes and back-palming, use a soft, unfinished card with an over-all back pattern showing no white margin, such as plaid 999 Steamboats. I think gilt edges are a thorough nuisance.

For the particular trick in this lesson you need a pack with some kind of picture on the back—one that is obviously either right or wrong side up. Magicians call a pack with that kind of pattern a one-way deck.

> *Where to Learn More:* Hoffmann, *Modern Magic;* Howard Thurston, *Four Hundred Tricks You Can Do;* Barrows Mussey, *Magic*

It is about an even chance whether this lesson is very necessary to you, or almost useless.

If you aren't accustomed to handling cards, but want to learn card tricks, you'll have to study it carefully.

If you play cards a lot, you will need only a paragraph or two to teach you all I have to say. Don't be insulted if I explain in great detail for people who can hardly tell clubs from spades. I hardly can myself.

The first point about handling cards is the same as the first point about handling almost anything in magic. Don't grab too hard.

Nothing betrays the bungler like clutching the pack in an iron grip. It makes the cards stick together, it tires your hands, and all of a sudden you're quite likely to spill the whole deck in every direction.

Dealing Position

A very common instruction for a card trick is, "Hold the pack in dealing position." This means just what it says: you hold the cards as if you were going to deal. Right-handed people deal with the right hand, and hold the pack in the left; and modern cards are made for their benefit, with the corner indexes in the upper left and lower right corners.

Fig. 6.   Dealing position

This means that even if you are left-handed you'll do better to hold the pack in your left.

The left edge of the pack is in the crotch of your thumb. Your thumb stretches part way across the back. Your fingers curl against the right-hand edge, so that as you push the top card forward to deal it, your finger tips can press, through the card, against your thumb tip. That will prevent more than one card from sliding out at a time. (*Fig. 6*).

Some people hold their left forefinger across the end of the pack instead of along the right edge with the other fingers. It seldom makes any difference which you do.

I shall be talking a lot about the top of the pack and the bottom of the pack.

The top has the backs of the cards showing. The bottom has the faces showing.

Now that you have the cards in dealing position, deal out a few rounds.

Don't hold the cards too tight.

And don't make your *right* thumb do all the work. Don't come over and strip each card off the pack with your right hand by main force.

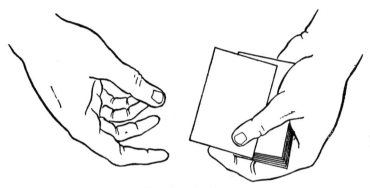

Fig. 7.   **Dealing**

As your right hand comes over, push the top card part way out with your *left* thumb. (*Fig. 7*).

Just to develop an easy motion, try dealing a few rounds with your left hand alone, tossing each card off by a swing of your wrist and a push of your left thumb.

Don't hold the cards too tight.

Have you learned to deal comfortably? Try a couple more rounds for luck.

The Overhand Shuffle

Now comes the matter of shuffling. If you're used to handling cards, you know how to do a smooth riffle shuffle. All the same, in a minute I'll give you a point to make it smoother.

If you haven't handled cards, a riffle shuffle is harder to learn than most sleights. You're probably in the habit of using the overhand shuffle.

To do an overhand shuffle, you hold the deck by the ends in your left hand, thumb across the near end, fingers (or at least the second, third, and fourth fingers) across the far end, with the bottom of the pack facing your palm.

Then you hold out your right hand palm up, with the fingers cupped and the thumb sticking nearly straight up.

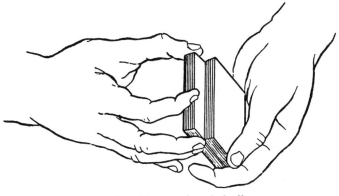

Fig. 8. The overhand shuffle

You drop a few cards from the top of the pack into your left hand; you may pull them down with your right thumb. Then a few more from the top of the pack on top of the cards in your right hand. Then a few more. Sometimes you may drop them from the top of the pack to the bottom of the cards in your right hand, or into the middle.

After you have done this a very few times, you will learn to shuffle quite fast. (*Fig.* 8).

What I said in the last lesson about acting natural is very true of shuffling. If you haven't handled cards much, you should use the overhand shuffle—and stick to it, even though later you learn the riffle.

But if you're in the habit of using the riffle shuffle, you shouldn't do the overhand shuffle.

Each way has its advantages. The riffle is neater, quicker, and more efficient. The overhand shuffle is much easier for a performer to turn to his own tricky ends. (For example, it is almost impossible to stack cards in a game except with an overhand shuffle.)

The Riffle or Dovetail Shuffle

Suppose you decide to be neat-handed and use the riffle.

Analyzed, the riffle is simply splitting the deck into halves, and dovetailing the ends or sides. In fact, magicians often call it a dovetail shuffle.

To split the pack, you might simply put it on the table and lift off half the cards. A good many people seem to wrestle with the two halves of a deck as if they were trying to look at all the faces of a pair of dice.

Magicians should seem straightforward. Don't fiddle like that. There are two right ways for a conjurer to start a riffle shuffle.

One is to hold the pack face down in the right hand, with your second finger at the extreme top right corner, and your thumb at the bottom right corner, leaving almost the whole top of the pack exposed. Curl the forefinger against the right middle of the top.

Now, come up and put your left hand in just the same position, but on the left side. The two curled forefingers will be touching.

Let your left second finger grab the top half of the pack, and simply separate your hands. (*Fig. 9a*).

Each hand should be holding one half of the deck—your left hand the upper half, your right hand the lower half.

Bring your thumbs close together, tilting the two halves of

the pack to form a tent. The ends of the cards held by your thumbs make the ridgepole. Your fingers hold the outer edges.

At first, you had probably better rest your fingernails (and indirectly the lower ends of the cards) on a table. Later, you can learn to shuffle easily in mid-air.

Straighten your two forefingers until the cards are bowed out from your hands. Keep on pushing until the ends of the cards begin to snap away from your thumbs. (*Fig.* 9b).

As the cards straighten out the ends will interlace, and you will find you have done a riffle shuffle—after a fashion.

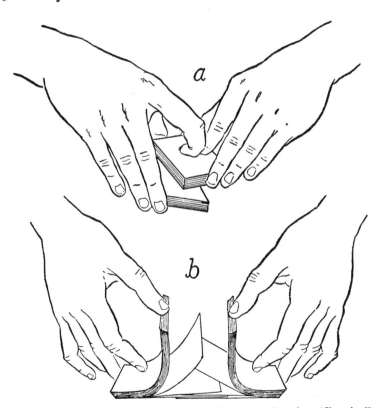

Fig. 9.   (a) First method of splitting the pack for the riffle shuffle; (b) Doing the riffle shuffle

You will probably have to practise for half an hour or more before the cards stop snapping off in fat bunches, and begin riffling smoothly one or two at a time.

Don't clutch the cards tight, and don't push very hard when you bend them.

With the ends of the two halves neatly dovetailed, you can either shove them together to square up the pack or spring them square with a "waterfall."

If you play bridge, you can probably do a waterfall. If you don't, but want to learn, here's how.

The "Waterfall" Finish

The two halves are dovetailed, with say a quarter of their length overlapping. Your thumbs are together on the overlap. Your fingers are at the outer ends.

You have to pick up the pack so that you can curl your fingers around to make clamps holding the outer ends of the two halves.

Push upward with the ends of your fingers until the cards form an arch.

Your thumbs push down enough to keep the overlapping ends of the cards from snapping out and coming un-dovetailed. Your arch should be nearly a semicircle. (*Fig.* 10a).

Now stop and listen to me.

If you don't, you're sure to try to squeeze the cards together, The way to do it is just the opposite—let go.

Keep your thumbs still; don't push. Simply relax your fingers and ease your two hands apart at the bottom, almost as if you meant to drop the whole pack.

If you do that gradually, the cards will come down singly from the top, springing together in a handsome waterfall. (*Fig.* 10b). At the end of the waterfall they will be almost squared up. But this is as hard to do evenly as a good riffle.

Once again, old bridge players will have to excuse me. I said

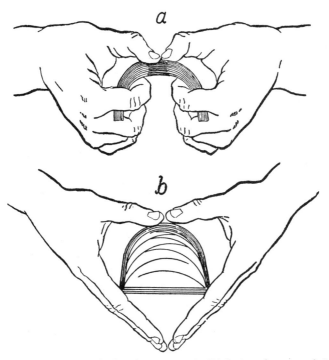

Fig. 10.   (a) Ready for the waterfall; (b) Doing the waterfall

there were two right ways of splitting the pack for a dovetail shuffle, and I've given only one.

Second Split for the Dovetail Shuffle

The other doesn't look so neat, but sometimes you need it for a trick. Hold the pack upright on end in your right hand with your thumb across the upper end. The top of the pack is toward your palm. Hold the lower end in a clamp made of your second, third, and fourth fingers curled around to the front, and your forefinger pushing against the top.

You really hold it just the same as if you were starting to

riffle. And that's exactly what you do. Push with your forefinger until perhaps half the pack riffles away from your thumb.

That leaves you with the bottom half sticking straight up, and the top half bent to the right. Of course, there's a gap between the upper ends of the two halves.

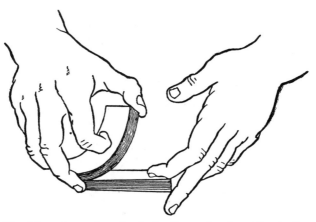

Fig. 11.   Second method of splitting for the riffle shuffle

Now come up with your left hand and clamp the free upper end of the lower half between your left forefinger on top and your left second, third, and fourth fingers on the bottom. (*Fig. 11*).

Do you see how you're about to get the same grip with each hand?

Carry your left hand away with the lower half, and put your left thumb across the other end of the cards.

There you are, ready to go into your shuffle.

One other thing that you will have to do often is to fan the cards out with both hands. Sometimes you will fan them face up, looking for a particular card. Sometimes it may be face down, so that people can pick a card at random.

Fanning the Cards

Just hold the pack in your left hand in dealing position, but with the cards sticking forward a little more. Bring your right hand out in about the same position, so that you can run the cards into it with your left thumb. Push to the right and a little away from you with your left thumb. You can help by "walking" your right first and second fingers along on the under side of the fan. (*Fig.* 12).

Fig. 12. Fanning

Don't hold tight. Easy does it. That's all there is to a two-handed fan.

The two-handed pivot fan and the one-handed fan are very pretty, but also quite difficult. Since they're just ornamental flourishes, I shall not deal with them here.

I think you've been patient with my shuffling and dealing about long enough. Let's try a trick.

As a matter of fact, we will try two. They're like Blackstone and the goat: the first one is harder to detect. It will put people in the right frame of mind to be fooled by the second trick, which is really a childish one if you stop to think.

They're also like Blackstone because they depend entirely on your acting. The trick itself isn't nearly so complicated as the coin effect in the last lesson.

Before you start to show the first trick, you must have your one-way deck arranged with all the back designs facing one way. That is, no card must be standing on its head when the pack is spread out face down. You understand I'm talking about the picture on the back, not about whether any of the cards face the wrong way in the deck. You don't want any of those, either.

Arrange your one-way deck one way before anybody is around; don't wait till the middle of the evening and then suddenly decide to show this trick.

Now you'll begin to see why I went on so long about shuffling. You can shuffle a one-way deck overhand as much as you like without disturbing it. If you want to dovetail shuffle, you must use the second method of splitting the pack. Try it once or twice and you'll see that the second method doesn't disturb the one-way arrangement, whereas the first turns one half end for end.

So you begin by shuffling the pack.

The acting in this trick is all that matters, and the main thing about the acting is that there mustn't be too much of it. The first trick should start with rather a ho-hum air—"Here's a bit of nonsense that may amuse you," so to speak.

That's the reason for all the shuffling and dealing. Even if you aren't used to handling cards, you must learn to appear to be. There's nothing in these two tricks except fanning, shuffling, cutting, and dealing. But the effects are so simple that they won't stand up under any extra fuss: you mustn't make hard work of them.

I'll go through the whole performance, except for the trick, just as I did in the last lesson.

The Card at the Number

Shuffle the pack. Then you can either fan it in your hands, or spread it face down on the table with a sweep of your arm. Ask somebody to pick a card, and not to let you see it.

I told you not to memorize my patter. Now I'll give you a few words *not* to say.

Don't say: "Please take a card, any card." That sounds like a green magician.

You can say, "Draw one," or "Pick one, and don't let me see it," or whatever you personally would say if you weren't a magician. But you mustn't sound like a phonograph record that you turn on whenever you want a card chosen.

Unfortunately, most card tricks involve having somebody choose a card. It's monotonous enough without any help from you.

Whenever somebody has to choose a card, make it seem as much of a new idea as you can.

Anyhow—someone draws a card, looks at it, but keeps it hidden from you.

Then he puts it back in the pack.

You shuffle. Sometimes it's possible to let him shuffle too, but you have to be an old hand at the game before you can develop that much nerve. For the time being, we'll go on without having you make it tough for yourself.

One reason you have to do this sort of trick casually is that the audience will then be casual, too. If you are very finicky, and make a great point of each step, somebody may ask to shuffle, or otherwise invent trouble for you.

If you just swing along in an easy, good-natured way, people won't think of things like that.

The card is back in the pack. You don't know what it is. You've shuffled and lost it.

Don't say much about that. Just move slowly enough and clearly enough to make it obvious. Probably, so far, you won't have said more than, "Take a look at one card—don't let me see it. Can I have it back? Thanks."

There's no reason for your audience to know that this is your first card trick. You're acting the part of a hardened old card sharp.

Cut the pack once or twice. And, for the love of Heaven, don't say anything about *that*.

Now ask your victim to mention a number from one to 52. Make it plain that you want a number, not the name of his card.

Otherwise, about two times out of five when you ask for a number he'll come back snappily, "I had the nine of spades," and your trick is done for.

On the other hand, don't tell him too much. Don't let him know what you want the number for.

Now you have the number without mishap. Take the pack and start dealing off cards from the top, face down, in a pile on the table. Count aloud as you deal.

When you reach his number, stop. Turn over the card at the number.

"That wasn't your card, was it?"

"No." It never will be.

All right. Put the pile back on the pack.

Now you can begin to boast just a little. You didn't see the card, did you? No way you could have kept track of it, was there? It must just be shuffled into the deck somewhere?

Fine. Let the man take the pack himself. It's all his from here on. Let him deal off the cards and count up to his number.

Don't say, "Count them off the same as I did." You'd much rather have him forget that you counted them off at all. If he doesn't forget, he still shouldn't be reminded.

He counts to his number and, sure enough, there's the card he chose.

End of first trick.

That was a pretty fair trick, but of course you did handle the cards, and he did have to say the number out loud.

Now he is to think of a number, and not tell anyone.

Next, he can take the pack away in a corner somewhere, count off that many cards, and put them in his pocket.

He is to put the deck back on the table, and keep thinking of his number.

You pick up a handful of cards off the pack, run through them quickly, look him steadily in the eye, and then give him a few cards to put in his pocket with the others.

You say (in substance), "I've outguessed you. I'm way ahead of you. Was your number odd or even?"

Suppose it was even.

"Even? All right, I've given you just enough cards to make the whole lot odd. Count them and see if I haven't."

You can do it every time. This particular trick you can even do twice running, if somebody insists it was just luck.

Now for the secrets.

You must have guessed that the first trick depended on the one-way deck. The principle is simply that if one card is turned end for end in the pack, you can find it from the back. This fact is so simple that you must hide it every way you can.

First, watch your man after he draws the card. Don't stare; that's rude. And suspicious looking. But keep an eye on him.

He may turn his card around, and save you the work.

More likely, however, he won't. Then you have to turn the pack around.

That's what you must hide. To hide it, don't furtively reverse the pack behind your back, or perform any other such nonsense. Hold it in dealing position in your left hand. Come up with your right hand and grab the far end of the pack between your thumb and fingers. Draw the deck forward out of your left hand, and casually wave the pack at the audience.

That automatically brings the other end forward. Then you can take the pack in your left hand again for the man to put his card back in. Or, if you like, you can spread the cards face down on the table again.

The only trouble with that is that your man might just possibly reverse his card after you lay down the pack where you can't turn it.

In your present stage of skill as a magician, that would be just too bad. A few more lessons and you won't mind a bit.

From here on, you can coast. The chosen card is back in the pack, and you can shuffle all you like (overhand or second-method riffle) without disturbing it.

Next, you cut the pack. The reason you don't talk about this is that on the last cut you must cut to the reversed card. Lift off all the cards above that one, drop them on the table, and put the remainder on top of the first pile.

You see what that does. It brings the chosen card to the top.

In nineteen out of twenty chosen-card tricks, your first act is to bring the chosen card secretly to the top of the deck. This trick is no exception: the one-way pack and the cutting are for that purpose alone. I shall teach you other, quicker, ways of doing it, but there is none where a little skull practice so completely eliminates hand practice as this.

The rest of the trick is all acting. When you count down to the man's number, the first card on the table is his chosen card, though of course he doesn't know it. When you put the pile back on the deck, his card is automatically at his number.

Big sensation!

Instead of one-way patterns, you can make a one-way deck by drawing a line with a rather soft pencil across the squared edge of one end of the pack. So long as the deck remains new and clean, you can spot a reversed card at a glance.

Mind Control

The second trick is all acting from start to finish. Better not try it on a second grade pupil. He's more likely to remember that if you add an odd number to an odd number the sum is even, and if you add an odd number to an even number the sum is odd.

Just be sure you hand the man an odd number; he can't win.

It would be possible to vary the trick by undertaking to make him win every time; you would give him an even number. But you dare not do it, because more than one quick repetition, at most, would set people to thinking about odd and even. And the whole success of the trick depends on their leaving their thinking powers in the checkroom.

LESSON 3.   The Lariat King

What Seems to Happen: Someone piles up two dice so that three of the twelve faces are hidden. With one toss of a rope you make as many knots as there are spots hidden on the dice.

What You Need: A pair of dice, the bigger the better. A rope, or heavy cord, about twenty feet long.

This trick, I believe, was combined by an English magician named Norman Hunter.

You notice I don't say invented, though perhaps I should. Using dice to make up a number that you want to know is an old idea, and tying a rope full of knots by magic is above voting age, too.

Inventing Magic

But on the whole, probably I should reconsider and call Mr. Hunter an inventor, because the *effect* is new. The idea of using the *number* of magic knots for a trick, instead of simply showing your ability to produce *knots,* makes a whole new effect so far as the audience goes.

And the audience is all that counts for a magician. With no audience, he can't possibly be more than a juggler. If the audience likes him, he's good, no matter what anyone says. If the audience thinks something is a new trick, it is a new trick, even if you do it with two odd pieces of a Mysto Magic set.

This is a very good thing for you. It means that nearly as soon as you start learning tricks you can start inventing new ones. Almost any little change will make a new trick.

If you did a card trick with a stack of calling cards, that would be a new trick for the audience.

Even if you only changed your patter, like Norman Hunter, and said, "How many knots shall I make?" instead of, "Look, I can make knots!," that would be a new trick.

Very likely, other magicians have devised the same new trick before you, but that doesn't make it any less fun. The best two coin tricks I do are my own invention. One of them had also been invented in Australia years before my time. It's so good it had to be discovered at least twice. Maybe the other one isn't quite so good, because nobody else uses it, as far as I know.

I called this trick the Lariat King because I wanted some handy name. Most of the standard tricks have a sort of stable name that all magicians know them by, and, in addition, different performers may use fancy titles for them on printed programs.

My only objection to calling this the Lariat King is that you may think you *have* to show it as a feat of roping. So long as you understand that you don't have to tell any one hard-and-fast story made up by somebody else, we can get on with the trick.

Of course, if you come from Texas and spin a mean lasso on your own account, roping will fit in perfectly. But you may just as well be a sailor making fancy knots and splices, or a shipping clerk wrapping bundles, or merely a private citizen.

The Lariat King

The trick goes like this. You come before your audience, trailing the rope and rattling the dice in the other hand.

Ask somebody to roll the dice a few times—and make sure the dice aren't loaded.

While someone is rolling the dice, you start coiling up the rope.

Tell the man to roll the dice "for keeps," but if he has any suspicions he can turn them any way up that he likes. Then he is to set one die on top of the other.

(Did you know that the singular of *dice* is *die?* Too many magicians don't.)

This means that three faces of the dice are hidden—the one against the table top, the one opposite it, and the one on the other die that covers that.

By now you have finished coiling your rope.

Wait for Slow Joe in the back to catch up.

Now is the time for you to tell whatever story you are stuck with—that you are not only a rope artist but a mind reader, or whatever your idea is. The thought you convey is that you are going to make as many knots in the rope as there are hidden spots on the dice.

Draw back your arm. Pause. Look toward the two dice guarded by your volunteer friend. Look at the rope.

Then, swish! Toss the coil across the room, holding on to one end.

The rope comes out all in knots. Give it to a second person to count the knots. You step back out of the way.

Let your first man pick up the dice and total the hidden spots. The magician wins again!

This trick is much harder to figure out than any you've tried yet. You aren't likely to be detected. So you can give it a more mysterious build-up, if you like to do things that way.

How the Trick Is Done

Your first act must be to learn the total of the hidden spots.

The most useful thing for a magician to know about dice is that the points on opposite faces of a single die always add up to seven. Two is on the back of five, three on the back of four, one on the back of six.

Therefore, the two hidden faces of the bottom die add up to seven, no matter which side is up .

The top face of the top die is showing, and you must catch a glimpse of it. Then the hidden face is seven, minus the spots you can see on top.

You needn't go through this calculation every time. The opposite faces of the two dice will total fourteen. Simply subtract the top face from fourteen, and that's how many knots you must make.

Now for the knots.

The way you coil the rope is the whole trick of making knots.

Hold the end of the rope in your left fist. Your thumb should be up, with the short end of the rope sticking up, the long end hanging straight down.

Bring the long end around forward with your right hand, up over your left knuckles, and down through your fist. That should form one loop, perhaps a foot long. The long end of the rope should pass to the right of the short end as it comes down through your left fist.

That loop is a perfectly normal one. You need it to make the knots, but you don't count it, and none of the other loops is made that way.

To make the rest of the loops, stick out your right hand, thumb down and palm turned to the *right*.

Take hold of the long end of rope, *from* the *left*, with your *right hand*. (*Fig.* 13a).

Now bring your right hand up and carry the thumb over to the left before you lay the rope into your left fist. This carries the long end of rope to the left, *behind* the first part of the loop. (*Fig.* 13b).

Make eight of these phony loops. You know beforehand that there must be at least eight hidden spots on the dice. There can't be more than six spots showing on top. Six from fourteen is eight.

You have to say something, perhaps ask the man if he has the dice all stacked up so that you can't see them. When you say "dice," you naturally glance in that direction. This is when big dice are a help, aside from the fact that they look showier.

You catch a glimpse of the top face, and subtract the spots from fourteen.

Then you know how many more phony loops you have to make.

Make them.

That leaves an end of rope still hanging down. Bring it up and slip it between your left second and third fingers. (*Fig.* 13c). If it's very long, make a few normal coils first.

This is the end you hold on to, the end which you mustn't let go.

The trick is really all done now. You know the sum of the spots, and the knots are as good as made. So you can boast all

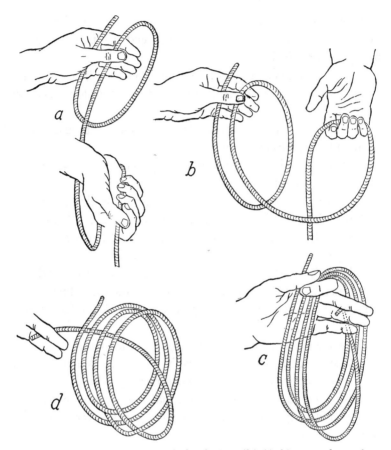

Fig. 13. (a) Starting to coil the lariat; (b) Making a phony loop;
(c) The lariat coiled and ready; (d) Making the knots

you want to (and think people will stand) about the miracle
you're going to accomplish.

You can ask your helper whether he knows how many spots
on the dice are hidden. If he doesn't, you can say this will prove
you have an X-ray eye and aren't just thought reading.

If he does know the total number of spots, tell him to think
hard of the number.

Any kind of nonsense you like, so long as Slow Joe in the back realizes that the marvel is about to happen.

When you throw the coil of rope across the room, give a good hard fling, then open your left hand.

But, for goodness' sake, *don't* let the outer end of the rope go from between your second and third fingers.

The toss pulls the outer end through the reverse loops that you have so carefully wound up, and thus makes as many plain overhand knots in the rope as there were loops dangling from your left fist. The first, honest loop doesn't form a knot. (*Fig.* 13d).

When you step back to let people count the knots, you can also make rather a fuss about keeping well away from the table. Be sure everyone realizes that you never touch the dice from beginning to end.

Make your helper add up the hidden spots.

If you're doing a children's show, or just enjoy low comedy anyhow, you can act hard of hearing and cause him to bellow the total at the top of his lungs.

Opportunities for this kind of horseplay are common enough, but don't rely on me to point them out. Performers who can use them will find them, and magicians of a quieter disposition should leave them alone.

Anyway, just because this trick is naturally mystifying, don't sit back and think it needn't be entertaining. A tiresome puzzling trick is more annoying in its way than a tiresome trick that you have the satisfaction of being able to see through.

LESSON 4.   The Afghan Bands and the Cut Turban

What Seems to Happen: You have a cloth ring, or an endless band about four inches wide and three feet long. You tear it lengthwise, thus getting two rings. You tear one ring again, and the two narrow rings you get are linked; the other tears into one big ring twice as large as the original.

For the second trick you cut a long strip of cheesecloth in half, knot it together, and restore it all to one piece.

What You Need: A strip of cotton cloth four inches wide by about three and a half feet long. (Magicians usually make the trick up in batches, and dye the cloth red.) Glue. A pair of scissors. A piece of cheesecloth, possibly a foot wide and twelve feet long.

Where to Learn More: Hoffmann, *Later Magic;* Carrington, *The Boy's Book of Magic*

These two tricks are good professional numbers. I put both in one lesson, first, because once you know how to make the Afghan Bands, there's nothing else to learn, and a three-year-old could not possibly fail with the effect; and second, because you are making progress by now, and can grasp a trick without quite so much long-winded explanation.

There is hardly any more to say about the effect of the Afghan Bands. You hold up your ring of cloth, made by simply glueing the ends of the cotton strip together. Run the circle around your hands two or three times so people can see that it's just a plain cloth band.

There are three little lengthwise slits to help you start tearing. Start down the middle slit, and simply tear your four-inch loop into two two-inch loops.

Take one in each hand, and hold them up so that Slow Joe in the back will know there are two plain separate loops.

Hang one of the two around your neck.

Run the other through your hands, just as you did with the big band.

And remember now what I told you in the first lesson: keep your elbows away from your sides and your hands up high. Slow Joe might be quite bright if he could see what you were doing.

Another point. This is the kind of trick that goes well with a fairly large crowd. If you have a living room or auditorium full of people, remember there is more than one person in the audience. Go down to the front of the stage (upstage is the back part; and you know how people dislike anyone they call "upstage"), or to the front of the cleared space where you are working. Walk leisurely from one side to the other, holding out whatever you have to show—at the moment, the single Afghan Band.

People are always pleased and impressed when they can see tricks close enough to touch—especially in a platform show.

However, the same rule holds on the stage as in taking a movie panorama shot: don't reverse and go back over the same view. If somebody calls you back, oblige him; otherwise, one swing across the stage is enough.

Return to stage center, fairly well down toward the front.

Start at the slit in your narrow band, and tear straight down the middle.

Nothing you can do will prevent the two thin bands from coming out linked together. You may play this for comedy by acting surprised and disgusted, or for a mystery by first explaining how it is mechanically impossible to link two separate bands. Any way that goes with your own personality will do.

Throw the torn bands to the crowd, and take the next one off your neck.

When you tear this, it will come out in one long circle—no credit to you, but it will.

Here, as everywhere else in magic, your acting can make the pay-off a riot, a baffler, or a dull thud.

How to Make the Afghan Bands

This trick, almost more than any other, depends on the work you do beforehand.

Get your strip of cloth, and fold it in half crosswise so that the ends lie together. Take the scissors and cut both ends together straight down the middle for about nine inches.

Now get out your glue.

Eventually, you must glue the two ends together so that they over-lap about two inches. But before you glue the left-hand half-ends together, *turn one around so that the inside comes to the outside of the loop.*

Then glue it.

Before you glue the right-hand half-end, give one of the ends a *complete turn,* so that the inside is twisted around to face in again.

Then glue that.

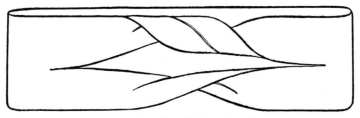

Fig. 14. **The Afghan bands**

After the glue has dried, snip center slits in the two halves. (*Fig.* 14).

There is nothing more I can tell you about working this trick. *Any* cloth or paper loop fastened together with a half-turn will tear into linked rings. A full turn makes one long ring. (And if you split that, you'd still get one long ring.)

As a matter of fact, a turn and a half will make one long ring with a knot in it. But enough is enough.

How to Work the Turban Trick

The next trick, the cut and restored turban, is a very old trick, a very good one, and a very even contest of wits between you and the audience. If you do it clumsily, you will be found out; if you do it well, your audience will be astounded.

It is often better to have some sort of excuse for using strange articles that don't make sense, such as long pieces of cheesecloth. So you may introduce this as a Hindu magician's turban, or a ghost's raincoat, or a government surplus. Or something.

Toss an end to somebody, and have him pull. Nothing wrong with the turban.

Next, clip one end of the turban in the crotch of your left thumb, with about six inches of the short end sticking up above your hand.

Get the same grip on the other end with your right hand.

That leaves quite a lot of turban trailing on the floor.

Grab about eight inches of the middle between your two hands, pulling the cheesecloth taut. This still leaves each hand dangling a long loop of turban.

There is a special way to hold the turban at this point, and here it is. Your two hands are held out horizontal, palms facing, thumbs up, as if you were showing the size of the minnow that got away (eight inches long). The ends of the turban are sticking up in the crotches of your thumbs. (*Fig.* 15a).

The middle stretch of the turban runs between the *second* and *third* fingers of each hand.

With the turban in this position, you can start your downstage promenade from left to right.

Over toward the right you ask someone to take the scissors and cut the turban square in half between your hands.

He does. The cut ends are as plain as day.

Next, you tie the cut ends in a square knot (or a granny, if you must). Pull the knot tight with a good tug.

There are some ragged ends (Irish pennants we called them in the Marine Corps) about the knot. Take the scissors, trimming the knot until it is neat.

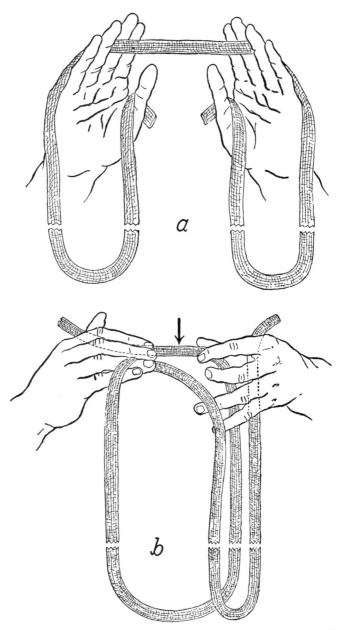

Fig. 15. (a) Starting the Turban trick; (b) Switching strands

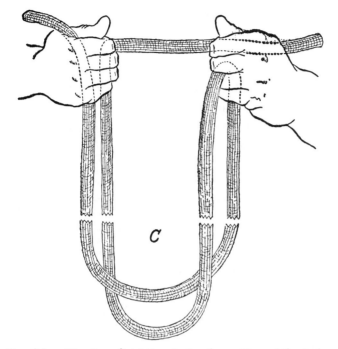

Fig. 15. (*Continued*) (c) **Ready for the cutting of the turban**

By the time you get through trimming, there is no knot left, and the turban is back in one piece.

So far as explaining the deception is concerned, I left you in the midst of a so-big gesture with a long loop of turban dangling down from each hand. Up to that point everything has been exactly as it seemed.

The trick is that you must get the man to cut off the end of the turban instead of dividing it in the middle. You make the switch as you go from the center to the right of the stage.

When you swing to the right you drop both hands by bending your wrists, and at the same time close your fingers to make fists.

The switch takes place just then. Your left second and third fingers drop the piece of the middle they hold, and instead scoop in the right-hand piece that is dangling from the crotch of your right thumb. (*Fig.* 15b).

With both hands now closed, all that shows is the short ends sticking up from your hands like a rabbit's ears, and a piece of turban held taut in the middle, ready to be cut. (*Fig.* 15c).

The swing of your body from center to right is a large movement, and the crooking of your left second and third fingers is a small movement. A large movement always tends to mask a small movement.

More important, just then you speak to the man you have picked as a helper, looking him square in the eye.

Very few people are watchful enough to notice small finger movements in the face of such distractions.

The net result is that you seem to be holding two loops, one with each hand, connected by a straight center piece that someone now cuts.

Actually, you have two overlapping circles of turban, with the end of the right-hand circle replacing the center or connecting piece.

Your helper cuts the turban squarely through the middle—he thinks. Four ends are unmistakably showing.

Both ends of the genuine turban are in your left hand. Your right hand holds a six-inch scrap of cheesecloth against the center of the turban.

Drop everything from your left hand promptly, before people have time to take stock and see what end should be where.

Hold your right hand up high.

Come over with your left hand to tie a knot.

To do that, swing the loose bit under the middle of the turban so that the two form a cross. Then make a plain overhand knot with the cut ends.

You simply have a scrap of cloth tied around the center of the turban; but to anyone who is expecting a square knot, this looks near enough like it.

Make quite a point of pulling the turban to get the knot tight. You're all right so long as it doesn't fall off entirely!

You may give an end of the turban each to two spectators to hold. This makes it seem as if there couldn't be any funny business.

Trimming off the ends of the knot with scissors is only one way of removing the tell-tale cheesecloth scrap, but it is probably the easiest. Just keep snipping away (don't cut the main part of the turban!) and throwing bit after bit aside until there's none left.

Keep first the fake knot, later the place where it was supposed to be, bunched up in your left hand.

When all of the knot is cut away, grasp the middle of the turban in your left fist as if you were still hiding the knot. Come down to stage center.

If you are having the ends of the turban held, tell the holders to get ready.

You need some sort of emphasis—a magic word like abracadabra, a warning like "Watch me!," "Here goes!," or anyway something to show that the moment has come.

Tell your helpers to give a yank.

Snatch your left hand back as if it were burned. Hold the pose. The turban is restored.

LESSON 5. Finding a Selected Card, I: Forcing

What Seems to Happen: A man in the audience chooses a card in such a way that you can't possibly know it.

What You Need: A pack of cards. There are also prepared decks, to be explained in the lesson.

Where to Learn More: Hoffmann, *Modern Magic;* Jean Hugard, *Modern Magic Manual;* Blackstone's *Modern Card Tricks and Secrets of Magic*

In a way, this lesson goes against the grain with me, because it only explains tricks instead of arranging a play for you to act. But if you're going to do card tricks, you have to know how to work them as well as how to show them, and I can't help that.

The standard magician's way of having someone take a card is to fan the deck face downward, and ask him to pick one.

Sometimes you have to do it this way, and you nearly always can; but watch out for two things.

Since it is a standard conjuring gesture, make sure people don't automatically expect to be bored the moment you fan the cards. As I told you before, don't say, "Please take a card, any card." You must take care that your invitation is casual and natural—*to you*.

A stout middle-aged banker with white piping on his vest can say, "Now if you will do me the kindness to select a card of your own volition——" A longshoreman at a union ball might say, "Grab one. Come on, what do you think this is, a sewing circle?" Probably you aren't in either class and you'll have to say something entirely different.

If you don't know what sounds natural to you, all I can say is that it's far better to sound too ignorant than to sound too fancy.

The second point to look out for is that people are often suspicious when asked to choose a card from a fan. They think you may be forcing one particular card on them. You have to make an exaggerated show of fair play with your fan—unless you are in fact trying to force one card. We will come back to that in a minute.

Another way to offer the cards is simply to hold out the deck and ask someone to cut off a handful, then look at the bottom card of his cut.

Another way is to let a man stick a pencil or paper-knife into the pack, and let him look at the card above or below the pointer. Whether it's the card above or below depends on the trick you are doing.

Still another way is to hold the pack out in dealing position and have someone lift up the corner just enough to peep at the index. This way looks very secretive and hard for you to beat, besides being quick and simple. Some of the slickest card manipulators in the business (including me) always use it. But it isn't so good on a platform when you want most of the audience to see what the card is.

Finally, we have the simple method of handing a person a pack and telling him to take a card for himself. This can make a great impression, sometimes helping to gloss over the fact that you don't let him put the card back in and shuffle it without help. Only if you do it too often you may slow down the act.

The card trick that all magicians dream of is to let someone hold the pack, choose a card, put it back, and shuffle, all without the magician's coming near. Actually, this trick can't be done. But there are many ways of coming close to it, cutting a corner here or there.

The other dream trick is to find a card that someone has only selected in his head, without ever touching it.

Surprisingly enough, this is more nearly possible than the other. It takes a lot of skill, and something much harder to get than skill—perfect timing, perfect confidence, the knack of making someone else unconsciously do what you want, and enough resources to make out somehow if you fail in this.

I shall give many more tricks in this and the next lesson than any one magician should use. In fact, most performers never use but one.

I suggest that you follow the fashion and try out different methods (skipping the mechanical ones if you don't want to buy special equipment). You will find you like one or two in particular better than the rest.

Stick to those, or it. Use it and use it and use it. Use it with friendly crowds and suspicious crowds; on the platform and with people looking over your shoulder; with brand-new decks and with blotter-like old remnants from the back of some drawer. In the end you will have that one method absolutely mastered. If you want to find a card, you don't give it another thought—the move is automatic, and it can't go wrong.

A good many very successful card workers are completely one-trick men. They depend wholly on a "set-up" (a prearranged deck), on a short card in the pack, on the side-steal palm. With their one trick they can get enough variety to put on a good show, and they can learn the trick so thoroughly that nothing will ever trip them up.

You need not have such a one-track mind as that, but neither have you got to use every trick in the book. Just look them over, take your pick, and remember that some of the other ways may help you out of a jam one day.

For example, if you set out to force a card, and miss, you can't very well start over on somebody else, leaving the first victim to sit there till the end of the evening.

But if you know one or two of the tricks in the next lesson, you can find the first man's card, do some entirely different trick with it, and *then* force the card you want on somebody more gullible.

If you finally decide to specialize in card tricks, you can get books that will teach you the near-miraculous mental effects I mentioned above.

The surest way of knowing what card a man picks is by making him take one that you know. The surest way to make him take a particular card is with a "forcing deck."

Forcing and Forcing Decks

"Forcing" is the magician's word for making someone unconsciously pick what you want, whether a card, number, handkerchief, or heap. A forcing deck is made up, say, of fifty-one eights of spades, with some other card on the bottom. It wouldn't do to have a man draw the eight of spades, and a moment later see another eight of spades on the bottom.

With this kind of forcing deck, you practically have to fan the cards when one is to be chosen. You can also spread them on the table with a sweep of your arm; only be careful that none turns over. Again, if you are careful, you can let someone stick a pencil into the pack.

But it is definitely not safe to hand the whole deck to someone and let him take out a card. Besides, in the course of time the secrets of certain tricks get around; and the simple forcing deck is one of those.

In fact, I hardly think you will find it worth while to add that kind of pack—or perhaps even any forcing pack—to your equipment.

The next step up in forcing decks is used chiefly by stage performers who can't take chances. Instead of fifty-one cards alike, the deck has seventeen each of three different cards, with the odd one on the bottom.

When you need three different cards chosen for something like the Rising Card Trick, you can either keep the three batches separate, and take care that one card is drawn from near the bottom, one from the middle, and one from near the top; or arrange the whole pack in a succession of threes, and ask the man to draw three cards together. Again the pack must be fanned for the choice.

The Svengali Pack

The best forcing deck I know of, and a really ingenious one, too, has to be riffled. You hold the pack in your left hand in dealing position. Put your right thumb at the back of the pack, your right second and third fingers at the front. Pull gently up and back with your right fingers, and riffle away.

As you do this, your helper is to poke his forefinger or a knife or pencil into the pack wherever he likes.

It happens that this is also the easiest position for forcing by sleight-of-hand.

But first let's deal with this almost foolproof forcing deck. The beauty of it is that you can riffle through the pack and show the cards all different. Riffle through again, and no one can possibly choose any card but the one you want chosen.

Half of the deck is perfectly ordinary—twenty-six different cards. The other twenty-six are exactly alike, not only in being the same card, but in that each card is trimmed just a hair shorter than the ordinary cards.

The ordinary cards are not arranged in any special way. Just put one face down on the table, then a short card on top of it, then another ordinary card, then another short card, and so on.

Experiment with the pack, and see what happens.

When you riffle, each short card crouches down and hides behind the long card in front. All the long cards are different; all the short cards are alike. When you riffle and show someone the faces of the cards, all he can see is twenty-six different cards. But when you hold the deck back up and riffle, the man's finger or knife is bound to come down on one of the short cards. I need hardly say that you give him the card below, not above, the pointer.

You can shuffle a pack of this kind without making much difference in the way it works.

These mechanical methods of forcing are nearly foolproof. The people who use them most are usually *not* beginners, too green to do anything else, but professionals who, for some reason, want the easiest and most dependable way.

I think you can have more fun learning to force a card with an ordinary deck.

Forcing Sleights: The Fan

The obvious way to force a card is also the hardest. You do it by fanning the cards.

You start off with the card you mean to force on top of the pack. Hold the deck in dealing position in your left hand.

Bring up your right hand to the end near you; grab the under half with your right forefinger on the right side near the corner, and your thumb on the left side near the corner. Pull the under half out, and drop it on top.

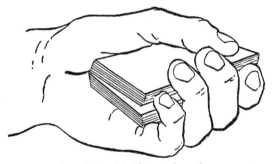

Fig. 16. **Holding a location**

Wait—not too fast! Before you slap the upper packet down on the lower, curl your left little finger over the card you want to force.

This means that you end up holding the entire pack in dealing position, but with your little finger dividing the halves. (*Fig.* 16). This is a position you will find useful in many card tricks. Try it over a few times. Don't grab too hard.

You needn't have your hand wrapped all the way around so that your little finger sticks into the break up to the second joint. For this particular trick, you hardly need do more than keep the break in the pack open by pushing the tip of your little finger against the side.

Now you have the card that you want to force in the middle of the pack, with your left little finger curled down on it. Next comes the hard part.

Walk up to someone and ask him to draw a card. As you speak, start fanning the pack from your left hand into your right. You can run through the first quarter of the deck rather slowly.

Keep watching your victim's hand.

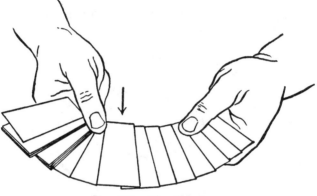

Fig. 17. **The fan force**

As he stretches his hand out, run the cards faster. Obviously, what you have to do is time your fanning so that the card under your left little finger comes along just as he grabs. (*Fig.* 17).

You must simply feed the one card into his hand, and then rock back on your heels just a little, so as to move the rest of the pack gently away from him without seeming to snatch it. Swaying back instead of pulling back is one of John Mulholland's many additions to magic. Go right on fanning the cards. There must be no jerks, no sudden break. Unless you seem simply to have run through the cards while he drew one, the force is not successful, even though the person gets the right card.

Some magicians find this force works best when they put on a bustling, pushing manner, and practically shove the whole deck into their victim's stomach. Others manage very gently, by pure timing.

Anyway, this is a hard trick to practise, because it depends entirely on how well you judge your victim's movements, and you can never practise except with a spectator to practise on.

More for the fun of it than anything else, I may mention that Nelson Downs used to force cards by fanning the pack behind his back. He did it mostly by backing into the spectator, and he said anyone could force cards that way if his feet were big enough.

The other two methods of forcing require neither big feet nor a live spectator to practise on.

Forcing Sleights: The Slip

In the first method, you hold the pack in dealing position in your left hand, but with the fingers curled over the top of the pack rather more than usual. You riffle the front end of the cards with your right hand, fingers at the front end, thumb at the back.

Your victim pokes a pencil or knife, or simply his forefinger, into the pack. The forefinger makes it a little harder for you to do, though it may look a bit more natural.

At the start, the card you want to force is on top of the pack. All four fingertips of your left hand have a grip on it. (But don't hold too tight!)

When your victim sticks the pencil in, relax both hands. Don't drop anything, but relax.

Then shoot your left arm straight out from the shoulder at him, carrying toward him the part of the pack under the pencil. He is supposed to take and look at the card under the pencil.

Actually, you have to stick out your left hand, instead of pulling back your right, so as to get the pack out from under the pencil.

Because, as you shoot out your left hand, the fingers close

down on the top card of the upper half of the pack—the one you want to force—and carry it forward. (*Fig.* 18). Thus, the top card of the whole pack slips off and becomes the top card of the lower half, which the victim then takes and looks at.

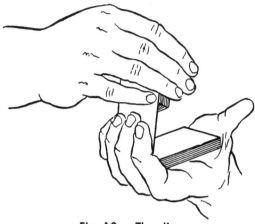

Fig. 18.   The slip

This method of forcing is called the slip. It's very easy, but you should run through it over and over until you can do it smoothly, with no jerks or loud snap as you bring the top card down.

Never forget: easy does it; don't clutch the cards.

Another Knife Force

The last method of forcing that I shall give you is fiendishly ingenious; Al Baker showed it to me.

It starts off like the method I have just described. But you must use a knife or pencil, not the spectator's finger. And the whole trick is practically the reverse of the slip.

You carry your right hand forward, not your left; and the chosen card is above the pencil, not below.

To start, put the card you want to force on the bottom of the pack. Then draw out about a third of the deck, and put it on top; but hold a break with your left little finger, the way you learned to do in the fan force. (Remember *Fig.* 16?)

Your game is to see that your victim sticks the pencil in close to the break you are holding, but *below* it. It doesn't necessarily have to be close, but it does have to be below.

When he sticks it in, take the pencil away from him by clipping it between your right second and third fingers as they hold the front end of the deck.

What you seem to do next is simply to hold out the upper half of the pack, with the pencil clamped underneath it, so that he can look at the card above the pencil.

Actually, you carry away only the part of the deck above the break you have been holding with your left little finger. The pencil is pulled out of the place where it was originally stuck,

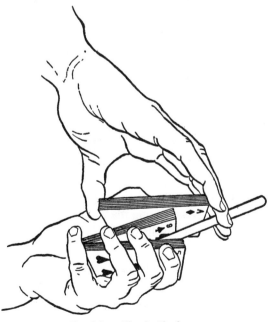

Fig. 19.   **The knife force**

but the upper part of the pack, moving forward, hides that fact. (*Fig.* 19).

Since the last card above the break is the one you are forcing, once again the spectator can't win.

Remember, it is just as important in forcing as in making a pass with a coin: *don't move the hand you don't want looked at.* In the knife force you must move your right hand forward, not pull your left hand back. In using the slip, you must carry your left hand forward, not swing your right hand away to the left.

You have been very patient about learning sleights. Now I will give you a trick to fix the force in your mind.

The Telephone Trick

The trick is so sensational that I am going to risk teaching it to you, even though you can't do it if you're one of those people who haven't a friend in the world. You need a helper, a person not from the audience, to perform the trick.

There is a long-standing prejudice among magicians against having confederates, plants, or stooges to help you. The only objection in my eyes is that you can't be ready at a moment's notice to do the trick (and that your stooge may not be much impressed with your powers as a magician).

None of that matters in this case, anyway, because you make no secret of your helper, who, furthermore, doesn't show up at the performance at all.

Somebody draws a card from the pack. Or three different people may draw. Let's say one man chooses.

Have him put his card in his inside pocket, then button up his coat.

Next, you give him a telephone number, have him call it, and simply ask the person who answers what card was chosen.

When he gets the right answer, and shows his card around, the trick is done.

Actually, as I don't need to tell you, the trick was done the moment the card was chosen.

You arrange with your telephone helper beforehand to be ready for the trick at about a certain time in the evening, and you give the name of a card (or three cards, if you're playing it that way) to be written down next to the telephone.

Then, when the time comes, you force that card, or those cards, on your victim.

Really, the whole trick is just salesmanship and build-up. All the emphasis is on long-distance mind reading and thought transference. This isn't a card trick at all. If you know anything about Dr. Rhine and extra-sensory perception, you can pull that into it. Anything—so long as you don't let people suppose that the trick hinges on the choice of cards.

Several "mentalists" (a rather flattering term for magicians who specialize in mind-reading tricks) have made reputations with this Great Telephone Trick. So, if you don't get the best out of it, the fault is yours.

There is another way of doing the effect, without forcing. You may hand the deck to the audience and let them make their own choice.

But you can't do more than one card at a time, because the tip-off is the name of the person you tell the victim to ask for over the phone. Charles Adams may stand for the ace of spades, Charles Baker for the deuce of spades, and so on.

That way, there is more chance for your assistant to do something wrong: so why not force the card, and be sure?

LESSON 6. Finding a Selected Card, II: Locations

What Seems to Happen: You can always find any card that is chosen. In the Spelling Trick you deal out a card for each letter of the name of the chosen card, which turns up at the last letter.

What You Need: A pack of cards. Prepared cards as described in the lesson.

Where to Learn More: S. W. Erdnase, *The Expert at the Card Table;* C. Lang Neil, *The Modern Conjurer;* Thurston, *Four Hundred Tricks You Can Do;* Hoffmann, *Modern Magic*

This is how you can find a card that you don't force. There are so many good ways of doing it that I could fill a whole book with nothing else. But, as you know, I'm trying to give you a large repertory of one-act plays, not to make a card sharp out of you.

So I shall only give you a few easy ways and one rather hard way to find a card.

Re-read Lesson 2.

Can you handle the cards without cracking or marring them? Can you shuffle smoothly—riffle or overhand—I don't care which?

Do you always remember not to squeeze the pack until the joker screams?

Can you hold the deck in your left hand, and riffle smoothly with your right?

Re-read Lesson 5.

Can you hold a break in the pack with your left little finger?

Good. You haven't much else to learn for the start of this lesson.

False Shuffles

You may have heard that gamblers can do a "false shuffle." It sounds very tricky.

Let me show you that some false shuffles could happen by accident.

First, an overhand shuffle.

Start with the pack in your right hand, ready to shuffle with your left. Use your right thumb to draw the top card toward you about a quarter of an inch. (*Fig.* 20).

Come down with your left hand, and pick up the bottom four-fifths of the pack to shuffle. Just casually shuffle the cards on top of those you leave in your right hand.

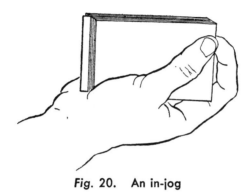

Fig. 20. An in-jog

But don't be so casual that the cards land every which way.

That original top card, sticking out a quarter of an inch toward you, makes what card workers call an "in-jog." It must serve to flag this particular spot, like a tab on a card index. If you throw the other cards around too much, you will need a bigger jog.

You have shuffled all the cards from your left hand into your right.

Now come down again with your left hand, and grab all the cards below the in-jog. (*Fig.* 21). Shuffle those on to the cards in your right hand.

The original top card is now on the bottom.

Pick up the whole deck in your left hand, and just shuffle anyhow, down to the last card. Drop that on top.

The original top card is back on top.

Now, a false *riffle* shuffle.

Let's say that you have some particular card on top.

All you need do to keep it there is to remember which hand holds the original top half of the deck. Then, in riffling, keep back the last card or two with that thumb until all the other cards have been dovetailed.

Again, say that your particular card is in the middle, and you want it on top.

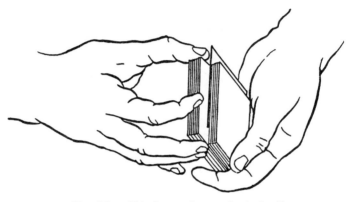

Fig. 21. "Under-cutting to the in-jog"

All you must do is break the pack above that card. Instead of holding back with the original top half, you hold back the last few cards of the original under half.

The Tap Location

Next, how to be as tricky as a gambler with the false shuffle.

Hand the pack to someone in the audience and let him pick out a card for himself.

Take back the deck and square it up neatly, but don't make a fuss about it. You're supposed to be sure it's squared; the audience isn't supposed to notice you're doing it.

Hold the pack in dealing position in your left hand. Have the chooser of the card thrust it in at the front. Don't let him push it more than three-quarters of the way in. (*Fig. 22a*).

If you forget to be gentle now, you may as well start over: clutch the pack and the trick won't work.

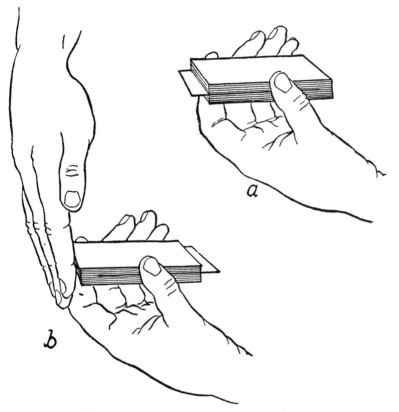

Fig. 22. **(a) Ready for the tap location; (b) The tap**

In fact, you had better change the hold of your left hand. Put your finger tips on the right-hand edge of the pack, and your thumb tip on the left-hand edge. You should be sufficiently ac- customed to handling cards so that you can make this change of position without fiddling.

You are holding the pack squared up, but with the chosen card sticking out perhaps an inch at the front.

Tap the front edge of the card with your right finger tips, driving it back into the pack. Better give several taps.

The last tap is a little stronger than the rest.

Unless you're freezing the cards in a grip of steel, the chosen card will go all the way through and stick out a fraction of an inch at the back. (*Fig.* 22b).

You may find that the card twists or sticks. The cure for that is, first, to tap at the exact middle of the front end, and straight back; second, not to give your final hard tap until the card is almost flush in front.

Now look what you've done!

You have the chosen card beautifully in-jogged.

Two quick overhand shuffles will bring it to the top. Or break above the in-jog, and one riffle shuffle will do the business.

Of course you realize that by using your head a very little you can just as easily bring the card to the bottom, where you can see it. With an overhand shuffle, in fact, it goes to the bottom before it goes to the top.

But if you only want to learn what the card is, you have a quicker way.

The Glimpse

Hold the pack in your left hand. Start off in dealing position, but then stretch your thumb as far to the right as you can. This will draw your fingers back under the pack a little, and collapse the rectangle made by the end of the pack into a parallelogram leaning toward your right.

Stretch out your arm to someone, and ask him to lift up a corner of the pack enough so that he can get a peek at one card. Make sure he knows there's just one card to a customer.

The only way he can do this is by pulling up the upper right-hand corner (from your point of view).

If you hold your thumb firm, the cards will bend crosswise, opening a break at the front, and staying closed at the back.

That's what you don't want. (*Fig.* 23a).

The moment he picks up the corner, relax your left hand. Instead of bending, the upper part of the deck will tilt up side-wise, leaving a break all along the right edge. The left edge stays closed. (*Fig.* 23b).

As he looks at his card, bend your little finger.

By crooking your little finger you have accomplished a card sleight, and a very slick one, too.

When the man lets go, press down on the deck with your thumb. The front end squares up as if it had never been disturbed.

But the fleshy tip of your little finger keeps the rear end of the pack wedged open below the card the man looked at. (*Fig.* 23c). Card workers call this "holding a little-finger break." It doesn't show from the front, it's the most natural motion in the world, and you can go from a little-finger break to half a dozen different finishes.

This time I said we were going to finish by seeing the chosen card.

You remember how a moment ago you slanted the pack to the right? Now you want to reverse the motion, and make the parallelogram slant to your left.

Swing your thumb away from you, along the left edge of the cards. Bend all your fingers toward the left, crowding the top half of the pack over against the ball of your thumb. (*Fig.* 23d).

The result of this motion, combined with the little-finger break, is that the top half (with the chosen card at the bottom of it) juts to the left of the bottom half, forming a step.

Turn your wrist, bringing the back of your left hand upward.

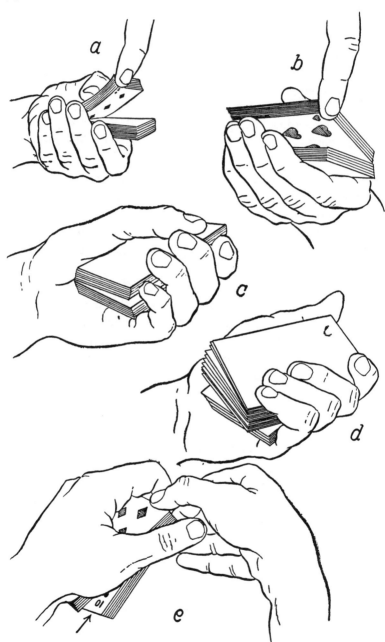

Fig. 23. (a) Wrong! (b) The right way; (c) Little-finger break;
(d) Crowding over for the glimpse; (e) The glimpse

If you glance down, you can just see the index of the chosen card sticking past the bulge of your thumb. (*Fig* 23e). That is why magicians call this move in its various forms "the glimpse."

You have the stages of the move clear in your head—offering the pack, break, glimpse. But if you divide it into separate parts like that, you will be detected.

After you get the break, start crowding the top half of the pack and turning your wrist simultaneously. It must be just one smooth motion.

And as you are taking the glimpse, come forward with your right hand. Grab the pack by the far end, right thumb on the face, fingers on the back; draw it forward through your left hand, squaring the cards and closing the telltale step.

Your right hand follows straight through, handing the pack (now face down by the simple holding out of your arm) to someone for shuffling.

I have taken a long time describing this because I want you to do it right. If you are smooth, easy, and casual, you can fool magicians with this form of the glimpse. The different moves must blend into one simple process: somebody peeps at a card, you square the pack, then immediately hand the cards out for a a good shuffle.

Don't be furtive and guilty about your stolen glimpse of the corner index. Your eyes would go to the pack anyway as you reach for it with your right hand.

The whole process looks (and is) so simple that you should do it rather faster than most tricks. Give the man plenty of time to see and remember his card; but from then on, zip!

The Spelling Master

Here is a superb trick that you can do with nothing but the glimpse.

Hand the pack out to be well shuffled.

You will have to use your judgment, and learn by experience how often to let the audience shuffle the cards. Some magicians are always doing it; others never do it at all.

I think too little is better than too much: constant shuffling, often by bunglers, slows up the show badly. Besides, you just make work for yourself. Half the time people wouldn't even think about shuffling if you didn't remind them.

But in this trick you want them to shuffle early and often. For one thing, the effect might be done by arranging the cards. (In fact, it is.) More important, all the shuffling is likely to make them forget that you ever handled the deck; and that turns a mere trick into a sensation.

So have them shuffle the pack.

Take it back just long enough to let someone peep at a card.

Then have them shuffle again.

Take the pack again, long enough to show people that you haven't stolen their card away—run through the deck face up, but warn them not to sing out or change expression until after you have gone well past their card.

Then hand the pack to the man who looked at the card. Stand well away from him, so that everyone can see you don't monkey with the deck.

Ask him what his card was.

When he tells you, ask him to spell out the words, including the "of"—for instance, N-I-N-E-O-F-S-P-A-D-E-S.

Have him turn over the card that stands for the last "S."

Apparently his card knows enough to come when it's called.

Since you know we are using the glimpse, I needn't tell you anything more about the trick up to the second time the cards are shuffled.

At that point you know what card the man chose, but you don't know where it is, any more than he does.

Hence your eagerness to be fair and aboveboard. Take the pack in dealing position in your left hand, face up. Give your little yarn about showing that the card was truly shuffled into the pack. Emphasize that you won't watch the man's face, and he is to let you go right on past his card.

Fan the cards into your right hand at a steady, moderate speed.

When you see the card that you originally stole a glimpse of, start spelling in your mind. If the card was the nine of spades, count the nine of spades itself as N, and spell straight along through to the end. (*Fig.* 24).

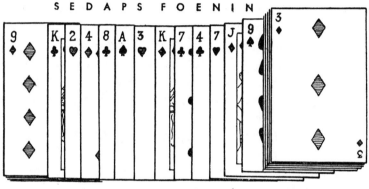

Fig. 24.   Setting up the Spelling Master

When you come to the final S, stop and look up.

Ask the man if his card is still in there.

As you speak, separate your hands. Carry away all the cards including the final "S" in your right hand. Keep the rest in your left.

When the man says yes, bring your hands together again. But put the left-hand bunch in front of the others.

The deck is now arranged ("set up") to spell out the chosen card.

Make the finish as impressive as you can.

There are many ways of doing the Spelling Master (the magician's familiar name for the trick you have just learned), but none simpler and few better than this. Later on, I shall teach you the best way of them all, probably the best chosen-card trick in existence. In it your helper spells out successfully the name of a card he has only chosen in his head, without even touching the pack.

We still have three more ways of finding a chosen card in this lesson. Two are mechanical; the last is pure sleight-of-hand.

The Stripper Deck

The first mechanical method is easy and ingenious, but getting to be rather well known. You are too likely to bump into someone who owns or has seen a pack like yours.

This kind of deck is the last word in the one-way principle. If you want to buy it at a magic shop, ask for a pack of "strippers." The back pattern is not one-way, and you can hardly tell there is anything wrong except by feel.

Strippers are trimmed to a taper, so that the whole pack is a tiny fraction narrower at one end than at the other.

You see what that does. If one card is turned end for end, you can strip it out by running your thumb and finger along the opposite long edges of the pack.

When several cards are reversed, you can lay the deck on the table, and put your right thumb and second finger on the long sides near the corners at the right end, your left thumb and finger in the same position at the left end. Part your hands as if pulling the halves of the pack apart for a fancy cut. The reversed cards strip right out, and if there are more than a very few, it does look quite like a real cut.

You can do various fancy flourishes, like separating the red cards from the black ones with one motion, as well as find any card that a spectator draws and puts back reversed. (You handle the deck just as you did with one-way backs.)

Strippers are foolproof in action, quick and easy to use. If you study them intelligently and learn the best ways of using them, you can make quite a reputation as a card worker with just that one secret.

On the other hand, as I say, a lot of people have seen strippers, or at least heard of them. Worse, you have to use your own pack.

"Whose cards are those, anyway?" is usually the first question people ask when you do a good trick. They are much more surprised if the deck is borrowed than if you bring it.

Furthermore, any meddlesome onlooker fooling around with your strippers may easily happen on the secret by accident.

He is much less likely to do that if your mechanical pack consists of just one card.

You may not see what good one card will do you, unless you always force it.

But stop and think for a minute.

Suppose you can always cut to one particular card by feel. That would mean that you could always find any card which was next above or below this one. Or suppose you have a dozen cards set up beforehand on top of the pack. With your mechanical card on the bottom, no matter how often the deck is cut, you can always bring your set-up back to the top.

"Mechanical" may seem a fancy name for the card you can always find. There are three main styles, all perfectly simple.

The Long Card

One is a long card. This means that the rest of the deck has a thirty-second of an inch trimmed off one end. Whenever you square the pack, and riffle with your right thumb, the long card juts out. It's not conspicuous, but you can feel it easily.

Shortening a deck to leave one long card is quite a chore unless you buy the outfit ready-made, or call on a printer who has a mechanical paper cutter. And like strippers, the long card may attract attention if anyone else handles the pack.

The Double Card

The double card is another form of mechanical locator. You need a deck with a white border around the back. Take one of the extra cards, trim off the border, and glue or rubber-cement the borderless card very carefully in place on the back of another card. Smooth it on thoroughly, and let it dry for some time.

When you riffle a deck with a double card in it, the vacant space formed by the extra thickness on the back will allow you to stop *bang* at the double card.

This kind of locator may be noticed too, but at least you don't have to work over the whole pack with a razor blade.

The Short Card

The last form of mechanical locator is probably the best, and certainly the simplest.

Instead of shortening the deck, you trim down one short card.

You may not think you can find this by riffling with your thumb; but just square up the cards neatly and try.

There's an extra slap as the short card goes by. You can always stop there on the first or second riffle. Yet no suspicious edges stick out of the pack, and no one handling the short card by itself will see anything wrong with it.

You can put the short card next to a chosen card in lots of ways.

Riffle with your right fingers instead of your thumb, stop when you hit the short card, and let your victim stick his card back in the pack there.

Have the short card on the bottom, take back the chosen card on top of the pack, draw out the under half, drop it on top. And so on.

Your short card will often do the work of an in-jog. You can work the Spelling Master without the glimpse. You can even force the short card itself after the fashion of the slip or the knife force, if you time the riffle just right, so that the pencil starts forward exactly as the short card snaps.

In fact, just about anything you can do by keeping track of one card you can do with a short card. There was a pre-Hitler German magician named Leopold Figner who built up a great reputation as a card performer and writer almost entirely by combining ingenious prearrangements and a mechanical locator. He used a long card, but I still think that, on the whole, the short card is better.

The Pass, or Shift

Finally, I promised you a sleight-of-hand method for finding a card.

This is really *the* sleight-of-hand method. It occurs, or can occur, in at least three card tricks out of four. There are ways of doing without it much of the time, but if you decide to learn it you need never be afraid of failing in a card trick. You can always wiggle out somehow with this sleight.

Magicians call it the pass or the shift. What it does is to shift the top half of the pack to the bottom. Obviously, that will bring a particular card from the middle to the top or bottom, or from the top to the middle (in case you're doing the old-fashioned fan force, for instance).

I know at least a dozen different ways to make the pass, some with one hand, some with both. Oddly enough, the oldest one of them all is still much the best.

A one-handed pass looks very tricky, and your skill may amaze people; but the one-handed pass is no good because it can be seen. All it will really do is impress on people how very hard magic must be to learn.

The two-handed pass shouldn't impress them at all; they must never see it.

Hold the pack in good old dealing position in your left hand. Actually, your fingers should be curled further over the top than they would in dealing; and you had better curl your forefinger around the far end, not the side of the pack.

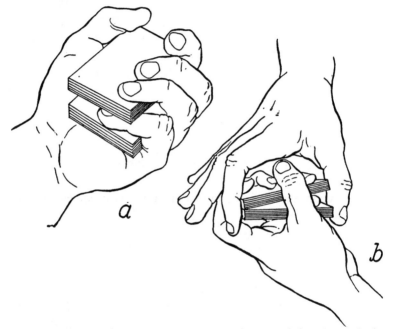

Fig. 25. **(a) Left hand ready for the shift; (b) Both hands ready for the shift**

Open a break with your right hand at the near end, and stick your left little finger in clear up to the second joint. (*Fig.* 25a).

That's the starting position for the two-handed pass; it should be as comfortable to you as signing your name.

Come up with your right hand, and put your forefinger at about the middle of the far end of the deck, your thumb opposite this at the near end.

With your *right* thumb and forefinger, take hold of the *lower* half—all the cards below your *left little finger*. (*Fig.* 25b).

That is the last movement your right hand should make from beginning to end. Your left hand does it all.

Straighten the fingers (not the thumb) of your left hand. (*Fig.* 26a).

That stands the upper half on its right edge. The left front corner comes up against the root of the little finger of your right hand.

Pull your whole left hand down, keeping your left thumb crooked.

This tilts the lower half up on its left edge. (*Fig.* 26b).

At this point, remember: don't lift with your right hand. Pull down with your left.

Now close the fingers of your left hand.

That drops the original upper half into your left palm. (*Fig.* 26c).

Raise your left hand enough to bring the two halves back together.

The pass is finished.

Run through it again, very slowly. The two halves must clear each other without brushing. Making the pass is quite easy after two or three attempts if you just do it anyhow; but that's no good. *There must be no noise.*

Are you getting the feel of it? Your right hand is just a pivot and a false front. Your left hand opens, drops, closes. Your left thumb is the hook that tips the lower half so that the upper half can clear it.

Don't grab too tight. Slow and gentle does it.

Other don'ts when you are first learning the shift:

Don't let your left forefinger stick out straight. It can be seen all over the room. (*Fig.* 27).

Don't use your right *second* finger as the front pivot unless you have tiny hands. The forefinger gives better cover.

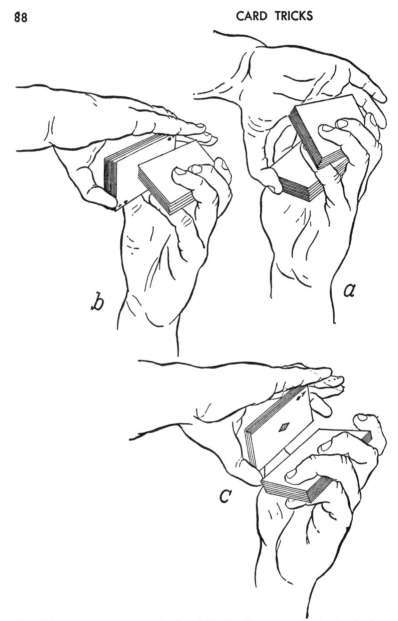

Fig. 26.   (a) First motion in the shift; (b) The top half clears the bot
tom half; (c) The top half has gone down

Don't bend your right second finger to help tilt the lower half. Let your left hand do all the work. (*Fig. 27* again).

Don't duck your hands as you make the shift. Remember, anything that moves attracts attention.

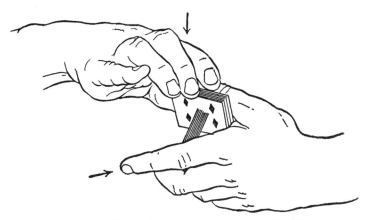

Fig. 27.   **Wrong! Never make the pass like this**

Don't close your eyes.

And, for goodness' sake, don't look at your hands.

You may think I'm very full of *don'ts* with very few *do's*.

I have a reason. The shift is like a spy service—necessary, but never mentioned. It's good for nothing if people even know it exists. There is no graceful way to do the shift—only an inconspicuous way. Anything that shows is a *don't*.

You can learn the shift well enough to use it with one long evening's careful practice. But to learn it so that you can depend on it and be comfortable with it may take a month or more of your spare time.

The pass comes about as close to the common idea of conjuring as any sleight I shall give you—a tricky movement that you practise for years, and perform faster than the eye can follow.

I told you to try the pass slowly. As a matter of fact, it's much **more** important to make no noise than to be fast. But since you're going to do the pass so cleanly that it won't show at all anyhow, the faster you learn to get through with it, the better. If you have a craze for speed, here's your chance. Just so you don't buy speed with noise. And don't be in such a hurry that you freeze the cards.

To cover the shift you'll have to use your wits somewhat. Not many magicians do the pass so perfectly as I hope you will; and, meanwhile, you must somehow hide it.

Cover provided by a large motion, such as sweeping your arms up and down, or pointing with both hands together, is worse than none. What you want is to make people look away from your hands.

You can simply watch their eyes, and make the pass when they aren't looking—a much easier method than you might think.

Or, you can stare somebody straight in the eye and ask him a question.

Speaking always draws people's eyes to your face.

Don't ever forget that. It will save your bacon time and again in every show you do. If they just won't look away, talk to 'em.

Well, I've had you working for weeks on the two-handed pass. The only thing I haven't done is convince you what it's good for. So here's one trick that consists wholly of making the shift four times.

The Red and Black Aces

Give somebody the pack, and tell him to pick out the four aces. If he finds more than four, he can keep the extras for his own use; you don't want them.

Take the pack back, leaving him with all the aces.

Now ask him to put an ace on the bottom of the pack. If it's a red ace, have him next put the other red one on top of the pack. In this trick suits don't matter, only colors.

Show the pack around with the top ace fanned out a little and the bottom ace in view. You want Slow Joe in the back to realize that you have the red (or black) aces on the top and bottom, and no fooling.

Take the pack in dealing position in your left hand, and lift off the top half with your right, fingers in front and thumb at the back end.

Have the other two aces, together, put on the lower half. Fan them out a little so that the corner indexes will show, and put the top half back in place.

You are now able to hold up the pack with your left hand in a crude fan, reminding Slow Joe in the back of the room, at one glance, that the red aces, say, are on the top and bottom, and the black ones together in the middle.

Close up your fan—but not in too much of a hurry.

First get your left little finger in between the middle two aces.

Ask people if they remember which color of aces was on the top and bottom. And as you ask them, make the two-handed pass.

When they tell you, warn them that they'll have to remember better than that, or the trick won't be any good.

Turn over the pack, and fan it out to show that they've got the situation backward. Red is in the middle, black on the ends.

Be patient about it, though. Give them another chance. Have your man pull out all the aces again.

Have him return the aces of one color to the top and bottom.

While he's thinking about the two aces that he still holds, make the pass.

With your right hand, quietly pick up the ace from the top of the lower half, and add it to the bottom of the upper half. (*Fig. 28*).

Hold out the lower half in your left hand; take his remaining two aces on top.

Put your hands together, drop the extra ace from the upper half back on the lower half, and stick your left little finger between the halves.

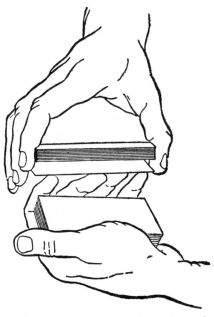

Fig. 28.   Picking the ace off the lower half

Ask them if they remember *this* time which color of aces was which.

As they look at your face, make the shift again.

They may be sure, or then again, after what has happened, they may not. Anyway, turn up the top ace, and show that it hasn't moved. Put it back on the pack. Get your left little finger in the middle again. Take hold of the pack with your right hand, ready for the pass.

Then turn your hands over to show the other ace in its proper position on the bottom of the pack.

A few lines back I told you that a big movement to cover the shift was worse than no cover. Well, here's the one exception. As you turn your hands back over, you can make the pass with almost no chance of being seen.

Ask people just once more if they remember where the aces

are. Then tell them you guess it's no use, you'll have to go on to some other trick.

Fan the pack face up: the four aces are together in the middle.

LESSON 7. Escapes

What Seems to Happen: Somebody ties your hands behind you with a piece of clothesline. Then you climb into a large bag with a drawstring at the top, which is pulled tight and knotted. You get out in about five seconds, with your hands still tied tight behind you.

Second, you are tied to a chair with many turns of heavy rope. You always get out in less time than it takes to tie you.

What You Need: About three feet of clothesline or sash cord. If it is new and stiff, soak it in water to soften it up. The ends should be finished off either in small, hard knots or by "whipping" (winding with thin cord). A big sack of stout cloth, such as canvas, large enough for you to get into, with the mouth turned in and sewn down to hold a drawstring. The drawstring may be clothesline, tape, or any stout line. The sewing of the hem that holds in the drawstring must be interrupted at one point for about an inch and a half.

For the second, about forty feet of stout rope. A solid chair. A three-fold screen, or, if you prefer, a large blanket.

Where to Learn More: Burling Hull, *Thirty-Three Rope Ties and Chain Releases; Gilbert's Knots and Splices;* Carrington, *The Boy's Book of Magic*

Probably the most famous, and certainly the best advertised, magician of all time was not even a magician, but an escape artist—Harry Houdini. As a result, everyone now thinks of escape tricks as the most sensational branch of magic.

To specialize in escapes is difficult, often strenuous, and some-

times dangerous. But the three tricks that follow will not give
you much trouble, though they look quite like muscular feats.

The Kellar Tie

The first one is known to all magicians as the Kellar Tie. You
can use it as a trick by itself, or as a frill to make the sack escape
seem harder.

Bring on your three-foot length of clothesline. You can toss it
to someone and ask him to give it a good tug.

The old books on magic would all say solemnly at this point,
"The rope may be handed to the audience for thorough examination, proving it to be quite unprepared in any way."

The trouble with this was that new magicians would often try
to talk like that, which sounded very silly from a twelve-year-old
boy. Also, it simply called attention to the other unfortunate
articles that could *not* be handed out for thorough examination.

Handing things out for examination is like having people
shuffle the cards—a good idea sometimes, if you don't make a
great fuss over it, but better done too seldom than too often.

Anyway, you have tossed out your rope. Pick as a target the
person you would like to have tie you up. For this trick you can
take someone who looks husky and reliable—say a sportsman
who knows a square knot from a granny. There isn't going to be
anything wrong with the knots, so you might as well make it look
good.

In fact, it's not a bad idea to choose *two* burly specimens,
rather than one. Let each take an end of the rope and pull.

That should make it obvious, without your having to say so,
that the rope won't stretch or come apart.

Come down front to stage center (if you're working on a
stage), and stand up straight at attention.

Call for the two volunteers to bring the rope with them. Have
one stand on your right, the other on your left.

Hold your right arm out to the front, shoulder high, and shut your fist.

Have the man on your right take the rope by the middle, and hang it over your right wrist. Swing your arm slowly from side to side, once, so that people can see.

Then have the man make a simple overhand knot, and draw it snug around your wrist. Both ends of the rope still hang down equally.

Swing your arm from side to side again.

Now have the man on your left make a second plain overhand knot, or, in other words, the second half of a square knot.

Get your two helpers at opposite ends of the rope, and have them pull hard. It can't hurt your wrist now; it will just tighten the knot.

Put your right hand behind your back, with the front of your wrist outward; put your left hand behind your back, with the back of the wrist over the knot in the rope. You want one end of rope coming out over your left wrist, and one hanging down below.

Do a smart about-face. (If you've been in uniform, you probably know that this works much better when you pull your chin well in.)

Stand for a minute with your back to the audience before you let your two helpers block the view.

Then have them draw an overhand knot snug around your *left* wrist, and finish it off into a square knot. Let them tug at the free ends again. As far as they are concerned, that is the end of the Kellar Tie.

About-face again.

You are able to reach out with your left hand to pat one of your helpers on the back, and thank him for helping you.

You can spin right around, and your hands will be tied as tight as ever.

You can hook your arms around a pillar, or through the top rail of a chair, and your hands will still be tied tight.

The Sack Escape

But if you're going on with the sack escape, keep your two helpers, and don't do any tricks. Ask one man to bring the sack forward and open it out.

If you had talked a lot of long words about examining the rope, you would now be stuck, because the sack won't stand being gone over thoroughly. You can make some fun, though, by having one helper put the sack over the other's head. If they are friends, they may go in for a certain amount of horseplay.

Anyhow, they will soon discover that there are no holes in the sack for you to get out of.

Have the two men help you into the sack, gather the mouth of it up over your head, and pull the drawstring tight.

They can tie it in all the knots they please.

Finally, they are either to set up the screen in front of you, or throw the blanket over you.

It's much easier for you to work behind a screen than under a blanket, only you must make sure that people don't think you get backstage help from behind the screen.

The wind-up is simply that you walk around the screen (or toss off the blanket) with your hands still tied tight behind you, and the sack hung casually over your arm, also behind you.

The secret of the Kellar Tie is perfectly simple if you will go through it with the rope. There is just one motion of your right hand to learn. Get your right hand tied in the middle of the rope —no trick about that. When the two helpers are through tugging at the ends of the rope, you will find that by simply closing your right fingers you can take hold of it two or three inches from the knot.

Do that, and swing your right arm behind you. One end of the

rope will trail behind; the other you are holding with the tips of
your fingers.

When you put your left hand on top of the right, do it with a
rubbing motion toward the right. Keep your right fingers closed
all the time. (*Fig. 29.*) This is a little hard to make plain, but
look at the picture, and try it once or twice; you will find you
have a loop of slack pressed tight between the front of your right

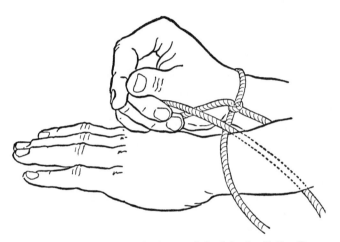

Fig. 29. **Picking up the loop of slack in the Kellar Tie**

wrist and the back of your left wrist, and also held firm by your
right second and third finger tips.

The other, free end of the rope hangs down below your wrists;
the one with the loop in it comes out over the top of your left
wrist, ready to be knotted.

If you let go of the slack with your right fingers, and instead
clamp them over your left wrist, you can hold your loop so tight
that almost no amount of pulling by the helpers will yank it out.

To release your left hand, all you have to do is pull it away.

Don't let go of the empty loop with your right hand altogether; the loop must be kept open to slide your left hand back in.

Of course you can tie yourself up tight again by merely pulling in the slack with your right fingers.

If the Kellar Tie is to be part of the sack escape, naturally you don't want any monkeyshines that show you can free your hands.

Stay tightly tied while your volunteers help you into the sack. You can even afford to totter about and fall against them in the process, to show how helpless you are. When they get the sack well up around your shoulders, you will have to release your hands. Another advantage of staggering and falling around is that your individual motions are harder for people to watch; and it distracts attention from the sack.

By this means, or some other, you have to get people looking away for perhaps ten seconds.

Although ten seconds is much longer than you would think, you may succeed in distracting attention for that long if you can think of something to talk to your helpers about. If you can't, then you must maneuver them between you and the audience; if they get in each other's way, so much the better.

What I am leading up to is that you must now do something simple but not altogether easy, and no one must be allowed to see it.

Without seeming to be untied at all, you must reach up through the break in the hem and pull down about two feet of drawstring.

Hang on to that slack, or you're really in the bag for the other team!

You can talk in muffled tones through the sack, telling your helpers to pull the drawstring up tight (that's why you have to hold on so grimly to your slack), and make a hard knot or two. Finally, they are to put the screen in front of you.

Make sure they have done that, and have gone back to their seats, before you let go the slack of the drawstring, open the mouth of the sack, and step out.

What you do with the sack may depend on what kind of knots your helpers tied.

If the knots are hard and complicated, you will simply have to tuck the slack back inside the bag, and loop the sack over your arm, with the mouth toward your body, before you tie your wrists up again in the Kellar Tie.

If they made only one simple knot, you can undo it, pull the drawstring tight, and knot it again without the telltale slack.

Tie your hands up, and come out in front of the screen.

Throw your chest out. Smile.

Finally, back up to a person in the audience (it needn't be your original helpers; give someone else a chance at the fun), and ask him to untie the knot around your left wrist.

Don't just take your left hand away, of course, or the loop of slack will show.

Instead, turn around to face front again, *then* bring your right hand out with both ends of rope dangling innocently from the wrist, and have still another person undo the last knot.

You can use the rope for a brief tug-of-war with your last helper.

Stand up straight. Smile. End of trick.

The Chair Tie

Our other escape, the chair tie, is neither so quick nor so neat as the Kellar Tie and sack escape; I wouldn't do the two one after the other.

Nevertheless, by the time you have shown the chair tie a few times, you can learn to make it into something big and startling. How big it is depends entirely on how good a salesman you are.

This effect is a real escape (as distinguished from a trick) because it is not so much a puzzle as a contest with the audience. Instead of the little one-act play that I have been talking about, in which puzzling things happen, you bring several people up on the stage, and defy them to do their worst. In a nice way, you invite them to spoil your show if they can.

That was what Houdini always did. He even backed up his
defiance of the public by offering $10,000 to anyone who could
defeat him.

This sort of thing, plus superb salesmanship on the stage,
made Houdini world famous. On the other hand, it never made
anyone love him. The crowds came to his show hoping to see
him fail. It was a pitched battle, like the circus wrestler who
takes on all comers.

You can give this kind of show, enjoy it, and be very successful. Only don't try to mix it in with regular magic. If you want
to use the chair tie as part of a conjuring program, you will
have to make it the final item. Otherwise, you get people into a
frame of mind that spoils their fun in such things as card tricks,
and doubles your difficulty in accomplishing the tricks, besides.
To repeat in a few words what I have been saying, salesmanship
in doing the chair tie consists of building up a conflict between
you and the audience—making it seem as if they had every advantage in crabbing the act, yet defeating them at last.

The chair tie works best with a large audience, for several
reasons. The first is that you want at least four or five men to
tie you up.

Ask them to look over the chair, sit in it, and generally make
sure it is strong, solid, and ordinary. This is one of the rare
times when you can afford to make a real point of having things
examined: it sharpens your challenge to the audience, and since
there is nothing wrong with any of the properties, you can't lose.

Your long rope should be lying handy, coiled up. Toss it to
your helpers, and ask them to test it. I say toss, and I mean toss.

You want everyone to realize that you aren't using a trick
rope; and, at the same time, you don't, if you can help it, want
them to get the rope coiled again before they start tying you.

Plant your chair in the center of the stage. Sit down with your
hands folded in your lap.

Now ask your helpers to tie you to the chair, tight.

Don't pick one man as the union representative, and talk to him; talk to them all at once.

There are two reasons why you want so many people on the stage: first, you seem to be badly outnumbered; second, they will get in each other's way. This, in turn, has the double advantage that the tying-up takes longer and seems more thorough, and that actually several men do a much poorer job than one man could do alone.

The reason you prefer not to have the rope coiled up before they start is that forty feet of rope will also get in their way. Pulling the whole length through knot after knot will take forever.

Naturally you don't say so, but your ideal is to have them tie one end of the rope to your ankle or a leg of the chair, and then just wind the rest around and around your body. You can't hope for anything quite so helpful, but the whole procedure of the trick is calculated to wear your helpers down into doing as nearly this as possible.

For instance, the second advantage of a large audience is that it gets impatient sooner; it doesn't tend to join in the intimate little game of tying you in knots; it wants the fumbling volunteers on the stage to get through with it.

When you sit down, slouch just the tiniest bit toward the front of the chair—not enough to be conspicuous.

Don't resist anything that your helpers want you to do, such as put your feet against the front legs of the chair. But don't volunteer any help, either.

Keep your hands firmly folded in your lap, unless the helpers insist that you part them.

As they get started with the tying, you should slowly, gently, fill your lungs with all the air they will hold. Set the muscles of your arms and legs.

Although you have to become tense, you mustn't act tense

about getting that way. You want to make yourself as bulky as possible all over, but you mustn't let the process be noticed.

The only advice you should offer your helpers is, "Make sure it's good and tight." You can even repeat this; it is the one thing the audience must have impressed on its mind.

You can also pass approving remarks about anything they do that seems to make it harder for you—tying the last knot around a chair leg out of your reach, for example.

Finally, the time comes when the helpers stand back to admire their handiwork. Incidentally, once you have performed this escape a few times, it is good salesmanship to have someone clock first the helpers while they tie you, and then you while you escape. You can cheat a little by starting to work while they are still setting the screen around you; don't shout "Go!" until they have all started for their seats.

The actual getting out is generally quite simple, though there are no invariable rules for doing it. Sit back straight in the chair; push your arms forward and away from you; let out your breath. Unless they have tied your hands specially, you are practically free right there.

If they have tied them specially, you may have to wriggle your arms under some of the surrounding coils, and go at the knots on your wrists with your teeth.

You will have to apply your own ingenuity and your own agility each time you show this escape; but the way the helpers have to tie you is so clumsy and inefficient that they haven't two chances in a hundred of holding you.

As you get free of the last coil, you can shout, "Time!" and rush around the screen, dragging the chair and festoons of rope noisily after you.

The more bustle the better in an escape trick.

LESSON 8.   The Egg Bag

What Seems to Happen: You show a small cloth bag, empty, and turn it inside out. When you turn it back, someone reaches in and finds an egg. The egg disappears again, and finally reappears.

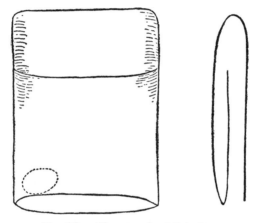

Fig. 30.   **The standard Egg Bag**

What You Need: A rectangular cloth bag about a foot deep and eight inches wide. Red or black flannel is a good material.

You can buy different sorts of egg bags at magic shops, or you can very easily get your wife or mother to make you one. In the latter case, you want a strip of cloth eight inches wide and almost three feet long. Fold down about ten inches of the cloth to form a pocket inside the bag, with its mouth toward the bottom. Stitch up the sides, run a line of stitching around the top to hide the fact that one side has a hem and the other a fold, and your egg bag is ready. (*Fig.* 30).

Two other ways of making the secret pocket are: to have it run all the way to the bottom, and sewn down half way across, leaving the mouth of the pocket half as wide as the bag (*Fig. 31*) ; or to have the lower two and a half inches of the bag made of coarse net. In this case, of course the pocket stops where the net begins, and it will be closed at the bottom perhaps two-thirds of the way across.

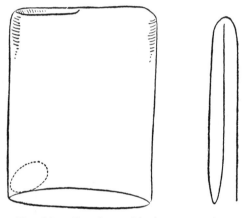

Fig. 31.   **Egg Bag with deeper pocket**

An egg. You can use a hard-boiled one, blow a fresh egg, or buy one of the imitation eggs sold at magic stores. To use a genuine fresh egg takes more confidence than I, at least, have got.

Where to Learn More: Hugard, *Modern Magic Manual;* Will Goldston, *Tricks of the Masters*

The egg bag is one of perhaps half a dozen magic tricks that are ageless, and may be called perfect. The trick is surprising, amusing, it looks simple, and furthermore it is simple. Yet, with just a little good management, you need never fear being found out. Magicians—especially comedy magicians—have made reputations with the egg bag for probably two hundred years.

So can you, with a little rehearsing.

I am going to give you the most usual modern comedy routine.

Once you learn that, and discover how to make people laugh at it, you can change it around to suit yourself.

There isn't even any law that says you must use an egg: you might use packages of fruit drops or a small bottle of cologne (to be given away afterward), and have a whole new trick.

For the present routine, though, put the egg in the secret pocket of the bag. Then stuff the bag, bottom up, into your coat pocket. Or you can have it lying around in a heap if it isn't where inquisitive youngsters might get at it.

Comes the time for the egg bag, grab the bottom of the bag in your left hand, so that the secret pocket (with egg) is turned toward you. Hold the bag up casually—not as if you were showing it off, but simply in a position where you can grab it.

Come up with your right hand, and take the near edge of the bag with your fingers inside and your thumb outside. You mustn't hunt around, but you must get hold of the egg through the cloth. It will rest in the curve of your fingers, while your second finger and thumb meet through the cloth. (*Fig. 32*).

Let go with your left hand, and slap the bag hard in your left palm four or five times to show there's nothing in it. (*Fig. 33*). Twist it up into a rope; let it go.

Then turn the bag inside out. Keep it bottom up, and, for Heaven's sake, keep the pocket side away from the audience.

You can hold the bag up by the two bottom corners. Give Slow Joe in the back time to realize it's inside out with nothing inside.

Turn it right side out again, and swing it carelessly (but not too hard, or the weight of the egg will make a bulge through the cloth) by a bottom corner in your left hand, while you get someone to help you.

When your helper comes up, turn the bag mouth upward, with the secret pocket towards you, the egg in the corner on your right. Hold the mouth open with three fingers of each hand inside, your thumbs outside, and your hands back to back.

This gives your right hand an inconspicuous hold on the egg, and also your hand covers the bulge that the egg makes.

Ask your helper to dip into the bag and see if he can find anything.

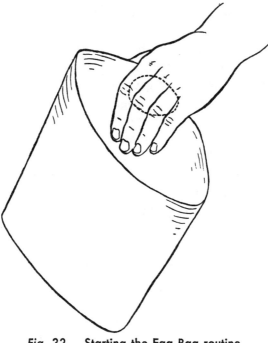

Fig. 32.   **Starting the Egg Bag routine**

No luck.

Have him try again.

No luck.

The third time never fails. Just before your helper dips, ease the egg down. It falls to the bottom of the bag, and he brings it out in triumph.

Incidentally, you will probably find it best to have him stand on your left. Then, when he puts his right hand into the grab bag, he has very little chance of catching the secret pocket with his finger tips; and with his knuckles he can't tell the difference.

Make your helper hold the egg up high. If you can do that sort of thing, ask him if he doesn't feel like cackling a little. Anything, so long as everyone knows he has found an egg in an empty bag.

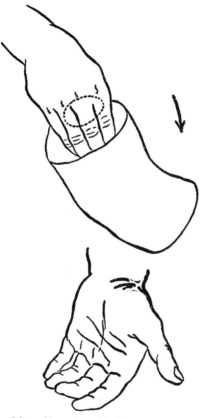

Fig. 33. Slapping the "empty" Egg Bag

Now comes what magicians call a "sucker gag." This means that some poor sucker thinks he has caught you cheating, but his pride bounces back in his face.

Anyone who is paying any attention at all sees you poke the egg into the bag, then sneak it out again and stuff it in your right trouser pocket. They are not much surprised, therefore, when you show the bag empty.

Unless your audience is altogether too well behaved for this trick anyway, some voice from the rear will yell, "It's in your pocket!"

That is your cue to turn your left coat pocket inside out.

Yells of, "The other pocket!"

Pull out your right coat pocket.

"No, your trouser pocket!"

Pull out your left trouser pocket.

Pandemonium. Shouts, whistles, and catcalls.

"Oh, *that* pocket. Why didn't you say so?"

Stand there, trying not to look too smug, until both the voice from the rear and Slow Joe in the back realize that all your pockets are empty.

"No, no," you say. "It's in the bag."

Fig. 34. "Exposing" the Egg Bag trick

Your helper dips in, and sure enough, so it is.

Now, in a fit of big-heartedness, you offer to show everyone how it's done. You hold up the egg, plunge it into the bag, and bring it out again, held in your palm by curling down your two middle fingers. Turn your palm toward the audience. (*Fig.* 34).

That, you explain, is how you made it disappear the first time : put it in and sneaked it out.

Then you put it into your pocket, sneaked it out the same way, and dropped it into the bag when nobody was looking.

Show each step as you explain it.

Perhaps I hardly need stop at this point to explain to *you* that when you first sneaked the egg out of the bag and into your pocket, you really tucked it into the secret pocket of the bag. I should warn you, though, that holding an empty hand as if it contained something the size of an egg wants practising. (*Figs.* 35a and b). It is very easy to forget and close your hand down to coin size. (*Fig.* 36).

Hold an egg in your fist, take a good look at it for size, and then try making that same size of fist with no egg.

That, of course, is what you do in "sneaking the egg into your pocket."

Your first explanation, with accompanying gestures, is perfectly straightforward (even if it isn't truthful).

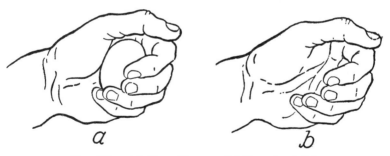

Fig. 35. **(a) Fist with egg; (b) Egg-sized fist**

Now you'll do the trick just once more so that the audience can be sure to understand it. Put the egg into the bag with a flourish, and slip it into the secret pocket. Bring your right hand out in an egg-sized fist, carry your hand half way to your trouser pocket, and then suddenly show it empty.

(Empty once; empty twice; empty three times—for Slow Joe in the back. Remember?)

Fig. 36.   Coin-sized fist

Beat the bag on your palm; slap it against your knee; turn it inside out, and then right side out again. Don't be in a hurry with all this, but don't leave the bag inside out and standing still for any length of time; after all, your helper is pretty close to you.

Have the helper try the lucky dip again.

Nothing there.

All this time, naturally, you have been holding the egg in your right hand through the cloth. Now let it fall to the bottom of the bag. Have your helper look up your sleeves. Still nothing.

Take up a stance with your feet a bit apart, a thumb in each top corner of the bag, and your fingers spread out.

Obviously, you point out, the only way to get the egg back into the bag is by sneaking it out of a pocket while nobody is looking.

In the first place, you hope everyone will be looking all the time. In the second place, will your helper please hold your wrists, and if he feels you trying to reach for a pocket, will he stop you?

You can squirm and strain toward your pockets for as long as you find it amuses people. Finally, you give up in disgust.

All right, so they have won.

But of course your helper looked in the bag, didn't he? Certainly.

No egg?

Absolutely not.

Well, maybe he didn't look far enough. And you reach in (hold your hand up, palm to the audience, first), and there's the egg.

For this particular routine, you can see that a plain bag is better than one with a net bottom. In fact, a net-bottomed bag takes a certain amount of practice to handle convincingly.

The bag with the pocket sewed half way across at the bottom is also handled a little differently. You can make the egg appear by tilting the bag, instead of just dropping the egg.

As I said before, this is just a sample comedy routine with the egg bag. Another, and one of the oldest, is to produce a succession of eggs.

A hundred years ago, magicians used an egg bag nearly twice the size of the modern kind, with a series of elastic pockets inside the secret pocket, so that you could actually produce a dozen eggs, one after another.

But by applying a little skill, you can get the same result with your modern bag and one or two eggs. I think you will come to agree with me that the lazy man's way is to practise a sleight instead of lugging equipment. Besides, a bag big enough to hide a dozen eggs behind a false side is not very neat or convincing.

Palming an Egg

The sleight is very simple, and one that you will always find useful; but I can't claim that it is easy to do perfectly after three or four attempts. You will have to watch yourself in a mirror, and be very critical of your own efforts.

The sleight is palming the egg. I suggest that you start learning with a golf ball, or some rubber ball a little smaller. Once

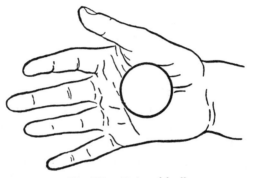

Fig. 37.   **Palmed ball**

you've learned to palm that, the egg will come easily enough; but at first, many eggs are rather big to be palmed in a small hand.

Look at the palm of your hand. There is a large bulging cushion at the base of your thumb. There is a much smaller bulging cushion running from the base of your little finger down to the heel of your hand.

What you want to do is to wedge the ball between those cushions. Once you find just the right spot, you can hold any small ball or anything having an edge, like a coin, almost without closing your hand at all. (*Fig.* 37).

In fact, some new magicians are so proud of being able to palm things that they spread their fingers out like a starfish.

I trust that you, however, will remember that you are trying to hide something, not to show how skilfully you can hold it.

All I can do is leave you alone with the ball until you find the right spot in your own hand. You will know when you get it, simply because the ball won't fall out if you turn your hand over.

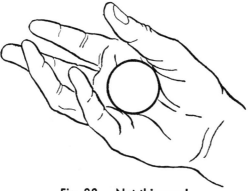

Fig. 38.   **Not this way!**

Here are three important don'ts. (*Fig.* 38).

1. Don't try to pulverize the ball. All you want is barely enough grip to hold it.

2. Don't swing your thumb over toward the little finger, as if to hold the ball with the thumb itself. The cushion at the base of the thumb does the work; try to squeeze it sideways, not at right angles to your palm.

3. In the same way, don't cramp your little finger inward as if you had arthritis. When you learn the right place and the right sideways movement of the thumb muscle, you should be able to hold a ball palmed while you pick up a teacup and crook your little finger.

Get the ball palmed in the right spot, with the right gentle muscle grip. Try handling things while you hold the ball palmed.

Try it some more. Your muscles have a memory as well as your head.

When your hands remember where the ball should go, you may learn to put it there with one motion.

Hold it with your fingers on one side and your thumb on the other. Then swing your thumb out of the way and roll the ball down into the palming spot. (*Fig.* 39). Take the muscle grip, and there you are.

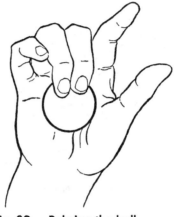

Fig. 39.   Palming the ball

With an egg, instead of rolling it you simply slide the big end into place by pushing on the small end with your fingers.

Try this simple motion of palming again and again. Don't be in a hurry, or you will tighten up. One smooth, gentle motion to the exact spot is what you should try for. You will soon learn to do it quite as fast as you will ever need to.

Now that you have learned to palm an egg in your right hand, try it with your left.

I think that you will be surprised at how much easier the skull practice on your right will have made the hand practice on your left. In any case, you aren't a good magician until you can palm equally well with both hands.

So now you can palm an egg. You're ready to put it in the bag again.

Egg Production Routine

Start out with the egg in the secret pocket, and the bag
"empty."

You go through the business of beating the bag and turning
it inside out. Then (when it is right side out again) hold it up
daintily by your finger tips. Let it be quite evident that your
hands are empty.

If you like, you can hold the bag in your teeth while you pull
up your sleeves a little.

Here you have to do some acting, because you must make
people realize that the trick is about to happen. I should say that
the best way was to give an expectant look down at the bag, then
up at the audience, then down at the bag again.

Hold it. (Remember Slow Joe in the back.)

Then an expression of surprise or satisfaction, or both.

Hold that.

Then lift your right hand up high, empty palm toward the
people, and swoop down into the bag.

Out comes the egg. Hold it up.

Broad smile, or startled look. Perhaps a little applause.

Then put the egg between your lips.

Make the most of your silly appearance with this ornament.
Generally, the more solemn you are, the more ludicrous you look.

It is a good idea to keep an eye on one particular onlooker—
not the one who laughs loudest. When you think he has had
nearly enough of your clowning, force the egg into your mouth,
and swallow it—people think.

Really, you put your right hand over the egg to push it in,
only instead you push out with your tongue, and palm the egg.

Puff out one cheek as you take your right hand away.

As you lower your right hand toward the bag, roll the egg
from the palming position into the curl of your middle fingers.

Take the bag in your right hand with your fingers (and the egg) inside.

Bring up your left hand, and poke the puffed-out cheek with a finger.

Puff out the other cheek, as if the egg had simply changed sides.

Chase the "egg" from side to side once or twice, and finally pinch in both cheeks between your left thumb and second finger.

That does it: down goes the egg with much gulping.

Meanwhile, with everyone's eyes on your face and left hand, you can slyly drop the egg to the bottom of the bag.

Both hands are empty as you hold up the bag again, ready for another dip with your right hand.

Well, well. Another egg.

Put it in your mouth, but don't stop for the low comedy. Palm the egg right out again.

Twice is enough to show your hands empty for the moment. Swallow the "egg" with one big gulp, pause a minute, and then reach straight into the bag with your right hand. Bring out the palmed egg.

That makes three eggs from the bag.

You will have to decide by experiment how long you can profitably keep this up. My guess is that six times will be a great plenty.

You needn't swallow all the eggs. If you have a dish or box (such as an ordinary grocer's carton for a dozen eggs), you can put your crop in that.

This in turn gives you two possible effects. You can wind up with the proper number of eggs, or you can wind up with the box empty.

If you're really going to produce the eggs, you have to put them in the box (or deep bowl) beforehand. You needn't bother to show it empty, even if you could, because there's no reason to: people don't know what the box is for.

If all the eggs are to disappear, simply don't fill the box first.

Each time you produce an egg, you carry your right hand out of sight behind the lid of the box (or down into the bowl). There you palm the egg, and bring it back into action.

You can reverse the deception once or twice. The first two times people have seen your right hand empty before you dipped. All three times they have seen the egg beyond any doubt.

So, the fourth or fifth time, you may simply bring up an egg-sized empty fist, leaving the egg in the secret pocket. Go through the motion of putting the egg in the box, carefully but very casually. Overacting at this point will ruin you.

You are then set to show the bag empty (which you haven't done for some time) before you produce another egg.

I said you could cut the clowning after you swallowed the first egg. This is because any simple act repeated more than three times has a tendency by itself to make people laugh. Just producing half a dozen eggs is all the comedy routine you need.

But in this trick, as always in any kind of entertainment, you must stop while they still want more.

LESSON 9.   Mind Reading

What Seems to Happen: People write questions, names, and this and that, on slips of paper. You read them without seeing them.

Working with a partner, you go among the audience, looking at things that people show you. Your partner, blindfolded, tells what the things are.

What You Need: A small pad of scratch paper, soft pencils. Matches and a good-sized ash tray. A large white handkerchief for a blindfold. Envelopes. A small sponge. Clear alcohol.

Where to Learn More: Theodore Annemann, *Practical Mental Effects;* Ottokar Fischer, *Illustrated Magic*

David Devant, the great English magician, once wrote a good little book called *Magic Made Easy*. In it is a chapter called, "What a Conjurer Can Do."

Devant breaks down all magic into seven classes. The seventh is "apparent mental phenomena."

Almost all magicians do at least one or two mind-reading tricks. Some of the best effects are done with cards and belong in another lesson. Here, I shall simply teach you several secrets for producing what is (so far as the audience goes) one and the same effect.

Then I am going to explain the work of stage mind-reading teams. I can't teach you how to do it, because you and your partner can only teach it to yourselves. But at least you will know how to go about it.

Reading folded, sealed, or wadded messages can be done single-handed or by a team. This is often used by fake spirit mediums, which, I suppose, is why magicians call these tricks "tests"—the pellet test, the billet test, the envelope test.

The Billet Test

The billet test is the easiest one to do. In it people in the audience write their questions (or the test names, words, or numbers, depending on the particular effect), on slips of paper from your pad. Then they fold the writing inside.

You collect the folded "billets," usually in a hat.

If you are working alone, you pick one from the hat, hold it to your forehead, and read off what is inside it. If people write questions, you read them and invent some kind of answer.

Unless you are quick-witted and clever—and when you think about whether you are clever, try not to kid yourself—I suggest you leave questions alone. Answering questions diverts people's attention from your trick to your skill at fortune telling; and you have to be good—or you'll be terrible.

If you are working with a partner, you collect the billets and hand her (or him) one at a time.

The "All-Alike" Gag

The simplest billet test is done by making your own forcing pack.

First, write something on a piece of paper, fold it, and have someone keep it.

Instead of passing out the paper for people to write on, you ask them to call out names.

For instance, ask for names of famous authors. A dozen different people will call out names, which you write down, one name to a slip. Fold each slip and drop it in the hat. When you have enough names, shake up the lot thoroughly.

Now hand out the hat. Have some innocent bystander ("a person without sense enough to get out of the way," as Mark Twain said) draw one billet.

Retrieve the others, and throw them into the fire, if there is a fire; otherwise, throw them away, but not where people can get at them.

Have the innocent bystander open and read out the billet he drew.

Have the custodian of the paper you originally wrote open and read off that.

Surprise, surprise. You knew it all the time: the same name on both slips.

To do the trick in this particular form you have to choose some class of people or things in which you can be quite sure that a particular name will be mentioned at least once.

If you take authors, you can count on Shakespeare or the author of any momentary best-seller. If political figures, the President.

Whatever name you decide on, write it down as the first step in the trick.

When you know that you will be performing at a given time and place, you can dress the effect up sensationally by sending a registered letter to yourself the day before at the address where you are to be. Sealed inside is the slip of paper with the name on it. People can even see where the impression of the postmark has come through the envelope. I owe this dodge to Ben Abramson, the eminent bookseller.

However you arrange that part, you stand up and ask for people to call out names.

Say you have decided on Mark Twain as the name you will force. Somebody calls, "John Milton."

You look him straight in the eye, repeat "Milton," and write "Mark Twain."

Keep this up until somebody does say Mark Twain. Conceivably, you may have to steer people in your direction—"Nothing but living authors today?," or "No Americans?," or whatever it may be.

If anybody gives you a name in the least out of the ordinary (such as Nietzsche), be sure you ask how to spell it, and make a great fuss about getting it right—all the time strenuously writing "Mark Twain."

In the end, you have ten or twenty folded slips in the hat, but they all say Mark Twain.

Have someone shake up the hat thoroughly, and draw one slip.

Then take the hat back, and burn all the rest of the slips, or throw them away offstage.

Now is your chance to put on an air of fierce concentration, nervous energy, and mystery.

Try to exaggerate in people's minds everything that you've done. Remind them that you have written down twenty different names. (Probably it was only fifteen, but twenty sounds better.) Before you even started, you knew what was going to happen; you gave the folded slip (or the registered letter) to be held by a reliable person. And so on and so on.

When you feel you have been as impressive as you can without growing tiresome (this is another good chance for you to judge by the expression of one of the less excitable spectators), have the man who drew the billet from the hat unfold it and read it out loud.

Take care that you are well away from the man who has your original slip when he opens and reads that.

So much for the easiest way of doing the billet trick.

The "One-Ahead" Gag

The next way depends on the "one-ahead" principle, which is probably used more than any other in message reading.

The effect is that a lot of different people write their own messages, fold them, and drop them in the hat. You pick the papers out at random, one at a time, read each message, and then get the person who wrote a certain message to acknowledge it as his.

The basic trick is simply this: you must find out what one message says before you start.

The easiest way, but one that spoils other people's pleasure in a mind-reading trick if they discover it, is to have a "plant" in the audience who will write down something you have told him. He can drop his question in last, on the top of the heap; or fold it in thirds instead of quarters; or mark it inconspicuously.

A more clean-cut way, if you have the nerve, is to pass the hat around for the first few slips, dip your hand in to stir them up, and clip one in the crotch of your thumb, so that it lies hidden inside your hand.

Ask someone else to go on passing the hat, while you stand on the stage with your back to the doings—so that you can't steal a peek, according to your story.

It shouldn't take you a moment to unfold the stolen billet (this should quite literally be played close to the vest), memorize the message, and refold the paper.

When you get the hat back, look around the audience. "Have we got everybody's?"

At that moment you can quite safely drop your stolen billet on top.

Set the hat on a table.

Great business of passing hand across forehead, wiping away conflicting mental influences, and concentrating.

Take out of the hat any slip *except* the one you know.

Hold it neatly by the tips of your fingers, and move slowly. This is mind reading, not sleight-of-hand.

Lay the billet against your forehead. Shut your eyes. Don't squint too much, or you'll be funny instead of impressive.

Announce the message that you know.

Ask who wrote it.

Either the plant or the man whose slip you stole will answer up.

Then open the slip you hold, and repeat the message you have just announced. Remember, you are supposed to be checking up on yourself by reading the first message out loud.

Actually, of course, you are hastily memorizing the new message.

Toss the message face down on the table.

Dip out another. Hold it to your forehead, and announce the message you have just learned.

Get the writer to acknowledge that. Unfold it, "read it aloud," and toss it on the table.

The last slip you do must be the one you learned beforehand. Of course, if you pick it up sooner it will break your one-ahead chain.

Some magicians believe in taking trouble to shift the stack of messages around so that all will be in the proper order; but I think the trouble is greater than the danger of anyone's checking up on you.

The Envelope Test

The one-ahead gag will work with the billets sealed in an envelope, too.

Then you must either use a plant or read one message without opening the envelope.

If that suggestion sounds like the result of too much alcohol, I can only say that it is. Alcohol brushed on the envelope will make it transparent.

You should use slips small enough to go in the envelope without folding, and make a point of having people turn the messages downward, out of sight, as they put them in the envelopes.

This is a very convenient trick for a team. Probably the "medium" will be blindfolded, and the performer will collect the envelopes.

It is a very useful thing for you to know that if you scowl while you are being blindfolded, and afterward raise your eyebrows, you can see down your nose from under almost any blindfold. If your partner puts the blindfold on you, there's simply nothing to it.

The medium sits there blindfolded, behind a table, with the little sponge soaked in alcohol ready—perhaps in a slightly open drawer.

The magician comes back with the hat full of envelopes, and snitches one out while his back is turned to the crowd. Possibly he may hold it against the outside of the hat, and drop it right side up in front of the medium as he puts the hat on the table.

One quick swipe with the sponge reveals the message.

Long before the trick is over the alcohol evaporates, leaving no trace.

Getting Impressions

Another group of methods for reading messages might be lumped together as the carbon-paper method. The principle is to use some kind of pad or smooth surface for people to rest their paper on while they write. Secretly, this resting surface records the message.

You can use a piece of cardboard made of two thin sheets glued together around three sides, with a piece of carbon paper over a sheet of white paper in the middle of the sandwich.

You can also rub the back of the sheet the man writes on with the end of a wax candle. Just by chance, you hand him a framed photograph to write on.

The candle wax comes off on the glass over the photograph, and if you hold the picture at an angle, you can read the message.

Both of these methods work better with a team, because someone has to go backstage to read the message.

Torn-Billet Reading

One of the most ingenious ways of message reading is so simple that it could almost happen by accident.

You need a slip of paper no larger than three by three and a half.

In the exact middle (measure to make sure) draw a circle an inch or an inch and an eighth in diameter. You needn't do it with compasses, but the circle should be fairly regular.

You also want a pencil and a small pad or notebook in your coat pocket.

The effect will knock them in the aisles if you sell it as pure concentration, thought transference. If you let it look like a mere message-reading trick, it won't amount to much.

Ask someone to take your piece of paper with the circle. Tell him that everything is planned to help absolute concentration, and if he doesn't honestly help you out he will be wasting his time as well as yours.

First, he is to think of something short and snappy, like a telephone number.

He is to think of it hard.

Then, so as to concentrate even his writing, and fix the number still more firmly in his mind, he is to write it down in the circle.

Next, he is to fold the paper in half with the writing inside. Then in half the other way.

Look him firmly in the eye. If his eyes show the slightest sign of wandering, reprimand him.

Finally, after you have stared him down, take the folded paper.

Tear it in half. Then put the halves together, and tear them in half the other way. Tear up the quarters.

Burn the scraps in the ash tray.

Take out your pad and pencil, and start concentrating again.

One letter and figure at a time, with great effort, you write down the telephone number.

The basis of the trick is the fact, which you have certainly noticed, that if you fold a piece of paper in four, and tear off a little bit out of the corner where there are no single paper edges, but only folds, you will find, on opening out the paper, that you have torn a good-sized round hole in the middle.

The drawn circle is intended simply to make sure your man writes in a small space at the exact center. When he folds the paper as you tell him to, all the writing occupies a corner segment half an inch across.

Take the folded paper in your right hand, with the corner where the writing is upward and to the right. (*Fig.* 40a). Tear the paper down the middle, and put the left-hand piece behind the right-hand piece—that is, the right-hand piece is toward you. (*Fig.* 40b).

The torn papers are now upright in your right hand. Turn them horizontal, keeping the crucial corner to the right. Tear them in half, and again put the left-hand bunch behind the right-hand bunch.

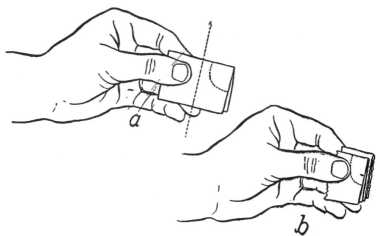

Fig. 40.   (a) Ready to tear the billet; (b) Ready for the second tear

Possibly you will need to tear once or twice more before the pieces are down to half an inch across.

At any rate, you end up with the all-important center bit directly under your right thumb. Draw it off the stack with your thumb, and hide it in the curl of your right middle fingers.

Dump the rest of the scraps into the ash tray, and touch a match to them. Be careful not to turn the inside of your right hand so that people can see the paper while you're striking the match.

Take the pad and pencil out of your coat pocket.

Get the hidden paper scrap between your right thumb and forefinger; put them on the face of the pad, and your second, third, and fourth fingers under the back.

You can't stay in that position long, so make the same movement with your left hand, clip the scrap, and unfold it with your left thumb and forefinger behind the screen of the pad. (*Fig.* 41).

Try writing something on the pad. As you do, read what is written in the unfolded circle.

Fig. 41.   **Reading the billet**

Look dissatisfied. Tear the first sheet off the pad, and crumple it up with the stolen scrap inside. Stuff it in your pocket, and try writing again.

This time, letter by letter, with several erasures and crossings-out, you contrive to write down the telephone number.

There are also a lot of message-reading tricks in which people have to write down numbers, add, subtract, and multiply. I don't think one in ten of these is any good, because they ask too much work of the audience; they are not clear-cut or straightforward; and they look like what they are, mathematical tricks.

If you discover one of these that you do like, most of your work in learning it must go toward selling it as thought transference, not mathematics.

Stage Clairvoyance

Now we come to stage mind reading by a team. Teams usually specialize and do no other magic; they make a full act, perhaps half an hour, out of having the performer pass among the audience, inspecting articles that people hand to him, while the "clairvoyant" on the stage names each thing.

The trick is over a century old, and such couples as the Floyds, the Zancigs, and the Sunshines have done wonders with it.

The methods are almost as many as the performers. A spoken code came first, and as long as ninety years ago electricity was put to work. Some performers would wire an entire theater with electrical contacts to go with metal heels on their shoes; the height of convenience that I ever heard of was a tiny radio receiver with earphones hidden in the clairvoyant's big turban.

Codes

If you want to start out in a small way, and be able to work anywhere, you had better try codes.

Pointer Codes

Pointer codes, to signal which is the required symbol among several written on a blackboard, are childishly easy to devise.

The clairvoyant will no doubt be blindfolded, which, as you learned a little while back, means nothing at all.

Say you are pointing with a stick to a row of names on a blackboard, of which the audience has picked one.

You can skip around at random. In that case, you may agree with your partner that you will touch the selected name third (or fourth or fifth).

You may touch the names strictly in order. In that case,

perhaps you will swing the pointer *up* to each name until you reach the chosen one; you swing *down* to touch that.

Number Codes

Number codes are also easy to devise.

For instance, the clairvoyant undertakes to "see" how many cigarettes are in a cigarette case brought up from the audience.

The performer brings the case up and lays it down on the table. Where he puts it gives the answer. He and his partner have mentally divided the table top into eight squares. The squares may stand for the numbers from one to eight, or the arrangement may be that the case, laid lengthwise in the first, stands for one, crosswise for two, lengthwise in the second for three, crosswise for four, and so on.

Probably the most ingenious, and by no means the easiest, of the number codes depends on timing. You signal by the pauses in which you say nothing.

If you and your partner have approximately the same pulse rate, you can use that.

You can practise counting together until you get the same timing with no mechanical help.

Or, each of you can wear a wrist watch with a sweep second hand on the inside of your wrist. But I think that's making it almost too easy.

To signal letters, you memorize a table made by writing the alphabet in six upright columns, five of them five letters deep, and the sixth containing only the letter *v*, like this:

	1	2	3	4	5	6
1	A	F	K	P	U	V
2	B	G	L	Q	W	
3	C	H	M	R	X	
4	D	I	N	S	Y	
5	E	J	O	T	Z	

You signal each letter by two numbers; first, the one that gives the horizontal line, then the one that gives the perpendicular. *E* is 5-1. *L* is 2-3. Just 6 is enough for *V*.

You can break your pauses any way you like: glance up, speak, scrape your foot.

One good effect is to write several columns of figures on the blackboard. The blindfolded clairvoyant, with her back to the board and the performer, adds each column.

Actually, the performer must mentally add the first column at a glance. Suppose it adds up to fourteen. He taps on the board with the chalk, pauses one beat, taps again, pauses four beats, taps again, and says, "Yes?"

Thereupon, the clairvoyant, who has been counting beats along with him, says, "Put down four and carry one."

Talking Codes

Talking codes are among the first things a skeptical audience will suspect, and, obviously, also among the hardest to memorize.

However, if you can learn to use one smoothly, and mix it up with other codes, you can put on a very good show.

All a talking code amounts to is an alphabet with a common word to match each letter—say "quick" for A, "please" for E, "now" for O, "fast" for U; and so on for the rest of the alphabet. The figures are signaled by ten of the same words; there is not much danger of confusion, since you ask for numbers when you want them.

"Careful" is a signal to double the letter or number that follows.

Once you have the alphabet code memorized, you must learn a set of abbreviations for all the common articles—H for handkerchief, W for watch, C for coin, and so on, as far as you want to carry it.

Real skill consists in knowing so many abbreviations that you can describe the most outlandish object with a very few code words.

Another effect that you can mix in is to dash about the room pointing to things, simply saying, "What's that?" each time.

You don't stop for elaborate description. Your partner merely says, "A ring—a handkerchief—a watch—a cigarette," and so on.

To do this you simply draw up a list of ten or twenty common articles that are sure to be in the audience. Objects can be repeated if you like.

Your job is to spot all the items on your list, and touch them in proper order, giving warning with a "Right!" or a "Careful!" if you can't find the next one in order.

Silent Methods

Magicians, always trying to make things harder for themselves, have even devised a second-sight act where nothing need be said at all.

Electrical signaling may play a part in this. Or a good way in a fairly small theater is to post a man with strong field glasses at a peephole in the wings. The performer turns a flashlight on each article, and the man behind the scene signals to the medium with any device from a radio headset to a thread tied around her ankle.

She may sit so that she can see him, and he can write the article in black crayon on a big sheet of paper.

I have only scratched the surface of mind-reading and second-sight methods. But if you come to grips with even one or two of them, you will find that you have nearly a lifetime career cut out for you.

LESSON 10.   Revealing a Selected Card

What Seems to Happen: You make as startling a display as possible of a card that someone has chosen and that you, theoretically, don't know.

What You Need: Several decks of cards. A thumbtack. A dagger or knife. An elastic. A sheet of newspaper. A spool of fine black thread. A stick of diachylon plaster, which you can get at drugstores.

Where to Learn More: Professor Hoffmann, *Modern Magic;* C. Lang Neil, *The Modern Conjurer;* A. Roterberg, *Card Tricks;* Harry Blackstone, *Blackstone's Card Tricks;* Ottokar Fischer, *Illustrated Magic;* Nelson Downs and J. N. Hilliard, *The Art of Magic*

If I let this lesson run on, it would fill two books the size of *Learn Magic.* But since you have already learned quite a lot about handling cards, you can pick up new effects quite easily; I shall hardly have to give you more than a hint.

And as you are becoming an actor in magic, I shan't have to remind you so often about letting people see what you are doing, and about letting them know when to applaud.

First, go back over Lessons 5 and 6.

As an exercise for your ingenuity, suppose *you* figure out the neatest way of having *two* cards chosen, and getting them both to the top of the pack, one above the other. You can do both of the following effects separately, but I think they are rather better together.

The Turned Card; Victim's Choice

Let's say that two people have drawn cards, looked at them, and put them back in the pack. By one of the methods of Lesson 8, you have got both cards to the top.

With a casual swing, you hold the pack a couple of feet above the table, and drop it.

One of the chosen cards turns face up on top of the pack.

Next, you put the whole deck in your second helper's pocket. Tell him to reach in quickly and grab a card.

Needless to say, he comes up with the one he chose.

To do the first part, hold the pack in your right hand with the fingers at one end and the thumb at the other, the top toward your palm.

Push the top card about half an inch to the right; your hand covers it.

When you drop the deck, the air catches the projecting top card, and flips it over.

The second part of the trick needs a certain amount of nerve, and a little experimenting.

I think you will probably find that your helper's upper right vest pocket is the best place to put the pack. You will have to test that, and also test how much you need to hurry the man.

The point, naturally, is that you want to make it impossible for him to pull out any card except the top one.

You may find it safer to put the deck in your own pocket; but I believe it is more surprising if you can work the trick as I suggest.

The Card Nailed to the Ceiling

The next trick is so old that it is practically new. It is quick and spectacular, but will spoil a good pack of cards, so you had better keep one just for this trick. (If good cards are spilled on the floor even once, they are done for; the grit ruins the finish.)

Somebody draws a card; it is shuffled back into the pack. You throw the deck straight up.

After the cards have fallen, the chosen one appears, nailed to the ceiling.

I think the simplest way of accomplishing this trick is to have a thumbtack in your left vest pocket.

Fig. 42.   Preparing for the Card Nailed to the Ceiling

When you have got the chosen card to the top of the pack, catch the thumbtack with the point between the tips of your left second and third fingers.

Then take the pack in your left hand in dealing position, but with the fingers curled to the middle of the top.

This will bring the flat head of the thumbtack against the middle of the chosen card. (*Fig.* 42).

With your right hand, slide the top card off to the left, and then put it right back in position, but *on top* of the thumbtack.

Press down gently until the point starts to come through. Then take your left fingers out of the way, and finish pushing so that the tack comes through its full length.

All you have to do now is hold the deck horizontal, and give it a smart toss at the ceiling.

After a few tries, you will learn to throw it so that it reaches the ceiling still more or less horizontal, and drives the thumbtack in.

This nails the chosen card to the ceiling.

The Jumping Cards

For another rather spectacular trick, invented by Cardini himself, you want a soft felt hat.

You drop the pack of cards into the hat, flick the felt with your finger, and the chosen card (or cards—you can just as well use several) jumps out like a shot.

When you put the deck into the hat, drop the chosen card on edge on one side of the center crease, and the pack on the other.

Flip smartly the side that holds the chosen card, and it will come sailing out.

The Transfixed Pack

For the next old favorite you want a knife—the wickeder looking the better—a piece of newspaper, and an elastic.

Review Lesson 6, and figure out how you can have two cards chosen, and bring one to the top of the deck, *and one to the bottom.*

The effect is simply that you wrap the pack in newspaper, then jab the dagger in at the edge.

When you tear open the package, the dagger is between the two chosen cards.

As I said, you must bring one chosen card to the top of the pack, and one to the bottom. No doubt you have already discovered that one way to do this is to have the two cards put back in the pack together, then to stick your left little finger in between them, and make the shift.

Anyway, there you are. Now bend the whole pack sharply

in half, downward. Bend the upper half alone sharply upward. (*Fig.* 43).

Make the shift. Now you have the two chosen cards together again, but they (along with the two halves of the pack) bulge away from each other at the middle. If you look at them from the edge, they are like a pair of parentheses ( ).

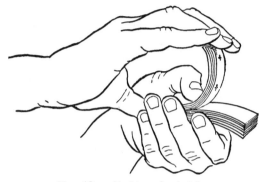

Fig. 43.   Making the bridge

The technical name for this move is "making the bridge."

I don't need to warn you that nobody must notice any of this.

Now wrap the deck in newspaper. A fairly small piece is better than too much; it makes a neater package. Put the elastic lengthwise around the bundle.

Run your left thumbnail over the side edge of the pack until you can feel the bridge. Punch that spot in a little. (*Fig.* 44).

Now, stop and remind people that they have drawn two cards, shuffle them into the pack, and lost them, and that no one could possibly find cards wrapped up in paper, anyway.

Get out your knife with a flourish. If you're on a platform, you can throw it once or twice, and let it stand on its point in the floor.

Toss the paper-wrapped deck in the air once or twice. Draw back your knife like a fencer ready to thrust.

Jab the dagger in at the spot you have marked with your thumbnail.

Bend the package back and forth a couple of times to remove the bridge. Then let one of your helpers have the whole business, with the dagger still thrust in. Tell him to break open the package, and see what he finds on each side of the knife.

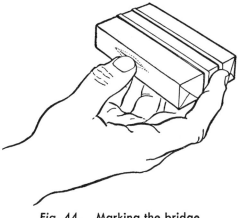

Fig. 44.   Marking the bridge

You want a fairly new pack for this trick, because the only danger is that the cards may not hold a wide enough bridge.

The Rising Cards (Three Methods)

Finally, we come to the Rising Cards, perhaps the oldest card trick there is. It wouldn't have lived so long if it hadn't been good. I shall give three ways of doing it, which you can combine or use separately, as you like; there are at least twenty more, besides which you can probably invent two or three of your own.

The name tells the story of the effect: the cards that people choose rise from the deck, or even float clean out of it.

First Method

The first and simplest method (once the card has been drawn, returned, and apparently shuffled into the pack) is to hold the deck face forward in your left hand; lay your right forefinger across the upper end; then raise your right hand.

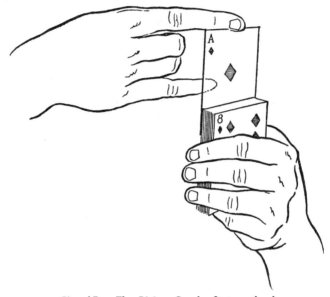

Fig. 45.   The Rising Cards, first method

The card comes up, dangling from the forefinger.

Of course you bring the chosen card to the top. With your right hand in the position I have just described, you will find that the knuckles of the second, third, and little fingers almost touch the card. Make quite a fuss about rubbing your finger on cloth to generate static electricity, or some such nonsense. Raise your right hand slowly and carefully several times from the upper end of the pack.

Nothing happens.

When you want the card to cling to your forefinger, simply straighten your right little finger. The tip, pressing against the back of the card, will carry it up as you raise your hand. (*Fig. 45*).

Second Method

Next, you hold the deck up in your right hand, and the chosen card rises of its own accord, not clinging to anything.

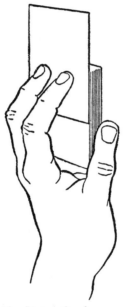

Fig. 46.   The Rising Cards, second method

Hold the cards back to palm by the long edges, your thumb on the left edge, your *third and fourth* fingers on the right edge.

Your first and second fingers rest on the top, and it is these fingers that, by a small walking movement, make the chosen card rise. (*Fig.* 46).

Hold your left hand a foot or so above the pack. As the card rises, you can move your left hand from side to side, and make the card swing to follow it.

Neither of these methods is very hard to catch, so they will be more startling if you follow up with the last, thoroughly professional, version.

Third Method

The effect is that you succeed in what, so far, you have only been trying to do—making the card float from the pack all the way up to your hand. There are several ways to do this, most of them suitable only for a big stage, with two or three assistants in the wings.

The method I give can be done anywhere, and once you have made your preparations, you can always be ready to perform.

First, you need about fourteen inches of fine black thread, or perhaps even better, of dark human hair. Tie a button to one end.

Get out your diachylon plaster, and with your fingernails dig a small piece from the end. Work it between your fingers until it gets rather sticky.

Thread the free end of thread on a needle, and run the needle from the inside of your coat to the outside at a point under the right lapel, somewhat above the top button. Pull off the needle. Make a knot in the other end of the thread, and shape the little pellet of plaster (which now becomes "magician's wax") around it. You can then stick the wax pellet under your lapel, and pull the rest of the thread back inside your coat. Let it hang straight down into your breast pocket.

If you are reasonably careful about how you stuff your wallet into your pocket, you can carry the thread for weeks without breaking it.

After you have got all this ready, you will hardly need to be told how to do the trick.

You bring the card (or cards) to the top of the pack.

With your right thumbnail, pick the wax pellet from under your lapel. As you stretch your right hand toward the pack, the

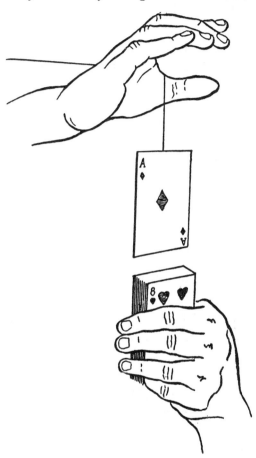

Fig. 47. The Rising Cards, third method

thread pays out until the button stops it. You must be fairly gentle, so as not to break the thread. Grab the deck for a moment by the end, with your right thumb on top and the fingers underneath.

This, of course, sticks the wax to the top card at the center of the end.

Now take the deck back in your left hand, the face toward the palm. Hook your right thumb under the thread.

Raise your right hand. (*Fig. 47*).

The card floats to that hand, which nips it, and holds it out to the person who drew it.

Before you actually give it to him, scrape the wax off the card. If you have worked the wax to the proper consistency, it will come off clean in one piece, ready to use again on the next card.

If you intend to have three cards rise, it is a good idea to make the third one look a little different.

Stick the wax on the back of the third card, and then stand the deck upright in a goblet or a highball glass. In dropping the pack into the glass, turn it upside down so that the wax is on the lower end.

If you have the nerve (and are using a hair rather than a thread), you can let someone hold the glass. Otherwise, you can set it on a table.

Now you have only to back away a little, and the thread, running over the edge of the glass, will make the last card rise without any help from your hands. (*Fig. 48*).

Probably the best excuse for backing away is to lean forward, pointing at the glass, and earnestly ordering the card to rise.

In all of these methods, even the best, you should avoid giving people a side view, because the card is supposed to rise from the middle of the pack, and a side view will show that it comes from the back.

As a matter of fact, it is quite possible to make the card really come from the middle; but in order to do that, you have to arrange a duplicate pack beforehand, and you should have an assistant backstage. Anyhow, you can learn all about those ways from the books I suggested at the start of the lesson.

The last of the three methods, being really quite a puzzle, will stand a good deal more mysterious treatment from you than the first two. If you have the thread always ready in your coat, start off casually with the first two methods. Then, in case any-

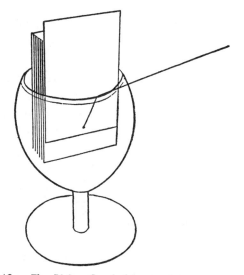

Fig. 48.   The Rising Cards from a glass

body gives you an argument, or you think conditions are good for the big smash ending, you can unstick your wax pellet and go to work.

The Mental-Selection Spelling Master

Early in the book I promised you a version of the Spelling Master in which the spectator would not even touch a card, but would just think of one, which would spell out correctly when he took the pack in his own hands.

Here it is.

To be exact, the effect is that you fan the deck face up, asking somebody to remember one of the cards he sees.

Then you look him in the eye for a moment, run through the cards very quickly, and hand him the deck.

Once he has the pack, you ask him what card he was thinking of, and immediately tell him to spell it out and deal one card for each letter.

There is no stalling or fiddling; even asking the name of the card is just a precaution to make sure he does the spelling properly.

The secret of this trick lies in forcing the spectator to think of any one card in a prearranged group of six. The six cards are set up so that any one of them would spell out; that is, the top one has ten letters in the name; the next has eleven; the bottom one has fifteen.

I could give you a fixed list of cards to memorize, but I think it will be more useful if instead you memorize the simple principles of the set-up. Then you can prepare for the trick in a matter of seconds, while people are busy discussing your preceding effect.

For spelling purposes, *diamonds* is an eight (the word has eight letters). This is the long one. You always start your set-up with two successive diamonds on the bottom.

Spades and *hearts* are just alike: six. You can mix hearts and spades, as you please, in the middle part of the set-up.

Clubs is five. The top card of the set-up is always a club.

Now for the individual cards. *Three, seven, eight,* and *queen* are the longest: five. The bottom card of your set-up must be one of these in the diamond suit.

Next come *four, five, nine, jack,* and *king:* four. The next to the bottom card must be one of those, also in diamonds.

Lastly we have the threes: *ace, two, six.* The top card of the set-up is one of those, in clubs.

Your set-up, from bottom to top, runs so: an eight-five, an eight-four, a six-five, a six-four, a six-three, and a five-three.

The word *of*, being the same for every card, makes no difference until later in the trick.

Run up six cards according to the formula, and put them on the bottom of the pack. Memorize the bottom diamond of the set-up.

Put six or seven indifferent cards below the set-up, taking care that none is a naturally conspicuous one. Aces, deuces, threes, and face cards are all conspicuous.

Make sure there are no conspicuous cards for five or six *above* your set-up. It isn't a bad idea to give a false overhand shuffle, leaving the bottom third of the deck undisturbed.

Turn the pack face up, and approach your intended victim. Stop in front of him.

Start fanning the cards face up from your left hand into your right.

As you do this, say rather slowly, "As I run these cards over, I want you just——"

Don't finish the sentence until you catch sight of the first diamond in the set-up, which you have memorized.

As that diamond comes into view, go on "—to think of one card, without even touching it."

Run leisurely, but not too slowly, through your set-up.

As you catch sight of the last club (the ace is a good one to use, because it is conspicuous), say, "Have you got one?"

Square up the pack, and get your left little finger between the set-up and the rest of the pack.

If your timing is smooth, there isn't one chance in fifty that the man will take a card outside your six.

Make the shift, or simply cut the pack, bringing the set-up to the top. The first card on the deck is now the ace, two, or six of clubs. The others follow in order.

Fan the pack facing yourself, and look intently at the cards, then into your helper's eyes, then back at the cards.

Take nine cards off the bottom of the pack, and put them on top.

Hand the deck to your helper. It is ready set up to spell any one of the six cards he could possibly have thought of.

If there is a better card trick, I don't know it.

LESSON 11.   The Thumb Tip

What Seems to Happen: You poke a lighted cigarette into your fist. It disappears.

You tear up a paper ribbon two feet long and an inch wide. In a moment it comes out whole.

You poke a colored handkerchief into your fist. It disappears.

What You Need: A thumb tip—a metal cap, shaped like the end of your thumb, and painted flesh color. (*Fig.* 49a). All magic stores carry them; indeed, they have become so easy to buy that this fact has done the trick no good.

A silk handkerchief. A small hemmed piece of the same silk, two inches square.

Two pieces of paper ribbon, the same size and color.

Where to Learn More: Stuart Robson, *Tips on Thumbs*

I said before that I didn't like to explain mere tricks when I might be arranging a play for you to act, yet here I go again. But there are certain pieces of apparatus that most magicians use, and I want you to learn to handle them right, not wrong.

It may not seem as if there were anything you could do wrong with a device as simple as the thumb tip. Actually, apparatus tricks need just as much care and rehearsal as sleight-of-hand.

Using the thumb tip is, in fact, a kind of sleight. I once heard Al Baker say that if you used it properly, your thumb tip could just as well be nickel-plated. He meant that you should never show it; and with good management you hardly ever need to.

Cigarette Vanish

To make the cigarette disappear, start with the thumb tip in your lower right vest pocket, with the open end up. Smoke your cigarette pretty well down.

When you want to get the thumb tip, hook *both* thumbs in your lower vest pockets.

This is something that John Mulholland taught me, which most magicians never know: if you have to put one hand in a pocket—vest, coat, trouser—put *both* hands in alike. That is a natural thing to do, and not at all suspicious; one hand at a time looks fishy.

At any rate, when you take your thumbs out of your pockets, the thumb tip is settled snugly on your right thumb. Take the cigarette from your lips, between your right first and second finger tips.

Keep all your fingers together, and the thumb out of sight behind them.

Hold out your left hand, palm up.

Close it into a loose fist, and turn it thumb uppermost.

Now, casually poke your right thumb into the left fist, as if to open it a little.

Pinch the thumb tip in the circle of your left thumb and forefinger, and leave it behind.

Lift the cigarette up part way toward your face, and take one final look at it. This will remind people that you actually have a lighted cigarette—and here it is.

Poke the cigarette into your left fist (and the thumb tip) with your right thumb and forefinger.

Stub the cigarette out, if you don't want a burned thumb.

Stick the right thumb deeper into your fist than the right forefinger, and pick up the thumb tip. (*Fig.* 49b).

Then draw back your right thumb, but leave the forefinger in your fist for a moment, as if tamping down the cigarette. (*Fig.* 49c).

Then carry your left fist away, following it with your eyes.

Remember Lesson 1. *Keep your right hand still.*

If you should still have a wisp of smoke in your lungs, blow it at your left hand.

Fling your hand open.

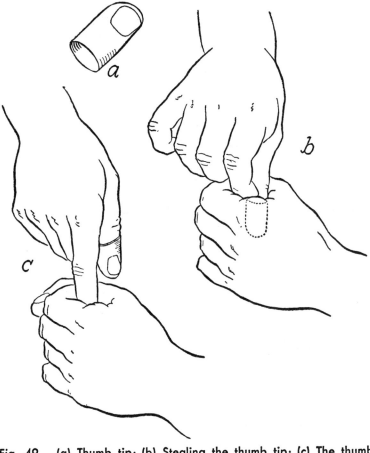

Fig. 49. (a) Thumb tip; (b) Stealing the thumb tip; (c) The thumb tip stolen

Pause. Remember Slow Joe in the back.

To show your right hand empty, just swing your palm around so that it faces straight to the left, and your thumb sticks out toward you, as if you were starting to salute (or, perhaps, thumb your nose).

The merit of this is that the thumb tip is still almost out of sight. Remember that the thumb tip is only inconspicuous, not really concealed if anyone looks hard at your thumb.

You can hook your thumbs in your vest pockets again, or you can leave the thumb tip behind when you reach for the package to get another cigarette.

The Torn and Restored Paper Ribbon

The torn and restored paper ribbon is done in various forms, with everything from a cigarette paper to a newspaper. The thumb tip is just about big enough to take the paper ribbon, so we shall use that.

Roll one piece of ribbon up quite tight and jam it into the thumb tip. Put the tip in its usual spot—your lower right vest pocket.

To start the trick, get the tip on your thumb. Hold up the ribbon at shoulder height, with a hand at each end, thumbs behind, fingers going over the top. You notice that the thumb tip is kept strictly out of sight all the time.

Swing once from side to side, so that everyone can see.

Then shift both hands to the middle of the ribbon, still keeping the same grip.

Tear the ribbon in half.

Hold your hands up and apart, with the two pieces of ribbon hanging down.

Lay one piece over the other, and tear both in half. Separate your hands again. You don't want people to say afterward, "Oh, he never tore it at all."

Keep on tearing the halves, and laying them together, until the pieces are nearly square. You must be neat but not fussy about it. In fact, the whole trick depends on neatness rather than on anything you could call dexterity. If you are messy about handling the scraps, they may not fit into the thumb tip. So long as you are neat, you won't need any special skill.

Finally, you have a small square stack of paper scraps, held in both hands, thumbs at the back, first and second fingers in front.

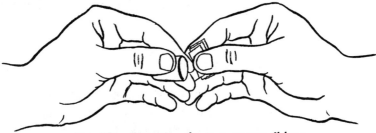

Fig. 50.   Restoring the torn paper ribbon

Catch the thumb tip between your left thumb and fingers, and withdraw your right thumb from it. (*Fig.* 50).

Now you can fish out the second strip with your right forefinger. Do that, and then use your right thumb to poke the torn pieces into the thumb tip.

Let go of the thumb tip with your left hand, putting it back in place on your right thumb.

You are now ready to start unrolling the restored strip, which you should do as nearly in one movement as you can, so that people won't think it is being unrolled but just pulled out.

For that reason, you may prefer one of two other ways to prepare the second strip. You can roll it up from both ends toward the middle; or you can fold it zigzag, in accordion pleats.

Experiment until you find the best size of strip and the best way of folding, so that you can finish by coming up with a single sweep of the hands, and a big smile.

Handkerchief Vanish

Making a handkerchief disappear by means of the thumb tip falls rather in the class of sucker gags.

To do it, you start with the little square of silk in the thumb tip, and the tip on your right thumb. Hold the handkerchief by one corner, in your right hand.

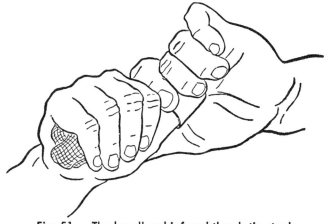

Fig. 51.   The handkerchief and thumb tip steal

Let everyone see the handkerchief; then press the corner flat between your two palms, and start rolling it into a ball.

When it is rolled into a fairly compact bundle, close both hands into fists.

You will have to experiment a little, because this is the critical point. You must, at the same time, carry away the rolled-up handkerchief in your right hand, and strip the thumb tip off your right hand into your left fist. (*Fig.* 51).

Stick out your left fist, and rather hurriedly stuff your right hand into your pocket, as if to leave the handkerchief. Don't look at either hand; look straight at the audience. If you watched your left hand, as you normally would, some people might be fooled after all. If you watched your right hand, it would be too obvious that you were faking.

Of course there will be yells of "It's in your pocket!"

You can now take your choice.

If you stuff the wadded handkerchief into the far upper corner of your trouser pocket, you can pull the pocket out and show it empty.

Or you can simply take your hand out of your pocket, and shake your head.

In either case, reach over and pull a corner of the silk from the thumb tip.

"No, it's still there."

Tuck the corner back with your right thumb, and carry away the thumb tip.

This time, you do follow your left hand with your eyes as it moves away from your right. Hold it. Remember our old friend in the back.

A tossing movement, and the handkerchief is gone.

LESSON 12. A Silk Routine. Part I

What Seems to Happen: You stand up bare-handed, and produce a large silk handkerchief.

You tie a knot, which disappears when you blow at it. You give a shake, and the knot reappears.

You lay three silk handkerchiefs loose on a chair. Three others you tie corner to corner, and put on another chair. You pass the knots from the second lot to the first; the three loose handkerchiefs come out tied together, and the three you tied before are now separate.

What You Need: Six white handkerchiefs of good silk, not much smaller than twenty inches square. They are better with fairly wide hems.

A candle in a candlestick. A large box of matches.
A spool of black thread.

Where to Learn More: Hoffmann, *Later Magic;* Hugard,
   Modern Magic Manual; Hatton and Plate, *Magicians'*
   Tricks; Blackstone's Secrets of Magic

Tricks with silk handkerchiefs are among the best you can do
in a show. Silks are pretty to look at, easy to handle, and, in
short, practically the ideal material for magic. But since you
generally have to get silk tricks ready beforehand, they aren't
quite so useful when somebody grabs you at school or the office
and says, "Let's see a trick."

You will notice that I have called this lesson a silk routine.
It's meant to be part of a show. You get things ready beforehand (though it hardly takes a moment), and then you run
smoothly through a series of small effects that follow one another naturally, and build up to a big effect.

To begin with, there has long been an argument between the
people who said that everything you use should be obviously
ordinary, and the people who said that you should always produce anything you need magically, and, if possible, make it
disappear magically when you are done.

The argument applies to this trick because you are going to
use silk handkerchiefs, which are very easy to produce magically. Should you do that, or should you simply take them out
of your pocket, as you would with any handkerchief?

I say this is a matter of your personality. John Mulholland,
who never does anything by accident, always has the handkerchiefs neatly ironed and folded in his coat pocket. It never en-
ters people's heads that anything could be wrong with them. On
the other hand, Ade Duval, the leading modern performer of
silk tricks, makes no pretense of being ordinary. Everything
happens magically with him, and he produces silks in all directions.

Make up your mind what sort of fellow you are, and plan your routine accordingly.

What I give here is a compromise: you produce three silks magically, and simply bring on the rest.

Preparing for the Act

Lay one of the silks flat on a table, and gather it up back and forth, accordion fashion, until it makes a long band, perhaps an inch wide. Then gather this up, accordion fashion, until you have a small square bundle. Don't let go, or you'll have your work to do over again!

Tie the bundle up crosswise with the end of your black thread. Leave fifteen or sixteen inches of thread dangling from the bundle, and snap the thread off at that point. The first time, you had better leave the thread longer, because you will have to fool around to get the right length for your own use.

Put the bundle in your lower left vest pocket. If you wear suspenders, run the other end of the thread in through the left armhole of your vest, and anchor it firmly to your suspender. If you don't, run the thread in at the armhole, and anchor it to the top button of your vest, out of sight under the buttonhole.

Tie three of your handkerchiefs corner to corner with small neat square knots, snug but not hard. The middle handkerchief will be tied by two opposite corners to its neighbors. (*Fig. 52*).

Lay the tied handkerchiefs out carefully on a table, so that there shall be no twists or snarls; then pick them up by the free corners nearest you, and gather them together. Shake them down so that the knotted corners are hidden as you hold the handkerchiefs up.

Lay them together over the back of a chair. Take special care that the knots don't show.

Roll another handkerchief into a fairly compact ball. Take a large box of matches, push the drawer half way out, and hide the handkerchief against the inner end of the drawer, so that if you were to close the box, the handkerchief would be pushed out.

Accordion pleat another handkerchief into a small bundle, and put it in the bend of your left elbow.

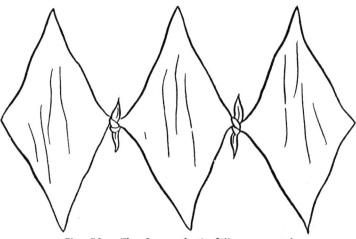

Fig. 52. The Sympathetic Silks prepared

The first part of this trick, I think, is better done in pantomime, with almost no patter.

Handkerchief Production (Elbow)

Come on stage with your hands palm outward. Look at each hand in turn. That's much better than elaborately showing them empty.

Take hold of your right sleeve at the bend of the elbow with your left hand, and pull it up a little.

Take hold of your left sleeve at the bend of the elbow with your right hand, and pull it up a little.

When you take your right hand away, carry the handkerchief in it.

This motion of pulling up your sleeves should seem a matter of convenience, to draw your cuffs clear of your hands. Pulling up your sleeves to show you have nothing hidden is rather old-fashioned, and should be saved for occasions when it really makes some difference to the trick.

You now have the handkerchief hidden in your right hand, but the last thing you want is to admit it.

Fix your eyes on a point in the air to your left. Poise your left hand as if you were about to catch a mosquito.

Make a snatch, and close your hand to about egg size. (Remember Lesson 8?)

Let a look of satisfaction come over your face. Then, quite casually, go through the motions of putting into your right hand the thing that your left fist holds.

Follow through with your eyes; this is just as important in producing a thing as in making it disappear.

Don't be in too big a hurry to open your right hand. When you finally do, of course there is the handkerchief.

Hold it up by one corner, and stroke it down with the other hand. Let people realize that one trick has been accomplished.

The Dissolving Knot

Take hold of two opposite corners, one in each hand. Swing the silk like a skip rope.

In fact, this does twist the handkerchief into a loose rope.

Now comes a move that is very easy to do, but hard to understand the first time, and hard to remember until you do understand it.

What people see you do is hold the handkerchief in your left hand; make a loop; reach through the loop with your right hand; catch the free end, and pull it through the loop to make a knot.

You must do this casually, smoothly, and rather quickly. Here's how.

Hold the handkerchief in the crotch of your left thumb, with about a third of the silk falling over the back of your hand, and the rest hanging straight down. (*Fig.* 53a).

Take hold of the lower end with your right hand. Bring it up *behind* your left *third* and *fourth* fingers; then *in front* of your left *first* and *second* fingers; and then into the crotch of your left thumb, and *across on top* of the upper end. (*Fig.* 53b).

Shift your left thumb to clip the new end instead of the upper end. (*Fig.* 53c).

Clamp your left second and third fingers together on the silk. Let go with your right hand.

Now put your right hand clear through the loop you have made. Put the hand through from *front* to *back*.

Grab the original upper end of the silk, which your left thumb has just released. (*Fig.* 53d).

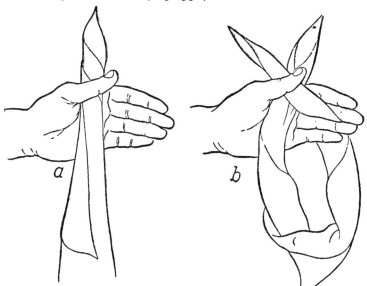

Fig. 53. (a) Ready for the vanishing knot; (b) The loop is made

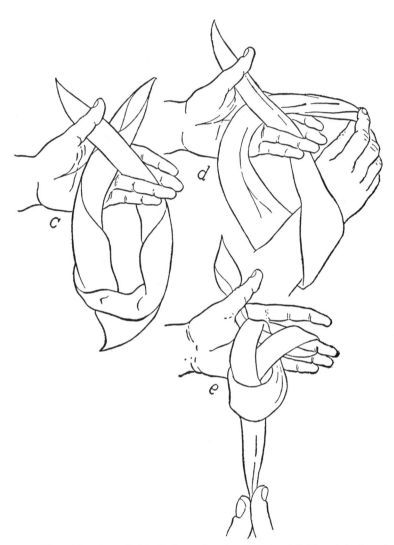

Fig. 53. (*Continued*) (c) Shifting the thumb grip; (d) The right hand
reaches through; (e) Tightening the vanishing knot

Pull this end through the loop, and draw it snug.

Don't for anything let go with your left middle fingers. (*Fig.* 53e).

If you have followed my description, held on in the right places, and pulled in the right directions, you will have in the middle of the handkerchief what looks like a plain overhand knot.

Actually, your left middle fingers, holding the middle of the handkerchief, have formed a bight or kink in the silk, and the knot is simply tied around that.

If you hold on with your right hand to the end you have just drawn through the loop, you can wave the handkerchief around by that end, or even mildly snap the whip with it, and you won't disturb the knot.

But if you hold the silk by the other end, a slight shake will undo it.

You can either shake the knot out in this fashion, or blow it out.

To blow it out, take the ends in your hands, holding the silk horizontal.

As you blow, lean back and spread your arms. That will pull out the knot.

Shaking in a Knot

You have conjured the knot away. Now to conjure it back.

For this it is necessary to have quite a big handkerchief. You will see why when you try the trick.

Wind your silk into a rope as before.

Then take it in your right hand, with about a third projecting up and away from you between first and second fingers, the rest hanging down. (*Fig.* 54a).

Give your right hand a circular sweep, to the right and up.

This will swing the lower end of the handkerchief behind your wrist, over and around to the front of your hand again.

Quickly, catch this end between your second and third fingers.
(*Fig.* 54b). Hold on with them as you open your hand out flat.

Your hand is now encircled by a loop of silk. Shake this off,
still holding on with your middle fingers. (*Fig.* 54c).

That makes a knot in the handkerchief.

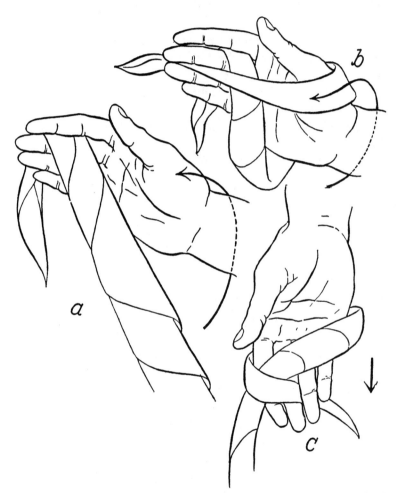

Fig. 54.   (a) Starting to shake in a knot; (b) Catching the free end of
the silk; (c) Shaking in the knot

If the handkerchief is too small, in the first place it will be very difficult to swing the lower end around your wrist and catch it; in the second place, if you succeed in that, the other end will fall out of the loop, and you won't have any knot for all your trouble.

These two knot tricks are quickly over, and are really just a sort of magician's passing remark. If you want to make more of them, wait until you have produced a second handkerchief.

In any case, you will soon learn to produce a knot with one quick shake of your right hand. This is one of very, very few moves in all magic that will baffle people if you do it fast, but will be obvious if you do it slowly.

Silk from Candle

To produce your second handkerchief, you want a candle in a candlestick on the table.

Pick up the box of matches in your left hand; take out a match with your right hand.

Close the box. Then strike the match and light the candle. Closing the box pushes the rolled-up silk into your left hand.

Set down the matchbox and throw away the match at the same time.

Now, you go through the same moves as you did with the first handkerchief production; only you snatch at the candle flame with your right hand, instead of at the air with your left.

The Flying Knot

If you want to make the vanishing and reappearing knot into a trick, rather than what magicians call a "flourish," now is the time. I first saw this done by a handkerchief manipulator named Rosinoff; with his skill it was very pretty indeed.

Tie a fake or "dissolving" knot in one silk, but don't disturb

it. Take the silk in your left hand by the end that will allow you
to shake the knot out.

Take the other silk in your right hand, ready to shake the
knot in.

Stand facing the audience, with both hands held high.

Look at the knotted handkerchief in your left hand. Look at
the plain silk in your right hand. Swing around, with your left
side part way to the front.

Now dip both arms toward the floor, and crouch a little,
exactly as if you were pitching horseshoes with both hands at
once.

What seems to happen is that you toss both silks into the air,
and when they come down the knots have traveled from one to
the other.

Actually, you snap the left-hand silk as you toss it, which
removes that knot. As your right hand disappears behind your
knees, you shake the knot in. Make the move on the downward
motion; don't try to do it on the upswing.

Catch the two silks as they fall, and hold one up high again
in each hand.

Applause.

Handkerchief Production (*Thread*)

Now you need a third handkerchief. If you had forgotten the
one in your vest pocket, I hadn't.

You have a loop of black thread dangling from the armhole
of your vest to your vest pocket.

Shoot your cuffs, or at least go through the motions, and then
settle your coat. As you do this, get your left thumb into the
loop of black thread.

Hold both hands about waist high, a little closer to your stomach than you normally would as a good magician. Turn the
palms toward the audience.

Swing to the right. Crouch just a little. Fix your eyes on a spot in front of you. The whole stance is just as if you were sparring open-handed.

Stare at that spot, and hold your crouch, until people have time to grow curious and perhaps a little excited.

Then snap both hands forward and clap them together.

The motion will yank the silk bundle from your left vest pocket into your left hand. Break the thread, or pull the silk out of the cross-tie, and separate your hands, spreading out the third silk. Now you have three silks to match the three hanging over the chair.

You are ready to do the Sympathetic Silks, one of the finest tricks with handkerchiefs that there is.

The Sympathetic Silks

Gather in your left hand the three handkerchiefs you have produced, holding them in a bunch near the top.

Go over to the chair, pick up the three from it with your right hand, and add them to the fistful in your left. Keep your left forefinger between the two lots.

The next move is perfectly easy so long as you keep track of what you are doing, and almost hopeless if you don't.

Your purpose is simply to count the six handkerchiefs, showing them all separate, and to put three back on the chair.

With your right hand, catch by the top corner the rearmost of the three handkerchiefs that were originally on the chair. Lift the silk up and a little back for about a third of its full height—not high enough to show the knot that secretly connects it with its neighbor. (*Fig. 55*).

"One."

Dip down with your right hand, and catch the second of the tied silks. Lift it up in the same way.

"Two."

Fig. 55.   Counting the Sympathetic Silks

The same with the third.

"Three."

Carry the three clean away, and hold them up high in your right hand.

Then toss them in a heap on the seat of the chair they came from.

Go back to your counting. Make just the same motions, never really separating the handkerchiefs. You have no knots to hide, but don't let that fact make you careless.

"Four. Five. Six."

Put one of these three over your left arm, and knot the other two together by their corners. Then, in turn, knot the third to a corner, making a chain of three.

The knot you tie is a special one, very easy to do when you know how. But you may have to read my description three or four times before you really get it.

Hold one silk between your left thumb and forefinger, with the palm away from you and the second finger raised.

Hold another silk by one corner between the thumb and finger of your right hand. (*Fig. 56a*).

Starting with this silk toward yourself, draw the upper corner away from you between the *left first* and *second* fingers, which are spread apart. Pull the corner forward until it dangles a little below your left thumb and forefinger. (*Fig. 56b*).

Let go with your right hand; come back; and reach forward under your left hand, between the left wrist and the left-hand handkerchief (which, as a matter of fact, is now on the right of the other handkerchief).

Nip the dangling corner of the right-hand silk between your right thumb and forefinger, and pull it back and to the right. (*Fig. 56c*).

This should make it slide off your left forefinger, and form a loop around the left-hand silk. (*Fig. 56d*).

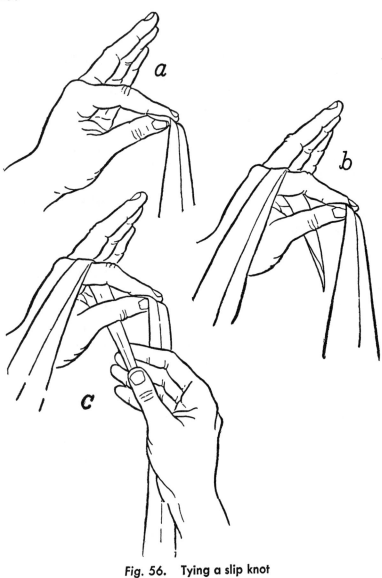

Fig. 56. Tying a slip knot
(a) Starting position; (b) The second silk in place; (c) Pulling the second silk under

Raise your right hand, palm outward, until its position exactly matches that of your left hand.

The two silks now form a twined X. The lower right leg of the X comes from the left-hand silk.

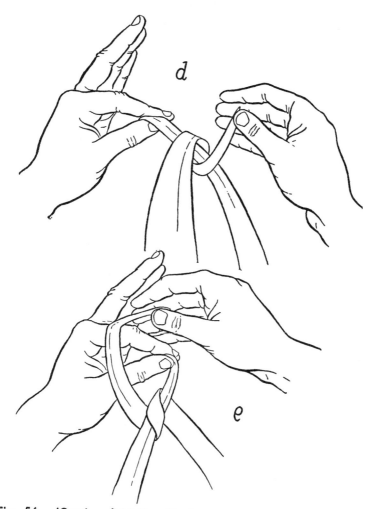

Fig. 56. (Continued) (d) The silks form an X; (e) Starting the second half of the knot

Swoop down and grab this loosely with your right second, third, and fourth fingers.

Now, with your right hand, repeat your original movement of carrying the corner of the right-hand silk forward between the left first and second fingers. (*Fig.* 56e; for the sake of clearness the picture does not show the fingers grasping the lower legs of the X.)

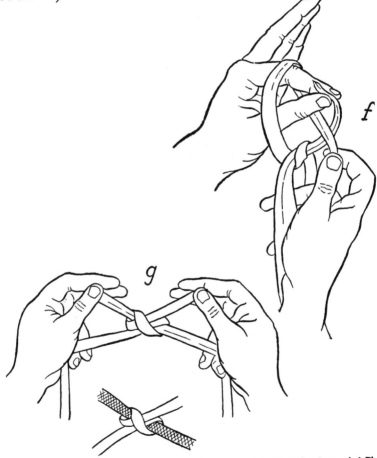

Fig. 56. (*Continued*) (f) Finishing the second half of the knot; (g) The final slip knot

Let go of the corner (but not of the part you hold with the rest of your right fingers); come back, and duck under with your right thumb and forefinger just as you did before. (*Fig.* 56f).

Swing down your *left* second, third, and fourth fingers to catch the lower *left* leg of the X.

Pull through once again with the corner you hold in your right thumb and forefinger. (*Fig.* 56g).

This is a very complicated description of how you do something very simple: keep the left-hand silk in a straight line, with the right-hand silk knotted around it. Once you get the right position of your hands, you can tug at the knot until it looks as hard as a pebble without ever bending the left-hand silk out of line.

Therefore, a comparatively gentle pull will undo the knot. You must next learn how to give this pull inconspicuously.

Once you have the three silks knotted corner to corner, grab the middle one around the middle with your right hand, so that the other two hang down side by side.

Then grab the other two handkerchiefs around their middle with your left hand. Turn your left side toward the audience; and as you do, raise your left hand and lower your right.

This undoes both knots at once, under cover of the two silks in your left hand. (*Fig.* 57).

Pile all three together into your right hand, and drop the heap on the seat of another chair.

You are all done with the trick, but the audience doesn't even know yet what's going to happen.

Go back over what you have done: laid three loose handkerchiefs on one chair, tied three more together tight, and laid them on the other chair.

Now, as solemnly or as comically as you like, pretend to pass the knots—not any part of the silks, but just the knots—from the "tied" pile to the "untied" pile.

Pause to let this sink in.

Then pick up the "tied" heap one at a time, and toss the silks in the air to show that they are separate.

Go to the other chair, catch a side corner of the top silk, and give a yank. The three, knotted together, form one long streamer.

Fig. 57. Slipping the knots

LESSON 13.   A Silk Routine.   Part II

What Seems to Happen: You poke a white silk through your fist, and it comes out red.

You roll up a sheet of paper, and poke three white handkerchiefs in at the bottom. They come out at the top green, blue, and red.

You put a handkerchief in a tumbler, hold a palm over each end, and—zip!—the handkerchief vanishes in a flash without being hidden for a moment.

What You Need: Four white silk handkerchiefs. If you are following my routine, you will use four of the six you have just been performing with. Two red silk handkerchiefs; one blue; one green.

A small and a large "dye tube," which you can buy at a magic shop. Both are metal. The small one is two inches long and an inch in diameter; inside is a length of black webbing, the ends of which are fastened opposite each other in the middle of the tube. The webbing is long enough so that you can push its center to either end of the tube. The big tube is four and a half inches long, an inch and a half in diameter. Some have crossed strips of webbing, like the small dye tube, only with two strips instead of one; others have a sliding metal cup three-quarters of an inch deep to do the job. The principle of both is the same.

A "pull." You can buy one or make it. There are many different forms for different purposes. You can get along with one made of a strap and a length of strong, thin cord. Stout fish line is very good. Buckle the strap around your left arm just below the elbow. Fasten one end of the line firmly to the strap. Run the line around your back and down your right sleeve. You are going to need a loop in the end about three and a half inches long. Adjust the length of the line so that when both arms are stretched as far forward as they will go, the end of the loop will be about at your right elbow. Make the loop permanent, with a very small knot, and cut the line off neatly.

A manila filing folder, or any piece of fairly stiff paper about that size.

A highball glass.

Where to Learn More: Lang Neil, *The Modern Conjurer;* Hoffmann, *Later Magic;* Hugard, *Modern Magic Manual*

Preparing for the Act

Take one of the red handkerchiefs, start with one corner, and work it into the smaller dye tube. Pack it in snugly so that nothing sticks out.

If the large dye tube has a cup, push it to the end of the tube so that the mouth of the cup opens *outward.* Then put in your colored silks from the *other* end, just as you did with the small tube.

Put the small tube in your right trouser pocket, with the open end (the one where the silk is not covered by the webbing) upward.

Put the large tube in the fold of the filing folder, fairly close to the right-hand edge (as the performer sees it) of the folder, with the open (or silk) end of the tube toward the left. The folder goes on your table, with the crease toward the audience. It is a good idea to roll one half of the folder inward so that when it is unrolled it will still have a curl. That lets the tube lie there comfortably without making the upper leaf of the folder stick up at an angle.

Buckle the strap of the pull around your left arm below the elbow, run the line around behind, and hook the loop over the button of your right shirt cuff.

With the tumbler handy, you are ready to start.

At the end of the last lesson, the knots had just flown from one heap of silk to the other.

Hand Silk-Dyeing

Now stand rather smugly with your hands in your trousers pockets. Grab the small dye tube in your right hand by curling the middle joint of your second finger against the closed (or webbing) end, thus pressing the open end to your palm.

Throughout the trick you must be careful—but oh so casual —in keeping the back of your right hand toward the audience.

Take your hands out of your pockets. Pick up a white silk by one corner between the thumb and forefinger of your right hand.

Hold out your left hand, palm up. Sweep your right hand, trailing the silk, from left to right across your left palm. As the silk brushes across, close your left hand gently on it, and raise the hand. In short, you have drawn the silk through your left hand.

Do this two or three times. The last time, drop the dye tube crosswise into your left hand.

The left hand would close on the silk anyway; only this time, keep it shut.

Hold your closed left fist (containing the dye tube) up, but follow with your eyes the silk in your right hand.

Now tuck the corner of the silk into the top of your left fist. With your right forefinger, give it a good push down into the closed end of the dye tube.

Bring your right hand below your left, and pull out a small corner of the red silk.

Poke some more in at the top. Pull some more out at the bottom.

Keep this up, alternating poking and pulling, until the white silk is all packed into the dye tube, and all of the red silk shows except the top corner, which you catch tight in the crook of your left little finger.

Give another poke at the top, and nip the dye tube between your right thumb and forefinger. As you raise your right hand,

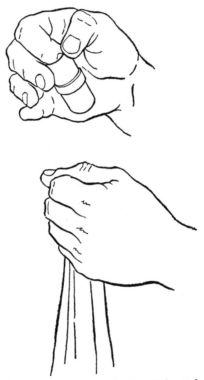

Fig. 58.   Stealing the hand dye tube

with the back toward the audience, the dye tube is masked. (*Fig. 58*). Curl the second, third, and fourth fingers around the tube, freeing your forefinger and thumb.

Reach down and give another tug at the red silk, but don't let go of it yet.

Give another poke at the top.

Another tug at the bottom; this time, carry the red silk away.

But still keep your left fist closed.

Look at the fist; then look around the audience. If you want this to be a sort of sucker gag, you can look very sly, and also very unwilling to open your left fist.

When you finally do, there is nothing left.

Stuff the handkerchief (and the dye tube) into your right trouser pocket, or drop it out of sight.

Silk-Dyeing (Paper Tube)

Now pick up your manila folder in your left hand, the thumb on top at the back edge, fingers underneath where they can grab the dye tube. Just bring your left hand forward—don't raise it too high.

The lower half of the folder will flop down. Take hold of it with your right hand at the bottom edge. Carry the bottom edge upward, and slide it under your left thumb.

Swing your left fingers (and the dye tube) back enough so that the original upper edge of the paper can escape and flop down in its turn.

What you have done is simply to show both sides of the folder without letting anyone see the dye tube.

Roll up the folder around the dye tube, and take it in your left hand. It should be rolled tightly enough to hold the gimmick (to a magician any hidden secret device is a gimmick or a fake) without too much pressure from your left hand.

However, you must relax your grip enough so that the dye tube will slide to the bottom edge of the rolled paper. Stop it from coming out by putting your left little finger across the bottom.

Take a white handkerchief in your right hand, and stuff it in at the bottom of the paper tube. It goes into the empty cup of the dye tube, which you now push part way up, forcing out the first colored handkerchief at the top. Tap the rolled paper against

your right hand until this handkerchief comes within reach. Dip
in with your right hand, and pull the silk slowly out

Show it around once, from left to right.

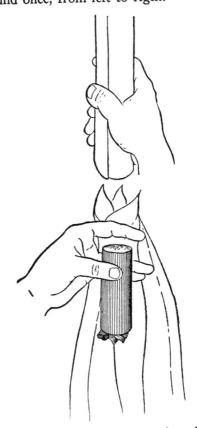

Fig. 59.   Stealing the large dye tube

Then stick the corner between your left second and third
fingertips, so that the silk partly hides the lower opening of the
paper tube. Poke in another white silk at the bottom, bring it out
at the top colored, and catch it too between your left fingers.

Do the same with the third handkerchief. Make sure you get
it packed in hard so that it won't leak back out of the dye tube.

Bring the last colored silk out at the top of the paper very slowly, then put it with the other two hanging from your left hand.

Relax your pressure on the paper, so that the dye tube can slide down until it is wholly behind the silks in your left hand. Nip it there with your left fingers and thumb. Take the rolled-up paper away in your right hand, following it with your eyes. (*Fig.* 59). Pause.

Unroll the paper with a shake. Empty.

Applause.

Drop the whole outfit—paper, silks, and dye tube—out of sight.

The "Lamp-Chimney" Vanish

The last step is the vanish of the handkerchief from the tumbler.

To do this, you must first settle your coat again, and straighten out the cuffs of your shirt.

Do your left cuff first, with your right hand; then your right cuff, with your left hand. This will enable you to unhook the pull from your cuff button, draw it out, and slip it over your right thumb.

Next, take the handkerchief in your left hand, and draw it once or twice through your right hand.

Finally, slip it through the loop, pull the silk through for half its length, and leave it in your right hand. Double the silk, and more or less wad it up. In the process, draw the loop off your right thumb.

Hold the wadded handkerchief at the finger tips of your right hand, the back of the hand to the audience, hiding the pull.

Pick up the tumbler in your left hand. Wait long enough for everyone to realize that it's an ordinary glass.

Then pop the silk in, and take the tumbler with your right palm flat over the mouth, and your left palm flat against the bottom. The silk, fluffing out, should hide the loop of the pull.

Hold the tumbler horizontal, and stretch your arms forward until the pull is taut.

Make sure everyone in the place knows you have a silk handkerchief tightly imprisoned in a tumbler, where they can watch it. If you don't say so, at any rate give them plenty of time to see.

Then take one step forward, and shoot out your arms, easing your right palm away from the glass a little at the back.

The pull will do the rest. If the line is short enough and the handkerchief not too big, you can even show this vanish with your sleeves rolled to the elbow.

The trick wants careful rehearsal. To use a big handkerchief, you must double it *before* you run it through the loop next to your thumb, so that only a quarter instead of a half of its length will project on each side of the loop.

The effect is better with a highball glass than with a water tumbler.

Once you master it, the silk vanish from a tumbler comes closer to real magic than almost any trick I know.

LESSON 14.   The Miser's Dream

What Seems to Happen: You catch half dollars all over the place.

What You Need: Thirty half dollars. A hat or a small bucket of some kind. You can borrow the hat, preferably a bowler. If you use a soft hat, you will need a saucer or butter plate.

Where to Learn More: T. Nelson Downs, *Modern Coin Manipulation* (Cheap edition, *Tricks With Coins*) ; Jean Hugard, *Coin Magic*

This is another trick as old as magic. Yet, with a clever performer, it is always new. It has one of the few really perfect
plots for a magical drama : no explanation is necessary, you need
make no excuses. You do just what anyone would do if he had
the power—collect money from everywhere.

Furthermore, the Miser's Dream will repay you for everything that you as a magician put into it.

Very likely the trick was first done soon after coins were invented; yet Nelson Downs won fame and fortune in the 1890s
with a vaudeville act that was nothing more than the old trick
done better. If your acting is good, the Miser's Dream will charm
people no matter how often they have seen it. Even if your acting isn't very good, the trick has such power that it will almost
go under its own steam.

You can safely show the Miser's Dream before you have ac-
quired much skill with your hands; yet no one has ever lived
long enough to acquire all the skill he could profitably use in the
coin-catching effect.

Downs earned his reputation by his acting; at the same time,
his skill was fantastic. He could let someone call a number, such
as fourteen, and with one swoop pick out exactly fourteen coins
from a hatful of half dollars. He could palm forty half dollars
with perfect grace. Yet he never let his ability tempt him into
showing off.

He realized, as you should, that he had a drama with everything in itself; and he stuck to that.

Coins for Magic

What kind of coins you will use is something to decide by
experiment.

Real half dollars have a convincing jingle, and always impress
the audience.

Real silver dollars are expensive and heavy, but even more

impressive, especially in the East, where you actually run the risk that people may remember the silver cartwheels when they have quite forgotten the trick. Dollars show up better on the stage than halves.

By the way, if you use dollars on the stage, people will always think they are half dollars; if you use halves, people will think they are quarters.

Quarter dollars are too small to be convenient unless you have quite tiny hands.

Magic shops carry "palming coins," which have certain advantages over the real thing. They are cheaper, lighter, and more sharply milled around the edges. Against this, you must remember that they sound tinny, are not nearly so impressive if people get a close look at them, and the newest type of palming coin, which may be all you can get, has no design, but is simply a flat metal disk, and bears almost no resemblance to a coin except in shape.

Palming coins come in dollar and half-dollar sizes.

You can also use foreign coins—for instance, nickel-plated English pennies.

Before you even start rehearsing the Miser's Dream, you will have to learn how to palm a coin. There are at least a dozen ways of palming, and I shall give you five here to start on. I am going to give the the easiest first and the hardest last.

Go back to Lesson 8, and review what you learned about palming an egg.

The Finger Palm

The easiest way is the finger palm. Lay the coin on your second and third fingers, near the crotch, and curl your fingers in gently. (*Fig.* 60).

That's all there is to the finger palm. You can finger-palm three or four coins just as easily as one.

To produce a coin from the finger palm, put your thumb on

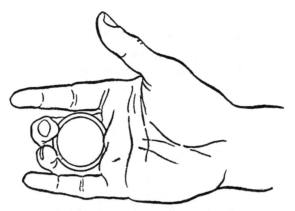

Fig. 60. **Finger-palmed coin**

it, and slide it up and forward until you have it between the tips of your thumb and forefinger.

Relax. Hold your hand as loosely as you can; it doesn't take much to hold the coin in place. And the whole art of deceptive palming is in making your hands look not only natural but casual.

The Thumb Palm

Next comes the flat thumb palm.

Lay the coin on the tips of your first and second fingers. Close the fingers.

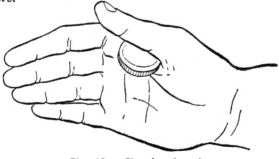

Fig. 61. **Flat thumb palm**

This turns the coin over, and brings it into the crotch of your thumb, where you simply clip it. (*Fig.* 61).

You reproduce it by merely reversing the movement—curl in your fingers, release the coin from your thumb, straighten the fingers.

The Regular Palm

The next method is where things begin to get harder—the regular flat palm.

Your experience in palming an egg will be useful to you now, because you will be able to find the exact spot to palm the coin.

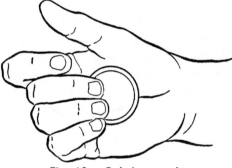

Fig. 62.   Palming a coin

Balance the coin on the tips of your second and third fingers. Close them into the palm, carrying the coin with them. (*Fig.* 62). What you will need to practise is hitting the right spot in your palm with one motion. The things I said about palming a ball or egg apply to a coin, only more so. Don't bend your little little finger and thumb inward; just move the thumb muscle sideways.

This you will have to practise, and no amount of advice can save you from having to practise.

But carry a coin with you, and practise at odd moments; you'll find it's fun.

To reproduce a coin from the regular palm, just let it drop to your finger tips, and put your thumb on it.

Finally, we have the two standbys of professional coin manipulators: the edge palm and the back palm.

The Edge Palm

The edge palm is just like the flat palm, with one important difference: the coin stands out from your palm at about the same

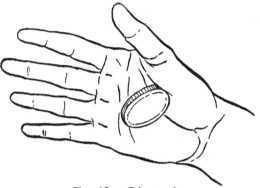

Fig. 63.   Edge palm

angle that your thumb makes with your hand once the coin is palmed. (*Fig.* 63).

Start with the coin on your second and third finger tips, just as you did for the flat palm. But, in bending them inward, curl the third finger more than the second, so that the second finger tip comes to rest on the edge of the coin. This lets you settle the coin in its proper position.

Palming Several Coins

For the simple purpose of palming one half dollar, the edge palm is no better than the flat palm, and has the drawback that the coin, sticking out from your palm, is rather more likely to be seen.

But when you want to palm four or five coins, either as a stack or one on top of another, the edge palm is essential.

To reproduce from the edge palm, curl in your second and third fingers, and nip the coin between them. As you straighten your fingers, move your second finger ahead of the third, so that you can easily catch the coin between thumb and forefinger.

After you can edge-palm one coin with either hand, try palming one, and then sliding another down outside it.

To get them snugly settled, you will have to release the first coin along with the second, and then press both of them together into place. Once you have learned this with two coins, you can almost as easily do it successively with any number up to six or seven.

To reproduce one coin from an edge-palmed stack, draw up the outside one with your third finger tip until you can catch the

Fig. 64.   **Reproducing coins from the edge palm**

edge with your second finger. (*Fig.* 64). From there on, the motion is the same as with one coin.

All fancy coin manipulation is a constant struggle against "talking"—the clicking or grating of the coins. To keep them from talking you must be perfectly gentle; never do anything sudden or violent.

Real coins talk more than palming coins.

The Back Palm

The last move of all is the back palm, and if you learn that, you will be able to do more than a good many magicians.

Back-palming cards is easy, as you will see in another lesson; back-palming coins is rather hard.

Luckily it isn't necessary to know the back palm; you can do the Miser's Dream very nicely without it. But it is an interesting sleight to play with until you master it. If you simply want to perform the Miser's Dream, and never mind about coin manipulation, you can skip this next.

At least when you are starting to learn the back palm, choose a coin that, as nearly as possible, just covers your second and third fingers at the first joint. For a good many people this means a dollar rather than a half dollar. In case of doubt, use the larger coin.

Take the coin between thumb and second and third fingers.

Bend the middle fingers until the nails are against the back of the coin.

Now bring your forefinger and little finger forward, pressing them sideways against opposite edges of the coin. Take your thumb away.

The coin should now be held between your *forefinger and little finger*. The natural tendency is to move those fingers to the front of the coin, pressing it against the middle fingers.

Don't.

Press gently sideways against the edges. If you take your middle fingers away, the coin must still stay right where it is.

So far, it's simple and easy. Now comes the catch.

Straighten all four fingers, so that the coin is hidden behind the second and third, and held by the first and fourth. (*Fig.* 65b).

The chances are three to one that when the joints of your

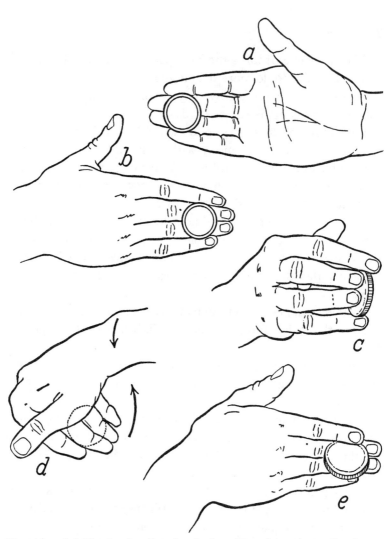

Fig. 65. (a) The back-palmed coin has been brought to the front;
(b) Back-palmed coin; (c) Transferring the coin from back to front;
(d) Wrist motion to hide the transfer; (e) The little finger lets go

middle fingers reach the place where they must clear your first and fourth fingers, you'll drop the coin. Don't think it's a mistake; it's just a difficulty.

Keep trying until you get it; and always remember that sidewise pressure of forefinger and little finger is what holds the coin.

So far, so good. There's worse to come.

The coin has disappeared, and your hand is empty. Then some bright youngster pipes up, "It's back of your hand."

What to do?

Draw back your middle fingers, so that the nails brush the face of the coin again. But instead of stopping there, carry them on until the tips can push against the far edge of the coin, turning it over on the pivot supplied by the pressure of your first and fourth fingers. (*Fig.* 65c).

Straighten your fingers again, and you have the coin in the same position as before, only at the front of your hand instead of at the back. (*Fig.* 65a).

The chances are at least five to one that you'll drop the coin when you first try to turn it over this way.

Keep at it.

Once you can do the movement fairly regularly, you will have to get up in front of a mirror and study the angles by which you can hide it.

Don't think, as your audience probably does, that you can spin the coin from front to back too fast for anyone to see it. If you even try to move that fast, you will drop the coin for sure.

The only good cover is to bend your wrist with a rolling motion, which you will learn more easily from two attempts before a mirror than from ten pages of instructions. (*Fig.* 65d).

You can—and should—make the movement quite slowly, merely keeping some part of your hand between the audience and the coin. This is what the rolling of the wrist accomplishes.

One last difficulty: getting the coin to the rear again.

It sounds perfectly simple. Just curl your middle fingers under again, and revolve the coin the other way. I won't pretend it's as simple as it sounds, because it isn't. You'll drop the coin dozens of times before you learn.

But keep on trying. In one of my favorite coin tricks, I back-palm five silver dollars, which I pick up in a single motion from an edge palm.

One thing more—but not a difficulty, thank goodness.

Unless you are actually going to show the front and back of your hand empty (whence the high-sounding official title of the sleight, the "continuous back-and-front palm"), it is rather better, once you have back-palmed the coin, to let go with your little finger, and clip the coin by the very edge between your first and second fingers. (*Fig.* 65e).

One advantage is that this gives your hand less of a cramped look. With practice, you can even hold two or three coins clipped that way.

The Miser's Dream

Now at last (probably after several days' work) you are ready to start on the Miser's Dream.

The first question is, what will you use to put the coins in?

For a hundred years or more, magicians seemed to think they might be imprisoned if they used anything but a high silk hat. I think that is still the most convenient receptacle; but unfortunately, silk hats are a rarity nowadays. You can never borrow one, and may not even be able to buy one.

Collapsible opera hats will do just as well, and take much less space to carry around, but they too are becoming antiques.

A hard black felt, a bowler, is good if you can find one.

A soft felt (fedora or homburg) is not nearly so good. Half the point of the trick is that people must hear the coins falling into the receptacle. The only way they can hear them in a soft hat is for you to put in a saucer, which looks foolish, and needs explaining.

Rather than use a soft hat, I would advise a small metal pail. You can use a child's tin sand pail, an Oriental brass bucket, or anything of this sort that you can find. For your own convenience, it is much better if the rim is beaded or rolled over outward, so that your thumb will have something to catch hold of.

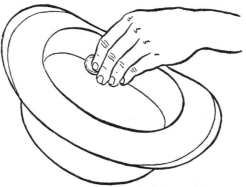

Fig. 66.   Ready for the Miser's Dream

Whatever container you choose, you must start the trick with your stack of thirty coins in your left hand. You can keep them in a pocket until you want them, or pile them behind something on the table. Get them from wherever you like into your left hand.

I shall assume you are going to follow tradition and use a hard hat. The movements are the same, whatever you use.

Grab the hat in your left hand, with the fingers inside against the sweatband, and the thumb reaching over the brim. This puts the stack of coins inside the hat. (*Fig.* 66).

You can show the hat empty if you want, but I wouldn't make a point of it. Why put ideas into people's heads?

Now stand with your left side to the audience. Look intently at a spot about three feet in front of your face.

Pause. Give people time to look where you are looking.

Then snatch at the spot with your right hand, and bring it back closed into a fist. Remember how you caught the silk in Lesson 12?

Open your right fist just enough so that you—and you only—can see inside.

Look pleased. After all, this is "found" money.

Make a tossing movement that brings your right hand just to the mouth of the hat.

At the same instant, let the bottom coin of the stack drop from your left hand. (Look again at *Fig.* 66). You must time the drop neatly; there is no other difficulty.

Lift your right hand as if to catch another coin. Halfway there, check yourself.

Take the first coin out of the hat, and hold it up with a smug grin.

Probably you won't say anything, but your acting should suggest, "I did too catch a coin."

Make the motion of dropping the coin back into the hat.

Actually, you palm it. Use any of the five methods you have learned—whichever comes easiest. Don't try to show off because, after all, the audience thinks dropping the coin into the hat is just a matter of course. Finding the coin is the trick; the rest of the time they should hardly be watching your hands.

As you finish the dropping motion, let another coin fall into the hat from your left hand.

Unless you are using the back palm, turn around to the left.

Pick another spot in the air, put your hand out to it, and daintily draw forth a coin at your right finger tips.

Look at it. Smile. Catching money is one sport that doesn't pall.

Palm the coin, and make the motion of dropping it into the hat. Let one drop from your left hand instead.

You can do this once or twice more; always fix your eyes on

some definite spot in space where the coin is to come from. And always *produce* the coin neatly at your finger tips. Don't just make a swipe, a fumble, and gradually wrestle the coin into view.

Too many young magicians spoil this sort of trick by muddling it. They don't build up people's expectation and focus it on a certain spot, nor do they satisfy the expectation by catching a coin there. They grapple with the coin rather than catch it.

Though perhaps you may not say a word, coin catching is divided into a promise—something over there!—and a deft fulfillment—here!

Don't catch coins out of the air too long. Four or five times is plenty.

Now start among the audience. Take a coin from someone's lapel, another from behind an ear.

You can be surprised at where the coins appear, but you must always give some sign of recognition before you actually bring the money out. Don't look in one direction, then reach in another.

Don't hurry. You can be brisk if that's your natural way; but making money is a trick good enough to stand on its own feet. Give people time to appreciate it.

The mechanics of producing a coin from people's clothes is quite simple, but you should rehearse it until you can work it neatly.

With the back palm, all you must do is take care that people don't catch a glimpse of the coin too soon.

With any of the other palms, bring your hand, palm down, to the spot where you want the coin to come out. The coin is already at, or should now be brought to, your finger tips, but still kept out of sight.

Tuck your fingers behind the lapel, into the cuff, or wherever it is, and then draw back your hand, holding the coin by its extreme edge.

Palming is so much harder than producing that most magicians just take producing for granted. Believe me, half an hour's attention to the way you *produce* a coin from the palm will convert your fumbling, amateur performance of the Miser's Dream into a real miracle.

Another point: pick places where something could possibly be hidden—behind a lamp, not off a wall; from someone's hair, but not off his cheek (unless you can learn to pinch it off a girl's cheek without seeming rude).

Now that your trick is well along, and people have come to take the dropping of each coin into the hat for granted, you may introduce a few comic variations.

If you give a quick look at Lesson 1, you will realize how you can push a coin through the bottom of the hat. Hold it in your right hand as you did when you first learned to make the pass with a coin; push against the crown of the hat, letting the coin slide back behind your fingers; drop one inside from your left hand to make the clink.

Again, you may hold the hat up high in your left hand, and throw a coin through the crown with your right hand.

To do this, of course you merely palm it. But take a tip from me, and palm it as you *draw back* your hand to throw, *not* on the forward motion. And don't drop the coin with your left hand at the exact instant when you throw with your right; wait a fraction of a second, so that people can shift their attention from hand to hat, following your gaze.

You can swallow a coin, follow it down your left sleeve with your right forefinger, and have it land noisily in the hat.

Look back at Lesson 8 and you will know nearly all you need to about the mechanics. Only don't put the coin in your mouth and push it out; palm it as your right hand travels toward your lips. Open and shut your mouth in a flash, then stick your tongue in your cheek.

You can toss a coin way up in the air—far higher than any ceiling—follow it up with your eyes, then down, hold out the hat, and catch the coin—clink!

I say again, palm the coin on the *down* swing. Your fingers must be extended and empty by the time they are flung up.

This is just as true of the back palm; besides which you would probably lose the coin with the violence of the toss if you didn't get it safely anchored first.

By now, you have probably expended the whole stack of coins from your left hand.

This is, after all, the Miser's Dream, and you are entitled to gloat a little. Dip your hand into the hatful of coins, shaking and jingling them.

Finger-palm five or six.

Reach into some safe hiding place—under a man's vest is good —give a shake to make the coins jingle, and bring them out in your cupped hand.

This leaves them in position to be finger-palmed again. Make the motion of dumping them into the hat, but actually keep them in the finger palm, and jolt the brim of the hat with your right wrist so that the other coins jingle loudly.

Go to somebody else in the audience, and repeat the production, only bring the coins out in a fan at your finger tips rather than as a clinking handful.

If you want to finger-palm them again, you can shake them gloatingly. Otherwise, hold up your right hand, and let them cascade into the hat.

One good production of several coins from the finger palm is to pull a small boy's nose with your right hand, holding the hat just underneath to catch the snootful of money. This will also work from the edge palm if you are able to do it.

The one flaw in the Miser's Dream is that it has no ready-made ending. There is no sound reason why you should not go on catching money all night.

So your own acting will have to provide a strongly marked finish.

You can pretend the hat is too heavy to hold any more. You

can say that if you keep on you'll just have to pay it all out in income taxes.

Somehow you must make a definite end, and let people know that they can applaud.

Just remember that in the Miser's Dream palming is a side issue. Your eyes, your timing, the deftness of your movements, are what make the trick.

LESSON 15.   Card Palming

What Seems to Happen: Mostly nothing.

You can make cards disappear and reappear.

You read a man's mind, finding a card you haven't seen him touch.

What You Need: For plain palming, cards with a high finish —bridge size, if you have narrow hands.

For back palming, soft cards with no white border on the back, such as 999 Steamboats or Bees.

Where to Learn More: Lang Neil, *The Modern Conjurer;* Downs and Hilliard, *The Art of Magic;* S. W. Erdnase, *The Expert at the Card Table*

Card palming sounds very difficult, but don't be fooled. It's easier to palm a dozen cards than one coin.

There's no hunting for the exact spot next to your thumb muscle; your grip needn't be so tight as with a coin; cards don't talk so loud.

But just because it is easy, some magicians never trouble to learn that there is also a right spot for palming a card.

Perfect card palming, like any other palming, should be smooth, but not furtive; bold, but not careless. First, however, you must find the spot.

Hold your hand out flat, palm up.

Lay a card on it running straight, lengthwise, right down the middle. Don't let it twist to either side, and don't put it closer to either edge of your hand. The outer left-hand corner (if you are using your right hand) should come over the cushion at the tip of your little finger.

Now you can palm after a fashion by simply closing all your fingers a little. Lots of magicians never go beyond that point.

But the secret of neat palming lies in that little finger tip. Bend it in just a trifle, and you will find that you have caught the card diagonally between the outer left-hand corner and the inner right-hand corner, which pushes against the bulge of your thumb muscle. (*Fig.* 67).

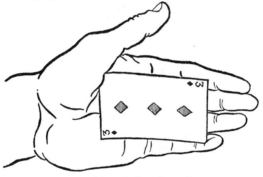

Fig. 67.   Palmed card

Just relax your hand, and hold the card by those two corners.

You don't bend the card hopelessly out of shape, and your fingers are together but not stiff. Let your thumb fall in the way that is natural to you.

Drop the card and palm it again a few times, until you get the feel in your little finger tip.

The Top Palm

Now for the process of stealing the card from the pack.

Don't let this expressive magical term make you feel or try to act like a thief. Perhaps you had better think of palming rather as a pick-up and delivery service.

The card you want to palm should be on top of the deck. Hold this in dealing position in your left hand, but get your thumb out of the way.

Bring your right hand forward, palm downward, and put the tip of your little finger on the outer right corner of the top card.

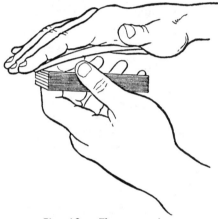

Fig. 68.   The top palm

Push away from you, sliding the top card perhaps a quarter of an inch ahead; then press down with your right little finger.

Of its own accord the top card springs into perfect position in your right palm. (*Fig. 68*).

This, again, is so easy that magicians often fool themselves instead of the audience: they bring up the right hand, palm off the top card, and move the hand away.

They might just as well hang out a sign saying, "Performer now palms off top card."

I hope you've been taking lessons from me long enough not to do anything so silly.

Bring your right hand up; palm off the card; then take the

deck by the ends in your right hand, sliding it from side to side as if to square up the cards.

Now you can, if you like, carry the pack away in your *left* hand, following with your eyes, and keeping your right hand dead still.

Or you can give the deck out to be shuffled with your right hand. To do that, hold the cards in a Y grip, your right fore-

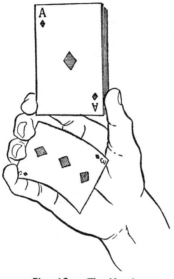

Fig. 69.   The Y grip

finger on the side close to the near end, your right thumb opposite, so that the whole pack is exposed.

The Y grip (so called from the shape your hand makes) is a very convenient one whenever you have cards palmed. (*Fig.* 69). Only if you want to use it then, remember to use it always.

Palming Several Cards

If you want to palm off more than one card at a time from the top of the pack, put your left little finger between them and the rest of the deck, as if you were getting ready to make the shift.

Then, when your right hand covers the pack, you can push the cards into palming position simply by straightening your *left* little finger.

You have just learned the simple top palm. There are also a bottom palm and a side-steal palm (which you can learn from other books if you ever need them), various forms of "color change," and the back palm.

Many magicians (especially the old-fashioned ones who stick to time-honored ways) use the top palm so that they can hand the deck out to be shuffled after someone has chosen a card, and it has been shifted to the top.

In addition, there are two marvelous tricks that depend wholly on the top palm. One of them I will teach you now, the other in the next lesson.

Williams' Card in Pocket

Give a man the deck, and ask him to shuffle it well. Let him keep it.

Tell him to think of a number from one to fifty-two, inclusive.

Tell him you are going to turn your back or leave the room, and during that time he is to count down to his number from the top of the pack.

He is to look at and remember the card at that number. For instance, if he thought five, he is to count down and look at the fifth card.

Then he is to put everything back just as it was. Explain that he mustn't reverse the order of the cards, because that would bring the one he saw to the top of the deck. You want it left just where he found it.

When he has finished, you turn around, or come back into the room, and take the pack from him—the first time you've touched it since the trick began.

You fan through the cards, occasionally looking him fixedly in the eye.

Finally, you draw out one card with its back to the audience. You don't show it, but simply put it in your pocket.

Then you ask what number the man had thought of—not what card, but what number. As I mentioned in Lesson 2, be careful about this, or he may sing out the name of his card.

Suppose he says eight. Very slowly and carefully, you deal off seven cards from the top into his hand.

The next one should be his—unless it's in your pocket.

Deal off the eighth card. Put it face down on the others in his hand, and say emphatically, "Now either I've got it in my pocket, or that's your card. Will you look and see if it is?" He looks.

It isn't his.

Slowly you pull a card from your pocket, and turn it over.

That's it.

You see that I've gone back to my old way of telling you all about the trick except how to do it.

This is such a stunning effect that I want you to get the plot firmly in mind before you begin to worry about palming.

So I have tried to describe the trick as the spectator sees it, only more carefully; and still I hope you won't see how palming could do you any good.

Do you give up? Or have you figured it out?

Here's how.

Everything is honest and plain sailing until the man hands you back the deck.

Then you fan the cards, and try to look as if you were reading his mind through his eyes.

Slide the bottom card over until it's behind the middle of the fan.

Pull that card out, and hold it up. Pause.

Put the card quite slowly in your pocket. Plunge your hand all the way in after it.

Palm the card, and leave your hand in your pocket for a moment, until people's attention can be steered to something else. Then, quite casually, and with no hurry at all, bring your hand back out with the card palmed.

Reach over and take the pack in your right hand, dropping the palmed card on top.

At the same moment, make an inquiring gesture, with your *left* hand, toward the man who chose the card, and look straight at him.

You see what has happened. Putting the palmed card (which originally came from the bottom) on top of the pack has moved all the numbers up one. Whatever card the man looked at is now one number further down in the pack.

Count off the cards, very slowly and carefully, into his palm.

When you reach the last card, point to it as it lies on top of the pack.

"This should be it, then."

Deal it on to the pile in his hand, and point to it again. Follow it with your eyes. "Will you look?"

As he looks, so do you, and everyone else will look too. That is the moment for you very gently and quietly to palm the top card off the deck. This, naturally, is his card. Don't dawdle, but above all don't hurry : put your right hand matter-of-factly into your trouser pocket as you await the man's reply.

No, he says, the card isn't his.

Of course not. Grandly you bring out his card at your finger tips from the pocket.

There are very few better card tricks or mind-reading tricks in existence than this.

Color Changes

A special variety of palming is the color change, or transformation, which magicians call by that name simply to distinguish it from other card sleights known as the top change, bottom change, palm change, and snap change. Actually, color has nothing to do with it; one card changes to another when you pass your hand over it, and that's that.

There are many methods; I am going to give what I think are the best two.

Clip Color Change

The first is called "the clip."

Hold the deck in your right hand, back to palm, the tips of your second, third, and fourth fingers along one side, the thumb tip at the other side. Your forefinger rests on the end of the deck.

Hold your left hand palm outward, so that people shall know it is empty.

Then, keeping the fingers together, draw your left hand three times toward you, lengthwise, over the face of the pack.

After the third rub, the card on the front changes to another.

The first rub is perfectly innocent, and gives you a chance to look at the front card and at your empty left palm.

On the second rub, your left thumb goes behind the pack, and your right forefinger pushes back the top card (or cards) into the fork of your left thumb. (*Fig.* 70).

As you draw your left hand toward you, palm the card.

On the third rub, leave the palmed card on the face of the deck; finish the motion cleanly, and turn your left hand palm outward.

There are two things to be careful of about the clip.

One, try not to let the repeated movement seem blurred or fussy; do it neatly and simply.

Two, unless you take special care the card may talk as it clears the near end of the deck.

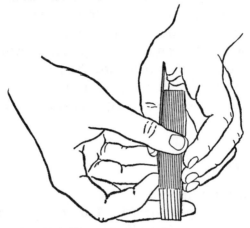

Fig. 70.   **The clip color change**

Erasing the Spot

The clip is not the best of the color changes except for one trick. That trick is so useful for keeping an audience in hand that I think you should learn it right away.

The deck has a three-spot on the bottom (any one but the three of spades).

You claim you can rub out the middle spot.

You do. But you are so clumsy that everyone sees you have merely carried away the front card, a corner of which still sticks out from your left hand.

If the audience is young or inclined to be boisterous, pandemonium will break loose.

Look as guilty as you can for as long as you can, and get the crowd as excited as you can.

Finally, you notice the telltale corner sticking out.

"Oh, that?" You show the card. "That's just the spot that I took out of the middle."

So it is—the ace.

This is the granddaddy of all sucker gags, and if you start your series of card tricks with it, none but a very bold crowd will dare give you any trouble for some time afterward.

Pick out the ace, two, and three of any suit except spades. Put the three on the bottom of the pack, the two on top of the pack, and the ace under the two.

Before you start your rubbing motion, separate off the top two cards from the deck with your right first fingernail. When you do the clip, carry away two cards instead of one.

Then, instead of drawing your hand toward you for the third time, move it clumsily across the pack from side to side, depositing the two-spot, and shifting the ace so that a corner sticks out in your left hand.

The rest is up to you and the audience.

The advantage of the clip color change for this trick is that you can control how many cards you palm.

The Side-Steal Color Change

For any other purpose, the side-steal color change is by far the prettiest I know of.

It, like some of the handkerchief knots, is perfectly simple once you get the proper starting position through your head. But you'd be surprised how often people turn the pack wrong way to, mystifying no one but themselves.

Lay the pack on the table in front of you, face up. Pick it up in your right hand so as to expose the whole face of the deck: put your forefinger at the extreme far right corner, on the end, and your thumb on the end at the extreme near right corner. (*Fig.* 71a).

Now turn both hands palm up.

Hold it. Look at your empty palms.

Turn your right hand over, and lay the deck in your left hand face up, in dealing position.

That's all anyone must see. But actually, as you put the pack in your left hand, your left finger tips hit the top card at about the middle, and slide it gently sidewise under your right hand. (*Fig.* 71b).

Palm the card in your right hand, and you are ready to make the color change by passing once over the deck.

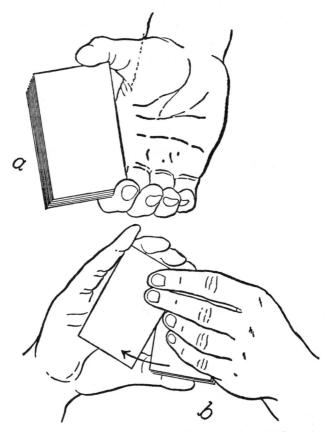

Fig. 71.   (a) Ready for the side-steal color change; (b) The side-steal

This steal wants some experimenting before you actually start hand practice. You will find it is neater not to slide the card straight out, but to push the near end further than the far end by giving a twist with your left first and second fingers.

Watch out for two things.

First, when you start to slide the card, don't frantically let go with your right thumb and squeeze the edge of your right hand against the face of the deck. Your right hand is at somewhat of an angle to the pack, and that is why I advise you to give the top card a twist as you slide it out.

Second, be very gentle, so as to defeat our old enemy, noise. The stolen card is likeliest to talk as the last corner clears the deck, just when you were thinking it was all right.

Reversing the Color Change

There is an excellent effect using the side-steal, which I shall give in the next lesson. Here is something half way between a trick and a flourish that I have always liked.

Do the side-steal color change extra slowly and carefully, giving people time to realize just what is happening.

Sometimes they will ask you to change the card back to what it was before. If they don't, offer to do so anyhow.

Suppose you have changed the king of hearts into the queen.

"This wouldn't be much of a trick if the king were on the back of the pack," you say, sliding the top card part way out and showing it. "Nor if it were here."

As you say that, you lift off the front card by the ends with your right hand, your thumb at one end and your middle finger at the other.

Actually, of course, the king *was* next to the bottom; so you must lift off not the bottom card but the bottom *two* cards.

The Double Lift

The move is known as the "double lift," and many magicians think it takes a lot of practice. As a matter of fact, you can pick up the edges of the two cards with your thumb, one after an-

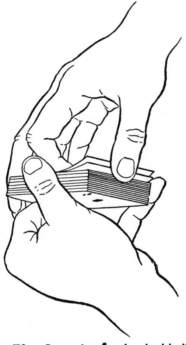

Fig. 72.   Preparing for the double lift

other, and then let them spring together. (*Fig.* 72). Bow the two cards slightly toward your right palm, and no one can possibly tell that they aren't one.

If you put the two back on the pack so as to overlap about half way to the right, you will find that your left finger tips are in perfect position to slide the lower one of the two cards into your right palm.

With your left thumb draw the front card, the queen, on to the deck, and you are all set to change the queen back into the king. (*Fig.* 73).

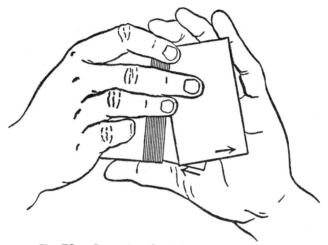

Fig. 73.   **Reversing the side-steal color change**

The Back Palm

Now we come to a flourish that was at one time considered the very essence of card manipulation. It really isn't important at all, but it's fun to do, and if you cut it short it makes a bright addition to a program.

Go back to Lesson 14, and look over the part about back-palming a coin. The motions aren't exactly the same, but the basic idea is.

Hold a card near the lower end at the center between your thumb and middle finger.

Bend your middle finger so that the card rests against the top joint.

Stretch out your forefinger and little finger so that they reach diagonally across the side edges of the card. (*Fig.* 74a).

Let go with your thumb, and straighten your second and third fingers.

Hold your hand out flat, all four fingers close together. (*Fig. 74b*).

There may be some stray corners showing, but you will have the card curved lengthwise and hidden behind your hand. Practise that until you can do it with no stray corners showing; it won't take you long.

Next, back-palm the card; then close your fist. (*Fig. 74c*).

Stretch out your thumb up the face of the card, and press down gently.

Straighten your four fingers, but *don't let go the edges of the card with your first and fourth fingers*. You want the card clipped on the front just the same as you have learned to hold it at the back.

To back-palm the card again, draw back your middle fingers to clear the outer end, and simply close your fist. You don't need your thumb for this.

As with the coin, you must be very careful about your angles and the rolling of your wrist. This is the only part of back-palming a card that is harder than back-palming a coin: the card is bigger and more conspicuous, so that the angles are more difficult.

That was pretty easy, wasn't it?

But don't think you're done yet. When you can do the "continuous back-and-front palm" with one card, you should go on and learn to do it with several.

Back-palm one card. Then take another between your thumb and second finger tip.

Close all four fingers, bringing the back-palmed card to the front, and with your thumb slide the new card on top of the first one.

Grip the two cards as one, and back-palm them together.

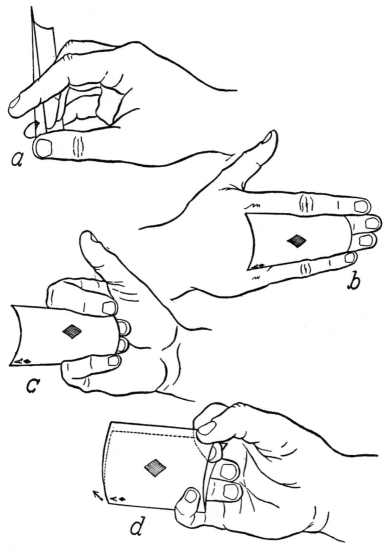

Fig. 74. (a) Starting to back-palm a card; (b) The card back-palmed;
(c) Moving the card from back to front; (d) Reproducing several back-
palmed cards singly

It isn't much harder to shift two cards back and forth from rear to front than it is to shift one.

To reproduce them one at a time, close your second, third, and fourth fingers; leave your first finger straight.

Put your thumb on the corner index of the front card, and push down, bending this card more than the one under it.

Now curl your forefinger so that it comes between the two cards. (*Fig.* 74d). Put your thumb against your forefinger, and the card will snap free at the corner from your little finger.

Open your fingers, and there you are, one card back-palmed, one held up between thumb and forefinger.

It isn't safe to lean too heavily on the back palm as the foundation of a trick. But here's one with a surprise ending that you can probably do.

Five-Card Vanish and Recovery

Stand with your left side to the audience. In your left hand, fan five cards, faces to the front.

Reach down with your right hand, and take one card away from the fan.

Make a tossing movement, down and up. On the down-swing, back-palm the card.

On the up-swing, follow with your eyes, and look quickly to the ceiling.

Pause.

If you want to show the back of your hand, you can. Don't try it unless you're sure of your skill.

Take another card from the fan, and toss that away.

Another.

Another.

When you reach for the fifth card, spread your left hand out nearly flat. Behind this cover, bring the four back-palmed cards to the front of your right hand, and palm them in your left hand as you take the last card in your right. (*Fig. 75*).

Move your right hand away, and make the fifth card disappear with a toss.

Hold the pose.

Reproduce the one back-palmed card. Then reach down behind

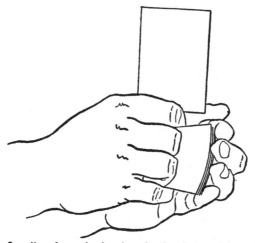

Fig. 75.   **Stealing from the back palm for the vanish and recovery**

your left knee with your left hand, and bring out the other four cards in as neat a fan as you can manage.

In all back-palming tricks, particularly with cards, it is very hard to resist the temptation to stretch the palming arm straight backward, and turn your back on the audience. Don't do it.

If the trick is to be any good at all, you must depend on a wrist movement alone for your angles. And when you are showing with people well to the side of you, you will just have to leave out back-palming tricks.

LESSON 16.   Two Great Tricks of Card Palming

What Seems to Happen: Two people draw cards. You bring
the first one to the face of the pack by slapping it. The second
one you produce wherever in the pack the chooser stops you.

You take ten cards in your left hand, and make them pass,
one at a time, up your sleeve and down into your trouser pocket.

What You Need: A pack of cards.

Where to Learn More: Lang Neil, *The Modern Conjurer;*
    Downs, *The Art of Magic*

I call these two tricks great, the first because Nate Leipzig
used the presentation I give, and anything he did with cards was
perfect; the second because it belongs to the list of immortal
tricks as old as magic and always young, along with the Rising
Cards, the Egg Bag, and the Miser's Dream.

Both tricks are simple. They are so simple that you may be
caught out unless you have a steady nerve, and can make people
look where you want them to, not where they want to.

Leipzig's Lightning Locations

Have two cards chosen. Bring them to the top of the pack,
and give a false shuffle that leaves them still there.

Most methods of bringing two cards to the top will leave the
second chosen card on top of the first. If this is so, you will have
to make some apology for changing the order of precedence.

Anyway, turn to the man whose card is (secretly) on top of
the deck. Hold the cards in dealing position face up in your left
hand.

Ask him if, by any accident, the front card is his.

No. (Of course not.)

Very well. The point of this trick—you explain, in substance

—is to show how fast you can find his card once you know what it is. You don't know what his card is, and you don't want to know just yet. But you will slap the pack with your right hand.

(As you say this, do so. Leave your hand covering the deck.)

The moment you hit it, you want him to call the name of his card out loud.

In the following fraction of a second, you will try to find his card from among all fifty-two.

As you say this, take the pack in your right hand, in position for the side-steal.

Gesture with both hands to emphasize what you say, and turn them palm up in the process.

All right. Does he understand?

Just then, with everybody looking at *him,* you quietly turn your right hand over, and execute the side-steal.

Keep the card palmed, and stare at the one on the front of the deck.

Ready?

Bang!

He can hardly get the words out of his mouth before you snatch your right hand from the deck, leaving his card on display.

So much for card number one. Card number two, of course, is now on top of the deck; but the less said about that the better.

Go to your second helper.

Point to the bottom card. He didn't by any chance choose that one, did he?

No.

Do a double lift with the top two cards.

Nor that one?

As he sees not the top card but the second card, he can only say no.

With the first card, you say, you chose where it should appear; but that isn't necessary either.

Hand the whole pack to your helper. Ask him to give you cards off the top as long as he feels like it. Whenever he wants to, he can stop.

The first card he gives you, face down in your left hand, is his. Take the other cards one after another on top of this.

When he stops, say, "This one" (pointing to the top one in your left hand), "or this one?" (pointing to the deck).

He will almost invariably say he means the one on the deck. Have him give you that card too.

Bring your right hand quietly up to the cards you hold, in position for the side-steal. Only don't turn your hands over, or move them at all.

"Are you satisfied with this card?" Look the man straight in the eye. "Do you want to go on any further?"

As you say this, do the side-steal; and then, without waiting, bring your right hand back to the left, and drop the palmed card.

"All right. You're satisfied with this one." Point to the top card with your right forefinger.

"Ready? What was it?"

Instead of slapping the top card with your right palm, snap it loudly with your second finger.

Turn it over.

Loud applause.

The Cards Up the Sleeve

Now we come to a grand old trick that almost anyone can go through the motions of; yet, if you can learn to do it well, you will be a real magician.

Count off ten cards from the pack.

Take the ten in your left hand and count them slowly, out loud, into your right hand, one in front of another.

Slide the fourth card a little bit below the others, making what would be an in-jog if you were doing an overhand shuffle. Don't pause or call attention to this. Count straight through, out loud, from one to ten.

Square up, palm the three cards above the in-jog with your right hand, and take the rest, also in your right hand, with the Y grip.

Stretch out your left hand, palm to the front. Look at it for a moment, then take the cards with that hand.

Reach your right hand into your trouser pocket. First shove the palmed cards into the upper front corner of the pocket. Then scoop up any change, or anything else you may have in the pocket.

Nip the bottom of the pocket between your first and second fingers, so that when you withdraw your hand full of change, the pocket will be pulled inside out.

The palmed cards, being now out of the way up in the corner, won't come out or show at all.

Dump the other contents of your pocket somewhere. Turn to face the audience.

Hold your left arm out straight at shoulder height.

Point at your left hand with your right forefinger as you explain that you are going to make the cards travel up your left sleeve (follow the motion with your forefinger), around behind, and down into your trouser pocket. For once, a magician admits using his sleeve!

Gesture at the pocket with your palm outward.

Push the pocket back in, daintily using only the first and second fingers of your right hand.

Now, all ready?

Stand up straight. Throw out your chest. Left arm at full length.

Look at the cards. Point.

Snap!

(You make the noise by brushing the corner of the cards sharply with your left thumb.)

Pause. People must realize, beyond any doubt, not only that the first step in the trick has happened, but also that your right hand is empty.

Don't say anything about it; just stand still until the fact of that bare right palm can sink in.

Reach into your pocket, knocking the palmed cards down out of their hidden corner.

Pull out one card.

"That's one."

Toss it on the table. You have seven cards in your left hand, whereas you should have nine. Now is the time for an easy, useful, and deceptive sleight called the false count.

The False Count

Try counting cards naturally from your left hand into your right, the order undisturbed—that is, stick each card from the left hand under the ones in the right. It is a quick, simple, noisy movement. The thing that someone watching you will usually count by is the noise as the left edge of the right-hand pile snaps away from your left finger tips.

Your left hand stays still; your right hand swings left and then right each time you take another card.

To make a false count, your right hand swings left and then right with a loud snap, but you don't take off the top card from the left-hand pile. You leave it there. (*Fig.* 76).

Try a real count several times over. Then sneak in a false one without varying the rhythm of your right hand or the snap of the cards. Keep the end of the cards pointed forward, so that the faces are hidden.

If you had ten cards, and false-counted one, you would seem to have eleven. Now you have seven, and on the third and fifth cards you miscount, giving what everyone thinks is a total of nine.

Stand up straight. Snap!

Another card gone. Make sure that the triumphant gesture of your right hand shows the palm empty again.

Out comes card number two from the pocket.

Miscount the seven cards in your left hand as eight.

Ready again. Snap!

Right hand empty. Card from pocket.

Fig. 76.   **The false count**

Count the seven cards as seven, trying hard to make your real count exactly like your false count. Jog the fourth card as you did on the first count.

Palm off the top three cards.

Take the rest in your left hand, and keep your eye on them.

Stand up straight. Snap!

Don't look guilty. Don't hurry. As a matter of course, put your hand into your trouser pocket.

Now stop. Fumble in the pocket. Look puzzled.

And bring your right hand out empty. Look surprised at the empty palm. Pause. Sudden dawn of intelligence.

"Oh. It must have caught at the elbow."

Give a little hitch to your left sleeve at the elbow with your right hand.

"There."

Again your right palm is certainly empty. Reach into the pocket.

"I thought so." Bring out card number four.

False-count the remaining four in your left hand as six.

Hold your left arm well out. An extra loud snap.

A slight gesture of surprise shows your right hand empty. "That must have been two at once."

So it was.

Count the last four cards as four, and palm off two.

"Sometimes, if I move fast enough, I can stop a card in *here* before it gets to my pocket." As you say "here," you reach inside the left shoulder of your coat, and leave the cards in the top of the sleeve.

Snap!

Hastily clap your right hand to your shoulder, outside.

"I think I caught it."

Don't put your right hand in; pull back the lapel with your left hand, so that the two cards show, sticking up out of your sleeve.

Bring them out, and toss them on the table.

You have two cards left in your left hand.

Turn them to face the audience, and remark what cards they are.

Lay them together, and palm the rear one by the side-steal. The front card stays unchanged.

Perfectly casually, your right hand goes into your pocket.

Snap!

"What was that card?"

Everyone shouts the name.

"So it is." Bring out the card, and show they are right.

The last card is a sticker. You can devise your own way of making it go.

For myself, I take it in my *right* hand and hold it well over to the *left*.

I make the motion of taking the card in my left hand, knuckles toward the audience.

Just before I close my left hand around the card, I back-palm the pasteboard in my right hand.

I follow my left hand with my eyes, keeping it half open as if to hold the card without bending it.

A moment later I turn my right hand over, bringing the card from back to front palm.

Pause. Snap of the left fingers.

People have just seen my right palm empty, so I simply put my right hand in my pocket for the last card.

"Four of hearts" (or whatever it was).

LESSON 17.   The Sponge Balls

What Seems to Happen: You show a ball of rubber sponge about an inch and a half in diameter. You pull it in two, which somehow produces two full-sized balls. You pull one of those in two again. You put two of the balls in your left hand and one in your pocket. You open your left hand and roll out three balls. You do this over and over, putting two in your hand and one in your pocket, and rolling out three again. You put a ball under each of two teacups. They both wind up under one cup. You pass the third ball under the cup too. Finally you give somebody two balls to hold, and make another ball disappear. When he opens his hand, he is holding three.

What You Need: A good-sized rubber sponge and a pair of sharp scissors. Cut four cubes, about an inch and a half square, off the sponge, and keep trimming down edges until the balls are more or less round.

Two teacups.

Where to Learn More: Hugard, *Modern Magic Manual*

Sponge-ball routines are one of the few really new additions to magic in the last fifteen or twenty years. They are ideal for an impromptu act over lunch with business friends, among a knot of people in a corner at a dull party, and that sort of thing.

They aren't hard to work, but your pantomime has to be good. You can't let a sponge-ball routine drag; it must be bright and brisk, with no pauses for slow-motion or impressive patter.

You have discovered by now that in teaching you most tricks I have tried to slow you down. I have emphasized the pauses much more than the movements.

With the sponge balls you must pause just long enough for people to see clearly what has happened—long enough for them to see, but scarcely enough for them to realize.

In short, you will have to learn by experiment just how fast you can work the trick, and don't slow down beyond that point.

You can palm a sponge ball just like any other ball; it is light enough so that you don't need a very firm grip.

If you prefer, you can nip a bit of the rubber in the fork of your thumb. Or you can use the finger palm.

The Basic Sponge-Ball Move

The only special move you need is the trick of squashing two balls together so that they look like one. This, of course, is the key point where sponge balls are different from solid balls.

Simply bring the ball from your palm (or the fork of your thumb) to a finger palm, and then roll it a little further forward still, but not far enough to show at your finger tips.

Reach out for the other ball with your fingers above and thumb, outstretched, underneath.

If you grab the ball firmly, it will mash together with the one in your fingers. You can hold the two together between your thumb and second finger; to a casual glance they look just like one ball.

The Routine

Start the routine with all four balls in your right trouser pocket.

Reach in, and crush *three* balls together tight.

Bring them out as one at your right finger tips. Show them rather quickly.

Then spread out your left hand and look at it. Without saying anything, you must emphasize that your left hand is empty, rather than that there is only one ball in your right.

With your left hand, make the motions of pinching a piece off the ball in your right. Let one of the three pop out full size.

Put it on the table with your left hand.

Pass the two balls, still held as one, from your right second finger and thumb to your left second finger and thumb. This time, your gestures are quite plain: nothing in either hand except one sponge ball.

"Pinch off" a piece with your right hand.

Put that ball on the table.

This leaves you with one ball in your left hand.

Make the pass with it, just as you learned to do with a coin in Lesson 1—palm it in your left hand as you make the motion of putting it in your right.

Remember the size of an expanded sponge ball, and don't close your right fist too tight.

Make a tossing movement toward your right trouser pocket, and fling open your right hand.

Don't be so brisk that people fail to see your right hand empty.

Reach in and bring out the fourth ball.

Make the pass casually and rather quickly, palming the ball in your right hand as you seem to put it in your left.

But this time, there really is a ball in your left hand, so your job is very easy indeed. Toss the ball from your left hand beside the other two on the table.

Hold your left hand out, palm up.

Pick up a ball from the table, and put it in your left hand, which you close.

Pick up a second ball, adding the one you have palmed in your right hand; show the two for a moment as one, and put that (i.e. them) in your left hand.

What little patter you use will come in here: "Two in my left hand. One in my pocket."

Pick up the last ball with your right hand, and palm it on the way to your right trouser pocket. Make the motion of pocketing the ball, but keep it palmed.

If you are working with people all around you—which, as I said, is when the sponge balls are at their best—you had better grab your right coat lapel as an excuse to keep your hand closed. I know that by this time you can palm neatly and safely; but with people at the sides there just is no such thing as safe palming.

In making the pass, too, you will have to modify my teaching in past lessons, and play it close to the vest instead of stretching your arms out grandly.

Open your left fist, and roll the three balls out on the table.

Do the routine over again.

"One, two in my left hand." (Add the palmed ball to the second one you pick up.)

"And one in my pocket." (Palm the last ball.)

Out they come rolling again—three.

You will have to judge by experience and by the particular crowd of people how often you should repeat this routine. My guess is not less than three times nor more than five.

You end up with one ball palmed in your right hand, and three balls on the table.

Set the two teacups mouth down on the table, with your left hand.

Pick up a ball from the table in your right hand, secretly adding the palmed one, and hold the two up as one.

Pick up the right-hand teacup with your left hand; put the "one" ball under the cup, and clap the cup down so that people

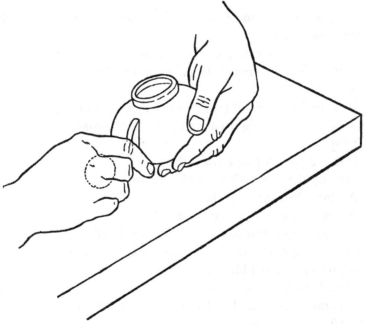

Fig. 77. Pretending to put a sponge ball under the cup

can't see the two balls expand. Don't seem hurried in putting it down—just prompt.

Pick up another ball in your right hand. Make the pass, pretending to put it in your left.

With your right forefinger and thumb, tilt the left-hand teacup away from you by its handle, just long enough to make a sort of shoveling motion of the left hand toward yourself. (*Fig. 77*). Then clap the cup down.

What you are supposed to have done, obviously, is put the ball from your left hand under the cup.

"One ball here. One ball here."

Presto!

Turn over the left cup with your left hand, and set it aside.

Pick up the right cup with your left hand, and show the two balls.

Pick up one of the two balls in your right hand, secretly adding the palmed ball.

With your left hand, set the cup over the ball on the table. Lift it again long enough to poke the two in your right hand underneath.

Pick up the other ball (which you haven't been using for some moments) in your right hand, and make the pass, closing your left fist.

Presto again. A toss toward the cup.

Pick up the cup with your right hand.

All three balls are together.

Ask someone to hold out his hand.

You pick up a ball in each hand, secretly adding the palmed one on the right. Put the ball from your left hand into the man's hand, which you tell him to close.

Then have him open it long enough for you to give him the two as one. Use your left hand to close his fingers tight over the ball.

Pick up the third ball in your left hand, make the pass, and make a toss with your right fist.

Bingo!

When he opens his hand, he has all three balls.

This routine, too, can be repeated, but I think it is a little dangerous unless you are very sure of yourself.

In the end, just grab all the balls and stuff them back in your pocket.

LESSON 18.   The Multiplying Billiard Balls

What Seems to Happen: You produce a solid red enameled wooden ball (known as a "billiard ball" in the magic trade, although it is a good deal smaller and lighter than any you will find on a pool table). It vanishes and reappears once or twice, and then multiplies at your very finger tips into two, three, and finally four.

What You Need: A set of three (or four) solid balls and a hollow half shell, which you will have to buy from a magic shop. Make every effort to get a turned wooden shell, not a metal one. The inch-and-three-quarter size of ball looks a great deal more professional than the inch-and-one-quarter. The inch-and-one-half size is all right.

Where to Learn More: Fischer, *Illustrated Magic;* Downs, *The Art of Magic;* Hugard, *Modern Magic Manual;* Burling Hull, *Expert Billiard Ball Manipulation;* Nevil Maskelyne and David Devant, *Our Magic*

In a way, the multiplying billiard balls, or Excelsior Billiard Ball Trick, is very much like the sponge balls—one small ball turns into several. Yet, in every essential respect, the two tricks are exact opposites.

Not only is the method different, but the whole presentation of the billiard ball trick is slow and graceful instead of short and snappy; deft instead of pell-mell.

Go back to Lesson 8 and Lesson 14, and refresh your mind about palming.

The Excelsior Billiard Ball Trick has been included in cheap magic sets for years, and a great many children have had magic sets; the three little red balls and shell are very well known.

To fool the magic-set owners, and keep a superb trick alive, you will have to do more than just roll the balls, one after an-other, out of the shell. Your palming and your timing are what will distinguish you from a child with a magic set.

On the other hand, you mustn't be carried away by your own skill.

Billiard balls are the most delightful things in the world to palm and play around with. The moment you pick one up you are strongly tempted to make the pass with it, reproduce it, swal-low it, juggle it, and carry on generally.

That is good exercise; but save it for your own amusement.

Don't ever forget what David Devant says about the billiard-ball trick: "To avoid over-elaboration, to know when to leave off, is a valuable asset to any artist, especially to an artist in magic . . . The manipulator finds the temptation strong upon him to linger lovingly over sleights, passes, and palms galore, whilst losing sight of the ultimate effect on the mind of his audi-ence. We do not remember ever to have seen an illusion with billiard balls in which the effect was not blurred by this sort of thing instead of being made to stand out in relief like a clearly cut cameo. On being asked afterwards what the conjurer did with a billiard ball the spectator probably replied—'Oh, all sorts of things.' "

In short, you must elaborate the billiard ball trick enough so that the precocious child with the magic set doesn't think he can copy you, yet not enough to confuse the effect.

I have kept the mechanical part almost as simple as it would be with a magic set. There are various kinds of "billiard-ball hold-ers" on sale at magic shops; some are wire clips to hold one ball, some are cloth tubes to give you three or four balls in suc-cession. I have never owned one, and I don't believe you need to, though they are handy things if you like to run your act that way.

The Conjurer's Clothes

The whole question of clothes and the magician is one that you must take sides on for yourself.

The older books about magic start with a chapter on the conjurer's dress. They usually assume that you will be wearing a tailcoat, and they go on to describe at least three sets of pockets that you can have built in (if you aren't too particular how your clothes fit). They also expect you to have an elastic around the bottom of your evening waistcoat, so that anything poked under it by a reasonably pot-bellied performer will not show much.

Even some recent manuals talk about "vesting." I am bound to say that I think it would be more surprising for a magician to produce from under his vest all the things he is told to hide there than for him to take a rabbit out of a silk hat.

I don't mean that you can't work the billiard ball trick, for instance, by vesting the ball. The one-ball clips will do, instead of an elastic to keep the ball under your vest. Or you can have one of the "Downs bag" tube holders sewn inside the lining of your coat at the side.

But personally I don't see why you need mutilate your clothes and stuff yourself out like a Christmas turkey when you can also steal the balls by putting your hand in your pocket.

Furthermore, in order to "get down" vested articles, you have to turn your back on the audience, or at the very least to turn sideways. That suggests concealment.

When you put a hand into a pocket, you can't conceal it, so there isn't the slightest need to try. Instead of making your steals unobserved, you just make them unnoticed.

I have already told you that when you put one hand in a pocket, you should, if possible, put both hands in your pockets at the same moment. That's the best way to make your steal unnoticed.

In the billiard ball trick you can't do this, because one hand is flourishing a couple of balls. Instead, you just have to make the action perfectly casual. Stick your hand into your trouser pocket as if you were too lazy to carry it on the end of your arm.

Once you put your hand in your pocket, *leave it there.* Don't bring it out until you actually need to do something.

After all my warning about billiard-ball passes and palms, I'm going to teach you two.

The Trap Pass

One is sometimes called the "trap" pass, because it works like a magician's stage or table trap.

Close your left fist and hold it out, thumb upward. Set a ball on the fist.

Bring your right hand up in front of the ball, palm toward you, and close the fingers to carry off the ball.

Just as your right hand seems to be taking it away, your left fist opens, lets it trickle down in, and palms it. (*Fig. 78*).

Follow your right hand with your eyes, and don't move your left.

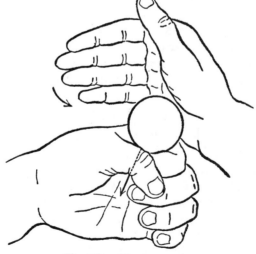

Fig. 78.   The trap pass

You can also approach the ball with your right hand from the left side, palm away from you, but I think it looks unnatural.

The Change-Over Palm

The "change-over palm" lets you show both hands empty when you really have a ball palmed. It's very easy to do, but

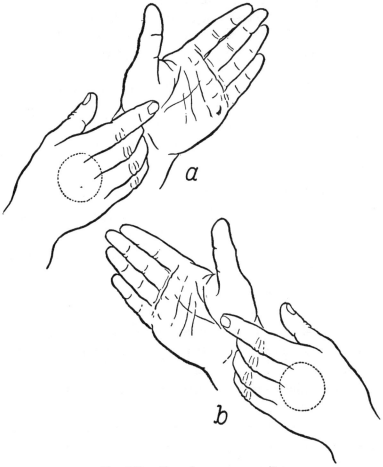

Fig. 79. The change-over palm

hard to work without giving a flash of the ball; so be careful
if you want to use it.

Say the ball is palmed in your right hand. Hold your left hand
up, palm to the audience.

Your right forefinger, pointing, should about touch the heel
of your left hand. (*Fig.* 79a).

Now you swing over to show the palm of your right hand,
pointing at it with the left forefinger.

This brings both hands for a moment palm to palm.

Roll the ball from your right palm over the heel of your
left hand and up into your left palm, where you palm it again.
(*Fig.* 79b).

One thing to watch out for, besides the angles, is the movements of your thumbs. They may too easily seem to waggle as
your hand shifts from empty to palming attitude.

Now to start the Excelsior Billiard Ball Trick.

The Multiplying Ball Routine

Put one ball, with the shell over it, in your left trouser pocket;
put the other two balls in your right trouser pocket.

When it comes time for the trick, put your hands in your
pockets. Palm one ball from your right pocket. Bring both hands
out of your pockets.

Produce the palmed ball. You can use the change-over palm,
and then make the ball rise on top of one fist by squeezing it,
or you can snatch at the air as you did with the handkerchiefs
in Lesson 12. Anyhow, produce it.

Pause. A billiard ball isn't very big for Slow Joe in the back
to notice.

Make the pass to your left hand, palming the ball in your
right, and go through the performance of swallowing, as you
did with the egg in Lesson 8.

With your right forefinger, trace the "passage" of the ball down your throat and into your left trouser pocket.

Bring out the ball with the shell over it. Hold it between your left thumb and forefinger, with the shell covering the front half (toward the back of your hand).

Look at the ball from all sides as if it puzzled you, taking occasion to let people see that you have nothing else in your hand.

Fig. 80. **Multiplying the ball**

Now the actual multiplication starts. The ordinary pose is with your left hand held out shoulder high, its back to the audience. On the stage this is fine.

For close-up work with people more or less around you, I suggest holding your hand, palm toward you, in front of your stomach.

In either case, you multiply the ball by the same motion. Bring your second finger down across your thumb, push against the ball as it sits in the shell, and swing your finger back, rolling the ball over your forefinger, and displaying ball and shell side by side. (*Fig.* 80).

The move is quite easy, but it wants a little more care when you also have (as you will in a moment) balls between your second and third, and third and fourth, fingers. Try it until you can do it neatly and rather quickly.

With your hand either outstretched or in front of your vest, then, roll the ball out of the shell.

Hold the pose. Look as surprised as you can.

Get the palmed ball in your right hand into finger-palm position. Come over with your right hand, and pick the solid ball from between left first and second fingers.

With the same motion, slide the finger-palmed ball into the shell.

Knock the two balls together. Separate your hands, holding a ball in each, and look at both.

Put the ball from your right hand between your left *second* and *third* fingers.

Stick your right hand in your trouser pocket.

Turn your attention to your left hand, as if wondering what would happen next. You should spend a certain amount of time over that.

Palm the last ball in your right hand, bring your hand out of the pocket, but hook your thumb in the opening.

Roll the next ball out of the shell.

Go through the same routine of sliding the finger-palmed ball from the right hand into the shell as you carry away the ball from between your first and second fingers. Knock all three balls together.

This time, replace the ball from your right hand between your left *third* and *little* fingers.

There is a move by which, if you like, you can show the inside of your left hand, and still not expose the back of the shell. You need your second finger free—no ball between it and your forefinger.

All you do is bring your second finger down against the edge of the shell beyond the tip of your forefinger. As you swing your left hand from side to side, bringing the palm outward, pivot the shell around with your second finger at the same speed. (*Fig.* 81).

Reverse the pivoting as you swing your hand back.

This move is particularly for the benefit of the magic-set boys, and if I used it at all I would do it only once in the routine.

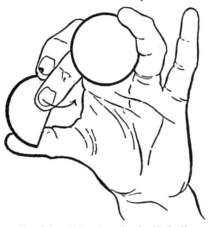

Fig. 81.   **Pivoting the half shell**

Magicians are fond of inventing moves to "disarm suspicion," and you should learn as many as you can; but remember that not arousing suspicion at all is even better than disarming it. Unless you have reason to know otherwise, you had better show the billiard ball trick as if nobody present had ever heard of such a thing as a half shell.

Roll out the last ball from the shell.

There you are, with four billiard balls in view, all five fingers occupied.

Pause to taste your triumph.

How you will finish the trick is up to you.

If you simply want to stop with the four balls—a natural and effective ending—you will need a fourth solid ball, which you can load into the shell.

Palm off the shell before you drop the four solid balls on the table or toss them to the audience to look at.

You can also make the balls disappear. This doesn't require the extra solid ball; but beware of fancy manipulations that will confuse the trick.

The one thing you daren't do is make the balls disappear by just reversing the way in which you produced them.

A good way is to "take" the ball from between first and second fingers in your right fist, actually rolling it back into the shell. Toss the "ball" away with your right hand.

Take the ball from between your left third and fourth fingers, knock it against the other two rather quickly and casually, and survey all three balls. Put the one from your right hand between your left first and second fingers, at the same time stealing the ball from the shell in the right finger palm.

Rub your left hand briskly once up and down your right thigh, and roll the nearest ball into the shell.

Stop short in surprise. Put your right hand in your trouser pocket, and bring out the palmed ball.

Give a nod—well, *that's* accounted for.

Put the ball back in your pocket.

Take the solid ball alone, from your left hand into your right. The ball in the shell is still in your left hand. Look at each ball in turn.

Turn your right side to the audience.

Toss the ball from your right hand high in the air, and catch it again at waist height, or lower.

Another toss.

As the ball goes up, your left hand drops its ball and the shell into your left trouser pocket, but stays out of sight behind your body.

Swing your right hand down for a third toss, but as you do, quickly shoot the ball across into your left hand, which instantly ducks out of sight again.

Follow the last, imaginary toss intently with your eyes.

The third ball, then, has vanished in mid-air. You have the "fourth" ball in your left hand. Make the pass to your right hand, palming the ball in your left, and toss the last ball too into nothingness.

LESSON 19. Thimble Magic

What Seems to Happen: A thimble appears on your forefinger, disappears, reappears on the other hand, changes color, and so on. Finally, you produce eight thimbles, one on each finger of each hand.

What You Need: Eight red thimbles, metal or celluloid. A blue thimble.

A "thimble-holder." You can make one from a piece of heavy cardboard about four inches by two, and a length of black elastic webbing. The idea is to have four thimbles side by side, mouth down, in such a position that you can slide four fingers in and pick up the thimbles with one motion. Sew the webbing to the ends of the cardboard, and catch it at three places between, making four flat loops for the thimbles. The cardboard should have safety pins or hooks to fasten the holder to the inside of your vest or coat. You can also buy metal thimble-holders of several styles at magic shops. These are probably more satisfactory if you find it convenient to get one.

Where to Learn More: Hoffmann, *Later Magic;* Hugard, *Modern Magic Manual; Thimble Magic*

Thimble tricks, like the sponge balls, are bright, brisk, and easy to do. They give you the satisfaction of performing real sleight-of-hand without much work; in fact, they're a lot of fun for everybody so long as the hall isn't too big.

You should work them more nearly at the speed of the sponge

balls than of the billiard balls, though you can be fairly deliberate if you like.

Silent and Talking Acts

All tricks of pure manipulation (which certainly includes
thimbles) are primarily pantomime tricks. Patter can add almost
nothing to the thimble trick; you may as well let your skilful
hands talk for you.

Nearly all the first-rate silent acts in magic are straight manipulation, like Cardini's, or else big, flashy stage shows that run
so fast they are almost acrobatics.

If you have been understanding as well as following my lessons, I believe you will find you can do pantomime tricks more
successfully than a good many of your fellow magicians. The
art of making the audience look the wrong way is called misdirection; and I have tried to teach you misdirection by eye and
gesture more than by patter.

Some magicians don't do a silent act for the excellent reason
that they are more entertaining when they talk. But a good many
performers are simply afraid to try it; they couldn't get away
with their tricks in silence.

Not that you must necessarily ever do a silent act. If you have
the skill to do one, though, you have the skill to tackle almost
any kind of magic show.

Quieting a Noisy Crowd

A silent act, or perhaps a silent part in a talking act, has another special value.

Loud, boisterous crowds can be an awful trial to a magician;
they are more interested in their own noise and their own wit
than in the show. They like to heckle and answer back.

You have your choice of outshouting these nuisances or quieting them. Strange though it seems, they are much easier to handle without words.

There is nothing for them to answer back to. Your very silence spreads to the crowd, partly because they, like you, have to concentrate their eyes on what you are doing.

Mind you, I don't say you can hold a talkative crowd with a series of fumbling, half-hearted manipulations just because you say nothing. I do say that a few striking tricks, done with smooth pantomime, will go a long way toward swinging a high-spirited crowd into the mood you want.

Now for the thimble trick.

The Thimble Thumb Palm

There is really only one sleight to learn, and there are no more than three or four, all told, that you *can* learn.

The characteristic thimble sleight is the thumb palm. You start with the thimble on your forefinger. Bend the finger in, leave the thimble caught in the fork of your thumb, and straighten the forefinger. (*Fig. 82*).

You are now a thimble manipulator.

It is sometimes useful to palm a thimble in the regular way, just as you would with a small ball; but that's nothing new to learn.

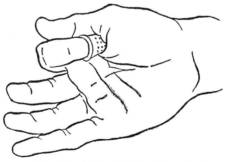

Fig. 82. **Thimble thumb palm**

You may also (as you can easily see) back-palm a thimble by holding the edges between your first and third fingers, with the second finger in front of the thimble to hide it. However, you will seldom need anything so fancy.

You can make a thimble vanish by using the pass in the old familiar fashion, with the thumb palm.

Deliberate Vanish

There is also a variation that is sometimes an improvement.

Put your right forefinger, wearing the thimble, against your left palm.

Close down your left fingers, one at a time, on the thimble, starting with your little finger.

Withdraw your right hand by a slight forward and upward motion, which will bring your right hand in front of the left for a moment.

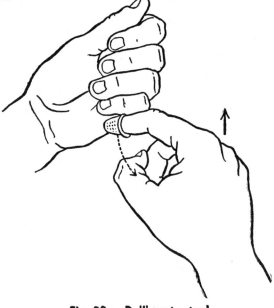

Fig. 83.   **Deliberate steal**

This means that the only way to get your forefinger out of your left fist is by bending it. That is the safe moment to thumb-palm the thimble. (*Fig.* 83).

Immediately straighten your right forefinger, and shake it at the audience as if to demand attention, or simply point at your left fist.

Make a kneading movement with your left hand, and the thimble is gone.

Thimble Routine

There are many different ways of loading for the thimble trick. Until you work out your own arrangement, try putting one red thimble and the blue thimble side by side, mouth upward, in your lower left vest pocket; another red thimble in your lower right vest pocket; and two in your right trouser pocket.

You can fasten the holder, containing the other four red thimbles, either under your vest on the left, or inside your coat near the right armhole.

Before you start the trick, dip into your left vest pocket and get the red thimble on your forefinger, the blue thimble on your second finger.

Curl your second finger, with the blue thimble, out of sight in your palm. Thumb-palm the red thimble at once, and stick your forefinger out straight.

Now you are ready to begin.

Point your forefinger sharply into the air, picking up the red thimble as you do so.

Surprise for everyone—yourself most of all.

Make the motion of putting the thimble in your right hand.

Under cover of this sweeping movement, thumb-palm the red thimble, and straighten your left *second* finger, so that actually the blue thimble goes into your right hand. (*Fig.* 84).

Stand and make a rubbing motion with your right hand.

Everyone expects the red thimble to disappear. Instead, of course, it comes out blue.

Fig. 84.   **Thimble color change**

Put the blue thimble on your right forefinger. Make the motion of popping the thimble into your mouth, but thumb-palm it as your hand travels toward your lips.

Go through the swallowing routine, and **repro**duce the blue thimble on your right forefinger tip from under your vest.

Make the motion of putting the blue thimble in your left fist. Actually, thumb-palm it.

The first red thimble was already in your left hand, so now the blue thimble is changed back to red.

Hold up the red thimble in your left hand with a look of satisfaction.

While everyone is watching that, dip into your right vest pocket, drop off the blue thimble, and pick up the red one. Thumb-palm it.

Stretch your right arm out and down, with the back of the hand toward the audience.

Rub your left hand, with thimble on forefinger, against your right sleeve at the elbow.

On about the second rub, thumb-palm the thimble.

A split second later, produce the thimble from the thumb palm in your right hand. Let just enough time elapse so that people will wonder for an instant where the thimble has gone.

Pass the thimble back and forth magically from hand to hand two or three times more, winding up with the thimble on your left forefinger.

Make a tossing motion toward your right trouser pocket, and thumb-palm the thimble.

Reach into the pocket with your right hand. Pick up the thimble from the thumb palm, and at the same time get the two thimbles in your pocket on to your third and fourth fingers.

Keep your second, third, and fourth fingers curled well into your palm, so that the new thimbles don't show.

Apparently, you have merely reproduced the one thimble from your pocket.

Make a sharp upward tossing motion with your right hand, looking way up as you thumb-palm the thimble.

When your eyes come down again, they meet your left forefinger, which suddenly produces the thimble.

While this is going on, work your right *second* finger tip into the thumb-palmed thimble.

All the hidden fingers of your right hand are now thimble-capped; only your forefinger is bare.

Take the thimble from your left forefinger and set it, quite openly, on your right forefinger.

Rub the thimble briskly against the front of your right thigh, and thumb-palm it.

Gone!

Reach with your left hand to wherever you have the holder. Get all four thimbles on the fingers, but curl in the second, third, and fourth.

The forefinger alone stands up, producing one thimble.

Go through your hand-to-hand toss once or twice.

Then don't thumb-palm the thimble that was supposed to vanish.

For a moment you look very foolish: so the trick is done with two thimbles!

Then straighten your right second finger. Three thimbles!

Fig. 85.   **The tourniquet with a stack of thimbles**

Your left second finger: four thimbles!

Right third finger: five thimbles!

Left third finger: six thimbles!

Right little finger: seven thimbles!

Left little finger: eight thimbles!

You can let it go at that, which is probably the best way; or you can gather the eight thimbles into a stack with your right second finger on the top and your thumb on the bottom.

Swoop down with your left fingers as if to close over the stack; but instead, simply let the thimbles drop into your right palm, and hold them there with your second finger on the end of the stack. (*Fig.* 85).

Hold your right hand still; move your left hand away, following it with your eyes.

Toss.

Gone!

LESSON 20.   Your Magical Outfit

What You Need: As much as you like to make or buy.
Where to Learn More: Hoffmann, *Later Magic;* Downs, *The Art of Magic;* J. F. Orrin, *The Conjurer's Vade Mecum;* Fischer, *Illustrated Magic*

As you have seen throughout this book, I think an amateur just learning magic is better off if he can do without much special equipment. Before you work up a regular set act, you may be called on dozens of times to show some tricks at a party or over the lunch table.

But after a while, you may grow ambitious for bigger things. You may want to make money out of magic, or at least to give a prepared show for your friends or for some charity.

You know more than enough tricks by now to give an excellent performance, even under difficult conditions. At the same time, when you can arrange everything to suit yourself, you may as well make the conditions easy instead of difficult, and also seize your opportunity to dress up the act.

Let me jump in here with a strong warning.

The monkey who said, "Neat, but not gaudy," had never seen the equipment at a magic store. Too much of the stuff that is built for magicians to put in their acts is simply horrible—ungainly shapes, lurid colors badly combined, tinsel and rhine-stones glued on at unlikely places.

I admit there are some acts and some audiences where these monstrosities are not out of place; but I hope yours won't be among them.

If a piece of furniture or apparatus is *not* faked, it may just as well look respectable as grotesque. And if it *is* faked, it can't afford to look anything but respectable.

Take, for example, the large class of tricks, not so popular now as they once were, called productions.

In spite of all the tubes and boxes that have been invented to be shown empty before you haul out half a stage full of stuff, the oldest receptacle of all—a hat—is still perhaps the best. The other containers look as if they had been specially built with a trick to them (which, in fact, they have), and you were merely defying the audience to discover the trick.

If you challenge them thus boldly, they are all too likely to succeed.

True, some devices are ingenious enough so that they aren't likely to be detected; but think how much easier it is simply not to stir up suspicion in the first place! If every article you use seems perfectly ordinary, people won't even think of examining things; if it looks like a magician's ready-built stage property, no examination will be enough to convince them.

The Magician's Table

The one property that is (for some unaccountable reason) comparatively free from suspicion is the magician's table. You can't go quite so far as the wizards of your grandfather's day, who spent half their time on the stage behind a high, massive contraption more like a desk than a table, which often had half a dozen devices to simplify the performer's work. Besides, your shows (like mine in the last ten years) may all be impromptu efforts where any table you find is merely a place to rest things on. But if you can have your own table, it may look small and innocent and still give you a lot of help.

The conventional magic table of the present day has a tripod foot, topped by a central column and a small round or rectangular top draped with a black velvet cover and colored fringe.

It is useful to have a chair at each side of the stage, too.

You can buy a ready-made magician's table for about twenty dollars. It will look slightly fakier than what you can make for yourself.

If you have a workshop, or enjoy handling tools, why not try building your own?

The two special devices still popular among modern magicians are the "black art well" and the "servante." The black art well is the reason why the velvet table cover is always black—practically never red, green, or blue.

Any form of central leg with tripod foot that you can manage will do for your table. It is a great help to have it collapsible for packing.

The easiest solution I know of is a music stand. Most music stands have a flat top set at a fixed angle; but you can also buy stands whose top may be set with a thumbscrew to any angle you like.

Make the angle ninety degrees, and you have only to contrive a suitable top.

The Black Art Table Top

If you are going to the trouble of making a table at all, you will certainly want a black art top.

"Black art" in conjuring is not a general term but a specific one. The name comes from an act presented by a famous magician named Robert Heller, the principle of which was that dead black is invisible against dead black. If you covered a man completely in black velvet, and had him walk across a not too brightly lighted stage whose backdrop was also black velvet, the man would not be seen.

The black art table top uses this principle to hide two or three holes, with secret pockets, in its surface.

The table top is covered with black velvet or felt; the holes, three or four inches across, are also lined with black velvet. The edges are masked by a pattern of yellow tape or braid, and from five feet away nobody would suspect anything wrong with the table.

Make your table top of plywood, whatever size you find convenient. An oblong fourteen by eighteen will give you more space to set things on, and fit into a suitcase no bigger than a round or oval top.

You must plan how you will attach the top to the base. If you are going to use a music stand, as I suggested a moment ago, you can quite easily anchor the plywood top to the metal rack. If you are going to use only the base, you will have to attach to the top a threaded socket that matches a thread on the leg of the base.

Next, plan the decorative yellow pattern that is to be laid out on the velvet cover.

One good pattern is a large diamond, the points of which touch the edge of the table top on all four sides. This in turn is divided into nine smaller diamonds. (Look ahead to *Fig.* 86). You can have a circle of circles, hexagons, or in fact any regular geometric pattern that looks mildly decorative and says nothing.

Scratch out your pattern carefully with a nail on the plywood.

Pick two or three of the sections made by the pattern—such, for instance, as the rear and two side lozenges of the diamond pattern—and cut a hole in the top that exactly follows the pattern. It is best to use a compass saw, but avoid boring a large hole to start the cut, because you want to save the piece of wood you have cut out.

It is also better, as you will see in a moment, to tilt the saw slightly inward as you make the cut, leaving a beveled edge all around.

Sandpaper down all the edges, including those on the wood you have cut out. Paint the whole top dead black.

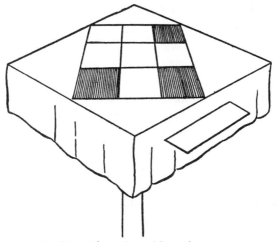

Fig. 86. Black Art table with servante

To cover the table top, you can use either felt or velvet. If you use felt, shrink it before you use it.

Take a white cloth as big as your piece of felt, and wring it out in cold water. Spread the felt on the wet cloth, roll the two up together, and let them stand for three hours or so. Then open up the package, and hang the felt up to dry. Give it plenty of time to dry, and then iron out any wrinkles that are left.

If you don't shrink the felt like this, it will eventually pull away from the edges of the black art well; it is also likelier to show spots.

Cover your table top with liquid glue. Lay on the felt (if that's what you're using), and squeeze it on hard and evenly with a roller (a piece of round stick or small pipe). Lay out your geometrical pattern again, this time on the cloth over the top, with tailor's chalk. Be sure you get the pattern in the same place as before.

Cut the material that is over the wells, starting at the center and cutting outward to the edge of the well. If the wells are diamond-shaped, simply cut two ways, from corner to corner. Fold down the loose fabric to cover the cut edge of plywood.

The wells themselves are simply pockets about four inches deep, of felt or velvet (depending on which the table cover is—there must be no difference).

The wells should be firmly anchored to the table top. One way is to turn the top bottom side up, turn the wells inside out, and tack a narrow metal or heavy cardboard strip through the cloth of the well to the edge of the board. Thus, when you poke the well right side out, the top edge is folded back and firmly held by the strip, which in turn prevents the tacks from tearing out.

Sand down the pieces of wood that you cut out of the well holes, and cover the top and edges with the same material as the rest of the table top. In that way, you can use them to plug any of the wells that you aren't going to use in a given show.

Now for the pattern on the table top. You can use yellow braid, fastened with tacks, but this makes rather a projection on the surface of the table. When you want to slide a coin or card into a well, the braid may catch.

The following method is recommended by Downs and Hilliard in *The Art of Magic*.

Use bright yellow, satin-faced ribbon three-eighths of an inch wide. Get a sheet of the thin rubber used by tailors, and called "mending tissue."

Cut the rubber into strips the width of the ribbon.

Put the ribbon face down on a table or ironing board; lay the rubber on the ribbon, and moisten it every three or four inches.

Give a quick touch with a warm flatiron to a moistened spot, and the rubber will stick to the ribbon.

Nothing but experiment will show you the right temperature for the iron. If the iron is too hot, or your touch on the rubber too slow, the rubber will melt.

Back as much ribbon as you need with rubber, in one piece; trim off any edges that stick out beyond the ribbon.

Now lay out your ribbon according to the chalk marks on the felt. Put a damp cloth over it, and press it with a flatiron hot enough to make the cloth steam.

This melts the rubber and cements the ribbon to the felt.

So much for the black art table top. Obviously, in order to hide the wells, the cover must hang down at the front and sides for six or seven inches. You can border it with gold braid or fringe, or have a deep fringe (with the velvet continued behind it) hanging from the edge of the table.

You will notice I say that the cover should hang down at the front and sides. If the table has no trick except the wells, the cover can hang down at the back, too.

But while you are building the table, you may as well have a servante in addition to the wells.

Servantes

A servante is simply a small shelf or bag (or holder of some other kind) out of sight behind a table or chair.

Most modern servantes are made of heavy wire or light strap steel, covered with black cloth. The frame can be round or oblong.

The round ones usually have an arm pivoted to a screw under the table, so that the servante can swing underneath out of the way.

The oblong ones have two arms going under the table. These should fit into screw eyes or guards of some sort, so that the servante will slide right out for packing. With this kind of servante, you can still leave the cover hanging down all around the table, and simply have two holes at the back for the arms of the servante to go through. (*Fig.* 86).

In any case, I think it is a good idea to keep the back part of the cover, and sew on snap fasteners. Then, if you have to work in the middle of a crowd, where you couldn't use a servante anyway, you can snap on the missing side, which will hide your art wells.

The other kind of servante that you are likely to find most useful is the chair servante.

These, like the table servantes, you can buy or make. They are usually help up by hooks that go over the top rail of the chair.

Throw a shawl over the back of the chair to hide the servante hooks.

You can use the table servante to get things from secretly, instead of having to carry them around in your pocket. But make sure you aren't too dependent on the servante. Being anchored behind your table much of the time looks suspicious.

You can get rid of things in servantes or wells. The chair servante is especially handy for disposing of things you are done with.

The wells, of course, are perfect for this.

Take, for instance, the color-changing silks in Lesson 13.

At the end of the trick, instead of having to steal the dye tube with your left hand behind the silks, you can simply spread the handkerchiefs across the table with your left hand (which also holds the rolled-up paper), and drop the tube down a well.

The Bottomless Glass

A useful property to go with the black art table is a bottomless glass, which you can buy from any magic shop.

The name describes it perfectly—a tumbler with the bottom cut out.

You can put an object the size of a watch, egg, or small handkerchief in the glass as it stands on your palm or the table. The object will be in plain sight, and there will be nothing to indicate any trick about the glass.

Cover the glass with a handkerchief, and you can steal the article inside by palming, or, more simply still, with the black art table. Just move the tumbler a few inches sideways, until it is over a well, and down goes the object inside.

The wells can also save you sleight-of-hand. Say you have an egg on the table.

Pick it up, closing your fist around it. Really, though, you kick the egg into the well with a push of your little finger, and just make an egg-sized fist.

Give a tossing motion toward the audience. Everyone ducks. but all for nothing.

The Mirror Glass

Another trick tumbler with various uses is the mirror glass.

This has a two-faced mirror partition down the middle. From a short distance it looks empty, even when there is something in the rear half. With the mirror glass you can do productions, vanishes, and changes.

Flying Silk

Just for instance, say you have a mirror glass with a silk in the back half, standing on a chair. On the black art table is a bottomless glass.

Roll up a small silk (to match the one in the mirror glass), and put it in the bottomless glass.

Cover each glass with a handkerchief, giving a half-turn to the mirror glass as you do. Move the bottomless glass over a well.

Hey, presto! The silk has traveled from glass to glass.

Candy Production

The mirror glass will allow you to change a tumbler full of sawdust into candies, which you can toss out to the crowd.

(Some such hand-out as this is practically obligatory at shows for children. The only trouble with the mirror glass is that you can't produce enough candy.)

With a circular wire or cardboard shape sewn inside the center of a double handkerchief, you can make the change with a full, unprepared tumbler. This gives you a bigger hand-out.

In that case, one well must be big enough to take a tumbler. A tumbler full of candy is on the table servante. The tumbler full of sawdust stands on the table.

Throw the faked handkerchief over the tumbler of sawdust, bringing your circular shape directly over the glass.

With your left hand you carry handkerchief and tumbler over the large well, and down goes the tumbler. The round shape, just the size of the glass, gives the impression that the tumbler is still there.

Your right hand, meanwhile, has stolen the glass of candy from the servante, and now comes up under the handkerchief as you lift it off the table and move forward.

Whisk away the handkerchief with your left hand, and there is the sawdust turned to candy.

Wands

You may think it funny that in teaching you magic I haven't said a word about wands.

Wands don't go with an offhand performance at a bridge game. They are really the badge of the professed magician.

If you come out carrying a wand, you are announcing that this is a magic show, planned to entertain people; they are entitled to judge you by your pretensions. You have to make good the implied promise of the man who carries a wand.

If you have read all the way through this book, and can do really well even a few of the tricks in it, then you may certainly venture to carry a wand at your pleasure. Whether you do or don't is a matter of your own choice.

For a good magician I can see no disadvantage in a wand except that you don't really need it, and it's something extra to pack.

The advantage is that you can palm things more easily in the half-closed hand that holds your wand; and when you pick up or put down the wand, you can drop the palmed article on a servante, or go through various other shenanigans.

There have been more mechanical wands invented than you or I ever dreamed of. To mention a few, there are appearing, multiplying, vanishing, floating, and rapping wands; wands to produce coins, handkerchiefs, eggs, cigars, and candy; wands that balance crazily, explode, or get too hot to hold.

If any of these amuses you, you may be able to find it at a dealer's. I shouldn't really advise you to bother with a trick wand unless it is something that will fit into a particular pet effect.

Programs

Now for one final word about giving a set show.

Arranging a program is something of an art, just like arranging a trick. You need a good opening and a good closing effect, and the tricks in between should follow one another smoothly and (at least to some extent) logically.

The first trick should be short and snappy, with a certain amount of flash. Producing a handkerchief as in Lesson 12 is a good starter, for instance. It has the advantage that you can work it in silence: there is something *happening* from the very moment you appear.

Save the best spectacular trick you have for the conclusion.

The Miser's Dream is a good one for that, oddly enough, because the end of the show helps to mark the end of the trick. You dump the coins out of the hat, bow with a pleased expression, and the evening is over.

The Chair Tie or some other escape, or the Vanishing Performer (see the next section), is good too.

Stage Management

When you have figured out a program, write it down.

Make a separate check list of loads and preparations.

Until the act has become second nature, keep a small typewritten copy of the program on your table, hidden behind something, where you can glance at it. Paste the loading list into the lid of your suitcase.

I am assuming that you know each trick perfectly, or you wouldn't put it into the act. Just the same, you must run through the whole show several times by yourself, doing each trick in full.

That is for two reasons: first, to help you memorize the act; second, to give it smoothness, and teach you the necessary stage management.

Naturally, you mustn't trip over black threads, knock things prematurely down art wells, or jar your dye tube off on to the floor.

More than that, and every bit as important, you must never have to hunt for anything. As you start each effect, you must go straight to the articles you need. They must be ready to your hand, and not buried under the débris of the last trick. If you have to step offstage to load up, you don't want to rummage through your pockets, and search table and chairs, before you remember that the billiard balls are carefully laid out in your suitcase.

In short, you must rehearse your act just as carefully as you rehearsed the separate tricks. Anything less doesn't entitle you to carry a wand and claim you're a magician.

One of the things a magician of your experience has learned by now is that anything which can go wrong does go wrong.

During the show you will deal with this however you can; but one step you should take before you leave home.

Carry with you everything you might possibly need, for show and encores. Don't count on finding anything ready for you. Maybe you can borrow a saucer for the Miser's Dream from the Ladies' Aid, and maybe you can't. If you're going to want a newspaper for the Transfixed Pack, take it along.

Scrub your hands and face thoroughly before you leave home; you may not be able to wash where you're going.

If you can find a chance beforehand to see the place where you'll be working, grab it. You may be able to keep them from seating people on the side; or you may have to change your program to suit the local situation. I once arrived for a show at a settlement house where the boxed-in stage was eight feet above the floor of the auditorium.

The vanishing elephant was about the only trick that would have been worth showing from that stage.

Part 3

How Stage Illusions Work

For you as a magician, watching other performers work is both a pleasure and an education. Naturally, you will never miss a chance to see a magic show.

Many of the acts you see are bound to be big illusion shows.

I hardly think you will have got to the point of sawing a woman in two by the time you finish this book; and I don't propose to teach you. Stage illusions are complicated and expensive to build and perform; they usually need two or three assistants. Home-made apparatus can seldom be much good on the stage—not, that is, unless you are an expert mechanic and carpenter.

Still, I think you should have some basis for judging the illusionists you see. This section is devoted to explaining (not teaching) the mechanical principles of the best-known illusions.

The Floating Lady

Some great illusions are almost as old as the smaller tricks like the Miser's Dream and the Rising Cards. As soon as magicians came in from outdoors, and began working in halls instead of at fairs, they began experimenting with the trick of making a person float in the air.

Robert-Houdin first showed the trick in 1849, and it was not new then.

As he did it, a small boy lay horizontally in mid-air, held up only by a walking stick erect under his right elbow. The secret of the trick was that the walking stick was iron, fixed firmly into the stage, and engaging at the top an iron harness that the boy wore under his clothes.

The next step, naturally, was to float a person without the walking stick.

The steel harness was still part of the trick, but the support was provided by an iron rod poked through horizontally from behind a dark backdrop. The rod connected with the harness.

The performer would pass a hoop over the floating figure to show that it was not supported. In this form of the trick, the hoop had to have a cut in it.

Then someone hit on the idea of using three iron rods from the back, instead of one. That way, you could pass a solid hoop slowly over the floating lady: assistants backstage withdrew first one end rod, then shoved that back and withdrew the middle one, then replaced that and withdrew the other end one. You could pass a solid hoop over the lady if you did it slowly enough.

Another method of supporting the lady was with sheets of plate glass reaching upward from the stage. With the right lighting, the glass was invisible. But there was great risk of a really nasty accident.

The form of the trick that you see nowadays was originally named "Asra." In this effect, the lady is "hypnotized," and covered with a white sheet.

The shrouded form rises from the table where it has been lying, and floats up and down. The performer passes a solid hoop over the figure from end to end. Howard Thurston even used to have children from the audience touch the lady as she hung suspended in air.

Then, swish!

The performer crumples up the sheet, and the lady is gone.

In the first place, as you may have guessed from what you

know of magic, the actual girl disappears at the start of the trick. The table or couch that she lies on is so built that she can sink down into it out of sight.

In her place a light wire frame gets covered with the sheet.

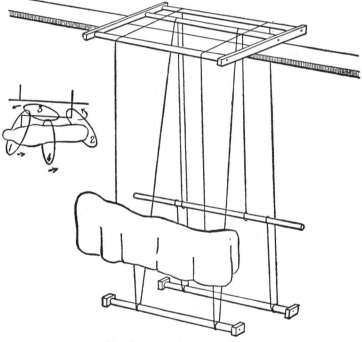

Fig. 87. The floating lady

The frame may have shoes attached that are allowed to stick out at the foot end.

The frame, in turn, is supported by an ingenious rigging of four very thin wires, two from above serving as a fulcrum, two from below bearing the leverage of the wire frame.

You can see much more clearly from a glance at *Fig.* 87 than from my description why this leverage arrangement is necessary. The wires are attached not to the frame itself but to a structure of rods projecting behind it to make a sort of gooseneck. The one rod that directly supports the frame is attached near where the girl's shoulders ought to be. It goes straight back for a few inches, then turns at right angles toward her feet, and turns at right angles toward the back again, at about the height of her ankles. Here it joins the rods that the wires actually support.

The purpose of the gooseneck is to let the magician pass a solid hoop over the floating form. He starts from the head, passing the hoop over both form and parallel rod. He brings the hoop to the foot end, pivots it around the feet, and carries it up clear behind the figure until he can pivot the other side of the hoop around the head. Then he passes it down over the form, but in front of the parallel rod, and straight off at the feet.

The final vanish is accomplished either by having the wire frame made to fold up, or by dropping it inconspicuously on the dark floor.

The Vanishing Performer

This principle of having the person actually disappear at the start of the trick, but be represented afterward by some sort of dummy, is used in a simple illusion called "The Vanishing Performer."

As a matter of fact, you may be able to build this for your own act, so I will describe it a little more carefully. You set up a black or dark colored three-fold screen, and in front of it a wooden stool a foot high.

You flourish a shawl about six and a half feet square. Then stand on the stool, holding the shawl up in front of you with both hands outstretched.

A pistol is fired, or you shout, and the shawl falls on the floor. You are gone.

There are two tricks: one to hold up the shawl, and one to let you get away.

The first is a black thread stretched across the stage from side to side at a height of seven feet three inches.

As soon as you mount the stool, you hook the corners of the shawl over the thread. You can devise your own way of holding them there.

The second is a hidden door with spring hinges in the center panel of the screen. The bottom of this door should be fifteen or eighteen inches from the floor.

Of course you have only to turn, leaving the shawl hanging by the thread, and duck through the door, closing it after you.

Then your assistant, if you have one, fires the pistol and breaks the thread, which drops the shawl in a heap.

Even if you are using this for a closing trick (and it is a good one), you will want to reappear from the back of the hall, running down the aisle to collect your last applause.

The Trunk Trick

The Trunk Trick is an old favorite.

The magician, with help from the audience, ties up his young lady assistant in a canvas bag, puts her in a large trunk, locks and ropes the trunk, and sits on it. A curtain is drawn or a sheet held up for a very few seconds, then yanked away.

The girl is sitting on the trunk, which, when untied and unlocked, reveals the performer inside the sack.

The preparation of the sack is very simple: the bottom seam is sewn up with a single thread in long stitches. The thread pulls out easily, leaving the bottom of the bag open.

The trunk has some sort of movable panel. Many different performers have devised their own ways of hiding and securing the panel.

Dr. Lynn, an English magician of the last century, arranged one end of his trunk so that a small steel ball, running in a channel, kept the panel tight shut unless the whole trunk were tilted at a certain angle. Then the ball rolled into a position that allowed the end of the trunk to fold inward.

An American method was to fake one of the panels in the top of a Saratoga trunk. A wooden strap that divided the top in half could be pushed sideways, revealing the catch.

In any case, the roping of the trunk is no obstacle to the girl's getting out, and furthermore it gives her time to escape from the sack and be ready to work the panel.

The unroping, in turn, gives the magician time to secure the panel and crawl into the sack. The audience forgets to include the time they take roping the trunk, and so the exchange of girl and performer seems to take no more than ten seconds.

The Mirror Principle

"It's all done with wires and mirrors" is a stock remark so common that it has now become funny. It is the companion wisecrack to "It's up his sleeve," and is usually just about as true.

But you have just seen that the Asra illusion *was* done with wires. And a number of other good effects are done with mirrors. The principle of all the mirror tricks (that is, of all the tricks where hidden mirrors are the explanation) is the same. Either a specially constructed box stage or—more often nowadays—a cabinet or box is used, which has interior sides and back just alike. Two mirrors are set at right angles, with their junction pointing straight to the front. Each mirror thus makes an angle of forty-five degrees with the eye of the spectator.

Consequently he thinks he can see the back of the box, when, in fact, the mirrors are reflecting the sides. (*Fig.* 88).

The oldest form of the trick used a three-legged table, with the center leg at the front, masking the front edges of the mirrors. A person could sit under the table, stick his head through a hole in the top, and thus apparently show a living, talking head

with no body. You will still see this rather crude trick sometimes in sideshows.

A better form was the old "Proteus" illusion—a cabinet three
feet six inches square and six feet high, elevated on four short
legs. Inside was a central pillar, with a lamp hanging from the
top.

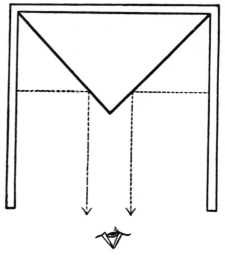

Fig. 88. The mirror principle

The cabinet was opened and shown empty. A man got in and
closed the cabinet.

In a second he was gone.

Two more men went in, one at a time, and did not come out.
The cabinet was opened and shown empty.

Finally, a fourth man went in; when the cabinet was opened
this time, there were four men inside.

The pillar, of course, concealed the front edges of the mirrors.
The mirrors swung forward like doors, so that the three men
could get behind them; the backs were painted to match the
walls of the cabinet. At the end of the trick, the mirrors were
simply folded flat against the walls, and that was that.

The two-mirror principle has sometimes been used to mask the support of the floating lady or the entrance and exit of a person through a floor trap leading into a cabinet.

Lost in the Crowd

Another familiar and effective vanishing-performer trick, which has several forms, depends not on wires, mirrors, and traps, but on the simple fact that audiences never notice anything unless it is called attention to.

The form of the trick that Houdini used was called "The Vanishing Horseman."

He rode a prancing charger on to the stage. He was dressed in a gaudy blue uniform, and was followed by a whole retinue of men in white uniforms.

Two of these men held up a huge fan in front of Houdini; in a moment they dropped it—and he was gone.

Houdini's bright blue uniform was made of paper; under it he wore a white uniform like his attendants.

The moment while they held up the fan was just long enough for him to tear off the blue uniform (and I mean tear it off), stuff it under the white uniform, jump off the horse to the rear, and mingle with the crowd of attendants. Nobody ever noticed whether there was one attendant more or less.

If you can muster enough assistants, you can devise your own way of vanishing by this method. The main thing you need is nerve; it's hard to realize that anyone can actually get away with such a barefaced trick.

Bullet-Catching

Another trick that needs nerve—but for a quite different reason—is the sensational bullet-catching effect. At least one magician, Chung Ling Soo (William E. Robinson), was killed because something went wrong with this trick.

The effect is simply that a pistol or rifle is loaded with a marked bullet, which a volunteer from the audience aims and fires at the magician.

Instead of dropping dead (unless he is unlucky, like Chung Ling Soo), the performer catches the original marked bullet either in his teeth or on a china plate held over his chest.

The method that was used in the days of muzzle-loading firearms depended on a trick ramrod, a plain wooden or metal stick. Over it at one end fitted a tube about two inches long, closed at the outer end. The tube fitted loosely in the pistol barrel, but tight on the ramrod.

The pistol was loaded with perfectly real black powder; then the magician sneaked in the tube, open end up. The marked bullet was dropped in next, and naturally went into the tube.

The ramrod, driven home, fetched out the tube with the ball inside. The magician stepped offstage on some pretext; he would get the bullet out of the tube, and either pop it in his mouth or palm it, ready to drop on the plate.

Now that Brownings and Garands have replaced the horse pistol, the magician resorts to a bolder substitution.

He hands out a number of cartridges, and has one bullet marked. This he exchanges, by palming, for a cartridge whose bullet is compressed out of graphite.

The explosion of the charge pulverizes the graphite, and the magician still produces the bullet (extracted meanwhile from the cartridge) in the time-honored way.

Alexander Herrmann made a great specialty of the bullet-catching trick, and came out of it alive; but the wear and tear on his nerves were worse than on those of the audience, who, after all, thought it was just a trick like the rising cards.

So it was, unless it happened to go sour.

De Kolta's Cocoon

"The Cocoon" was one of the many brilliant tricks that made the reputation of Buatier de Kolta.

He brought out an oblong wooden frame about two and a half feet deep, with paper pasted over one side. This he showed around; there was nothing wrong with it.

Next, he stretched a cord across the stage, tying one end to a hook, and running the other through a pulley at the opposite side of the stage. He hooked the frame to the rope, and hoisted it up by drawing gently on the pulley end.

Then he sketched a cocoon in charcoal on the paper that covered the side of the frame toward the audience. When he tore away the paper, a monstrous cocoon came to light inside the frame.

De Kolta took down the frame, leaving the cocoon hanging there until he could put a stand under it.

Thereupon, the cocoon opened, and a girl with butterfly wings popped out.

Really, the whole point of the trick was the offhand way in which de Kolta tossed around the frame, hanging it from a thin string as if it weighed nothing.

Actually, the cocoon was a steel shape, covered with canvas. It was hitched to four very thin wires that went up overhead, and were counterweighted backstage.

After showing the frame around to begin with, the magician set it on the stage, and the cocoon was promptly raised into it from a trap; naturally, the paper hid the cocoon.

When the frame was hoisted up on the cord, the counterweighted wires took care of the heavy cocoon until de Kolta was ready to produce it.

Two tricks very similar in working, but quite different in

effect, were invented respectively by Chung Ling Soo and the late Arnold de Biere: the Oyster Shell and the Costume Trunk.

The Oyster Shell

The Oyster Shell might perhaps better have been called a giant tridacna, since it was about five feet across. It rested on a low platform, and sat at an angle tilted toward the audience. The performer raised the upper shell to show the inside empty.

He closed it again, and then grandly opened it, to help out of the shell a girl whom he called the pearl in the oyster.

When the shell was first shown empty, the girl lay down under the lower half. She was hidden behind a painted gauze roller-curtain that formed the bottom of the shell.

Once the shell was closed the girl let the roller-curtain snap back, and was ready to jump up the moment the magician released her.

De Biere's Costume Trunk

De Biere's Costume Trunk Trick was more elaborate, and a good deal more ingenious.

On a low platform stood what looked like an ordinary traveling trunk. Actually, the lid came off altogether, and the sides proved to have no bottom.

De Biere lifted up first the top and then the sides, revealing a stack of three trunk trays, which he separated and showed full of costumes.

Reassembling the trunk, he invited the audience to choose a national costume (which he forced).

Then, bang! Out of the trunk sprang a girl dressed in the chosen costume; no sign of the trays.

The bottom drawer of the trunk played the largest single part in the trick. It was anchored permanently to the platform, and its bottom, which could be lifted out, rested only an inch or two from the top of the drawer.

Under it was a piece of canvas covering a hole in the platform. This sagged enough to that the girl could hide between the high bottom of the third drawer and the slack canvas.

The second drawer was a shade bigger than the bottom one, and the top one was biggest of all. Both of these also had bottoms that would lift out.

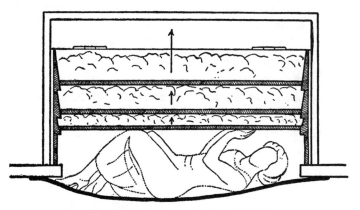

Fig. 89.   The costume-trunk trick

What happened when it came time for the girl to appear was that she stood up, pushing the loose bottoms of all three drawers up ahead of her. The costumes in the drawers went with the bottoms, and all crushed flat into the lid of the trunk. (*Fig.* 89).

The Goldfish Bowls

One trick that has gone from a famous stage effect to a simple little parlor performance, and back again, is the production of goldfish bowls.

In one form of the trick, the magician waved a shawl around, then threw it over his left arm and shoulder, holding the arm square in front of him.

When he drew off the shawl with his left hand, he was holding a glass saucer about eight inches in diameter and two inches deep, full of water, with goldfish swimming in it.

He repeated the production twice more.

The equipment began with rubber covers that fitted tight over the mouths of the bowls; the old-fashioned magician's dress suit did the rest.

One bowl was put in each of the two "loading pockets" inside the breast of the coat, right and left. The third bowl was slung under the coattails in a bag open at one side.

The shawl, draped over the magician's whole left side, made it very easy to bring out the bowls, pull off the rubber covers, and make the production.

But the bowls weren't very big, after all, and the rubber covers had a habit of slipping and giving the magician a pocket full of water. Conjurers had begun to neglect the trick when Ching Ling Foo put it back on the map.

Ching Ling Foo was a real Chinese, from whom Chung Ling Soo copied his name and act.

Ching wore a Chinese robe, on the order of a mandarin coat, and wherever he went, even offstage, he walked with a slow, pompous, straddling gait. He was a wonderful performer, and in a moment you will see one reason why.

His goldfish bowls were at least twice the size of the old-fashioned kind, and quite deep. His production was neater; he didn't muffle himself in the shawl so much.

The reason for his straddling walk was that in the show he carried the bowls slung between his knees.

Since he couldn't walk naturally in the trick, he walked unnaturally all the rest of the time.

Anyone who gives that much attention to magic is almost bound to be good.

Ching's goldfish bowl trick was not very useful to Occidental magicians. In the first place, they didn't know how he did it; and in the second place, they couldn't use his method in a dress suit anyway.

But once he had done the trick, they had to do it too, or be left behind. (Sad to say, most magicians are like sheep; they can't see anyone do a good trick without wanting to imitate it. I hope very much that you won't suffer from this disease of the profession.)

So, somebody quite ingenious devised a way of producing not a shallow bowl but a globe, as deep as it was wide, and putting it on a tiny side table. There was no rubber cover and no straddling.

You could produce as many bowls as you had side tables, because that was where the bowls were hidden. Each table was draped with a fringe just deep enough to hide the bowl; at a touch a simple mechanical arrangement dropped the fringe to the level on which the bowl stood. The shawl, of course, hid this motion.

Since it is important to keep people from thinking of the tables as part of the trick, careful performers generally carry a wet sponge where they can get at it with their right hand. As you stand in the middle of the stage, imitating the shape of the bowl with your left arm, a squeeze of the sponge makes a very convincing "spill" from the bowl that isn't there yet.

Finally, a clever mechanic has devised a method of producing a whole stack of fish bowls, rising one on top of another to a height of perhaps three and a half feet.

Under the bottom bowl is a little round board platform—just a piece of plank painted black.

Attached to this by spring catches, and sitting over the stack, is a stout black cloth tube with a ring bottom and a cross-handle over the top bowl. A central plunger in the bottom of the platform, if pushed, trips the catches and releases the cloth cover.

The stack is stood out of sight on a rest with a recess for the plunger. It is picked up behind the shawl, or some other cover, carried forward, and set down smartly on the stage.

This releases the black cover, and when the shawl is removed, there stands the stack of bowls, precariously balanced, and ready to be picked up one at a time.

The Rapping Hand

The history of the fish bowl trick is the reverse of another old stager, the rapping hand.

This is a wax or wooden hand, life size, which rests on a plank or piece of glass.

No one is near it, yet it lifts up the middle finger and taps smartly. It will answer questions by rapping once for "no" and three times for "yes." It will spell, or do anything else that can be done by taps. I never heard of one that would answer in Morse code, but if both magician and audience were radio operators, it might be a good idea.

This trick was considered pretty hot stuff in the early days of spiritualism, but was gradually abandoned because it didn't seem impressive enough to justify the build-up. At first, it was worked by electricity, with a piece of iron hidden under the velvet cuff at the wrist of the hand, and an electromagnet in the plank or table top underneath.

Turning on the current would draw the wrist down and so raise the fingers of the hand; breaking the current would drop it with a loud rap.

The first improvement was to do away with the electromagnet, and rest the hand on a sheet of plate glass.

The magician's old (not to say a trifle doddering) friend, the black thread across the stage, was responsible for this. The thread ran between the backs of two chairs at opposite sides of the stage, and up over the wrist of the hand. A pull by a hidden assistant would draw down the wrist, and when he let go the thread, the finger would rap.

This is where the trick left the stage and moved into the parlor. You can now buy a rapping hand that you lay on a board not very much bigger than a writing tablet. You can stand anywhere, right in the middle of the audience, if you like, and the hand goes on rapping.

The whole trick is in the board. It has two battens across the bottom to reinforce it. One of these will move sideways a little under pressure, and when it does it pushes up a tiny black pin through the top of the board. With the hand in the right place, the pin will make it rap loudly. The pull of your fingers under the board is so slight that even if someone looked below and saw it, he might hardly notice.

The Talking Skull

A first cousin to the rapping hand is the talking skull, which moves its jaws instead of rapping.

The skull is made of papier mâché, and is therefore very light. Usually, the thread across the stage makes it talk, but the most recent development is to show the trick, like the rapping hand, on a small board that you carry around.

A pin in the back edge of the board takes the place of the movable batten.

The Merry Widow

A simple production illusion, and all the better for it, was Carl Hertz's "The Merry Widow."

A small platform stood on the stage, with a pole rising from the center to support a kind of domed sunshade or canopy.

Curtains were hung around from the sunshade, forming what the English call a bathing tent.

In a moment, a tall girl came out, wearing a huge "Merry Widow" hat (whence the name of the trick), and carrying a long staff.

The platform was so built that people could not see underneath. The moment the curtains were hung, the girl came up through a trap from behind.

The really ingenious part of the trick was that the hat was hidden in the tent canopy. The girl's staff was the tent pole.

There are two classes of performance that more or less blend into each other, and are known collectively to magicians as "cabinet work." They mean, not rosewood inlays or dovetailed drawers, but the kind of tricks done inside a cabinet, in the dark.

The modern cabinet is not a cabinet, either, but a framework of pipe on casters, with canvas top and sides, and a draw-curtain in front.

The Spirit Cabinet

So-called "spirit effects" are generally done in a cabinet. There may be members of the audience sitting inside with the performer, or he may simply be tied up tight and left alone.

Slates are written on, bells are rung, tambourines jangled and tossed out through the curtain; ghostly shapes or lights appear. Since the magician is usually offering to duplicate "spiritualistic" performances by trickery, he won't bother with such inferior and obvious performances as hollow voices saying they are happy beyond the grave.

The other kind of cabinet work is escapes. Houdini and his wife always did their trunk trick in a cabinet, and he used the cabinet in general for any escapes where he did not want people to see him do it.

The relationship between spirit tricks and escapes is even closer than the fact that both use a cabinet. Spirit tricks in general break down into a mere escape, with some extra provision for the performer to tie himself up again.

The Kellar Tie, for instance, is excellent for spirit work. That is, it will make a beginning. In a cabinet act, the magician will usually have himself lashed or manacled hand and foot, or perhaps tied to a wooden post in the cabinet.

The devices that will free you entirely or leave you with an extra hand at liberty to make the "manifestations" are innumerable—from the dodge of stepping back out of a circle of sitters, giving your neighbors each other's hands to hold when they think they are holding yours, on up through fake handcuffs, posts, pillories, all the way to manipulation with your bare toes.

There are a lot of books of spirit effects, which you can look into if they appeal to you. Personally, I have always thought it was a poor sort of magic that had to be done in the dark, when you might as well be showing off your wonders in the glare of the footlights.

Escapes you already know something of. Both the chair tie and the sack escape would go nicely in a cabinet.

The Milk Can Trick

Of the more sensational stage escapes, depending on faked apparatus, I will just mention the milk can, which Houdini made famous.

The can looks like any ordinary creamery can, with a mushroom top, a comparatively small mouth, and a bulge below. The usual can, however, is cylindrical; the escape milk can is slightly conical, tapering inward toward the bottom.

The top can be fastened with hasps and padlocks.

The audience (or rather their "committee") are asked to examine the can. In the time they have available, they won't find anything wrong.

The can is filled with bucket after bucket of water. (Houdini claimed that he once nearly drowned from the fumes when he did the trick for some brewers with beer instead of water.)

The performer gets in, the lid is locked on, and the curtain of the cabinet is drawn.

I hardly need to say that in a matter of seconds the performer is out of the can, which remains locked and full of water.

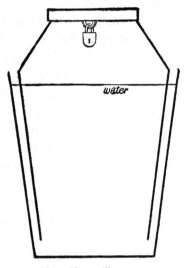

Fig. 90.   **The milk-can escape**

Essentially, the secret of the can is that it is two cans, one inside the other. The can with the neck, lid, hasps, and padlocks is bottomless. Outside it goes a can that reaches only to the shoulder, where the neck of the can starts to slope inward. (*Fig.* 90).

There are spring catches of some kind to hold the two together.

Once the magician is inside, he trips the catches, and pushes the inner can straight up over his head. The water stays in the outer can while the magician climbs out and slams the inner can down in place again to engage the catches.

The milk can escape verges on the popular class of sensational tricks that may be lumped together under the name of "blood-thirsty."

The first, simplest, and in some ways the best of all these, was the original Indian basket trick.

The Basket Trick

The magician showed a large round basket with a small mouth. His young assistant would get in, sometimes first being tied up in a net. It was quite evident that the boy filled the whole basket.

The magician threw a cloth over the basket, and then rushed at it with a long sword, which he plunged through and through it.

There were loud yells, and the sword came out dripping blood.

After some chanting and carrying on, the magician would jump right into the basket with both feet, and sit down inside. No sign of a corpse anywhere.

Eventually, the cloth (which was left over the basket all this time) would slowly rise, and the boy would come out safe and sound.

In this form, the effect was an example of pure showmanship, with almost no trick at all. By intentional clumsiness the boy could seem to fill the basket very full, but actually there was room for him to curl around in the bulging outer edge, facing outward so that his knees would not be in the way.

The magician then enjoyed a fairly wide choice of where to thrust the sword without hitting anything. The boy had a sponge dipped in red ink, which he dabbed on the blade as it went past.

With the boy curled in that position, there was plenty of room for the magician to sit down in the basket. The fear and excitement that he could work up were the only real mysteries of the trick.

If you don't mind yelling, jumping around, and carrying on outlandishly, you can get away with the Indian basket trick in its genuine form. But it is hardly the thing for a city slicker in evening clothes. Accordingly, a European seventy-five or eighty years ago devised a stage method.

He had an oblong basket about two feet square and five or six feet long, which he set on the usual low platform on the stage.

He made a girl lie down in the basket, closed the lid, and stuck the sword through from the front in various places.

Screams. Blood.

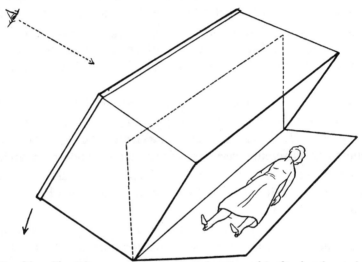

Fig. 91.   The "Japanese box" principle as used in Stodare's version of the Indian Basket Trick

Then he tilted the basket over toward the audience, raised the lid, and showed there was no one inside.

A moment later the girl reappeared from elsewhere in the theater.

The stabbing, as in the original basket trick, was a matter of care on the magician's part. The disappearance was mechanical.

The basket had two bottoms, permanently fixed at right angles to each other, and pivoted at the corner to the rest of the basket. The normal position was with one bottom upright along the front side of the basket, and the other bottom in its natural place —at the bottom.

But if the girl got into the basket while it was thus arranged, and the basket was tilted over forward, the two bottoms would stay still, so that the one formerly at the front now made the bottom of the basket that the spectators saw, while the girl lay behind on the other. (*Fig.* 91).

The Sword Cabinet

The next step in bloodthirstiness was the "sword cabinet." This you still see occasionally in sideshows, or even (in an improved form) on the stage. It is simply a small wooden cabinet, just large enough to contain a girl, and with a large assortment of slots cut in the top, bottom, and sides.

After the girl gets in, swords are poked through the slots from many different directions, and left there. It doesn't seem as if a cat could wriggle safely among the maze of blades.

When the swords are pulled out, the girl is alive and as frisky as ever.

The sword cabinet can be worked in various ways. In one, the cabinet has a false bottom and back, and the real bottom is made of heavy sheet rubber. The false back has a pair of spring doors.

While the magician is sharpening up his swords, the girl backs through the spring doors. She sticks her legs forward under the false bottom; the rubber bottom underneath sags enough to give her room.

The swords are so arranged that one goes from top to bottom, passing between her knees, two from front to back, passing just over her head as she sits in her lowered compartment, and two from side to side, passing nowhere near her at all.

Sawing a Woman in Two

Finally, we have perhaps the most famous of all stage illusions: Sawing a Woman in Two.

You must have seen it or heard of it, so I needn't describe it at much length. In substance, the girl is put into a long, horizontal wooden box. Usually, her head, hands, and feet stick out through holes in the ends. The lid is put on the box.

Then the magician saws the box in two across the middle with a two-man cross-cut saw or even a buzz-saw.

After appropriate ceremonies, the box is shoved together again, opened, and the girl emerges unharmed.

There are almost as many methods as there are performers. Obviously, however, you have to use two girls—not one to saw up and one to restore, but one for the head and one for the feet.

How you hide them is a matter of choice. One way is to have a false bottom in the box, rendered less conspicuous by a rather deep platform stand that the box rests on. One girl is hidden under this false bottom.

The girl who openly gets into the box puts her head and hands through the holes, and draws her knees up to her chest. The girl who was hidden sticks her feet up through a trap in the false bottom, pokes them out of the holes at the end, and then contrives to sit up and lean forward, with her head between her knees. (*Fig. 92*).

Zinc sheets are slid down to seal off the open ends of the two halves as the box is sawn through.

Thurston used to have the girl whose face stuck out roll her head from side to side with each stroke of the saw. It looked unpleasantly real.

When the sawing is finished, and everyone has had a chance to be properly horrified, the two halves of the box are shoved together again, made fast, and the box is opened—but not until the girl whose feet stuck out has been able to wriggle back into her first position under the false bottom.

I'd rather be a magician than his assistant, any day.

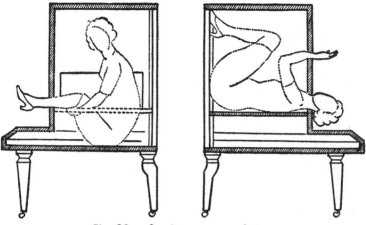

Fig. 92.   **Sawing a woman in two**

Index

Names of tricks are capitalized. Tricks are listed both individually and under the categories of ball tricks, card tricks, coin tricks, escapes, illusions, mental effects, and silk tricks.

A CATALOG OF SELECTED
DOVER BOOKS
IN ALL FIELDS OF INTEREST

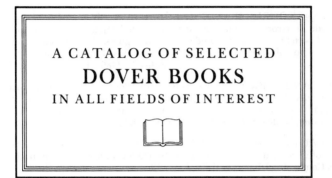

DOVER BOOKS

IN ALL FIELDS OF INTEREST

DRAWINGS OF REMBRANDT, edited by Seymour Slive. Updated Lippmann, Hofstede de Groot edition, with definitive scholarly apparatus. All portraits, biblical sketches, landscapes, nudes. Oriental figures, classical studies, together with selection of work by followers. 550 illustrations. Total of 630pp. 9⅛ × 12¼.
21485-0, 21486-9 Pa., Two-vol. set $29.90

GHOST AND HORROR STORIES OF AMBROSE BIERCE, Ambrose Bierce. 24 tales vividly imagined, strangely prophetic, and decades ahead of their time in technical skill: "The Damned Thing," "An Inhabitant of Carcosa," "The Eyes of the Panther," "Moxon's Master," and 20 more. 199pp. 5⅜ × 8½. 20767-6 Pa. $4.95

ETHICAL WRITINGS OF MAIMONIDES, Maimonides. Most significant ethical works of great medieval sage, newly translated for utmost precision, readability. Laws Concerning Character Traits, Eight Chapters, more. 192pp. 5⅜ × 8½.
24522-5 Pa. $4.50

THE EXPLORATION OF THE COLORADO RIVER AND ITS CANYONS, J. W. Powell. Full text of Powell's 1,000-mile expedition down the fabled Colorado in 1869. Superb account of terrain, geology, vegetation, Indians, famine, mutiny, treacherous rapids, mighty canyons, during exploration of last unknown part of continental U.S. 400pp. 5⅜ × 8½. 20094-9 Pa. $7.95

HISTORY OF PHILOSOPHY, Julián Marías. Clearest one-volume history on the market. Every major philosopher and dozens of others, to Existentialism and later. 505pp. 5⅜ × 8½. 21739-6 Pa. $9.95

ALL ABOUT LIGHTNING, Martin A. Uman. Highly readable nontechnical survey of nature and causes of lightning, thunderstorms, ball lightning, St. Elmo's Fire, much more. Illustrated. 192pp. 5⅜ × 8½. 25237-X Pa. $5.95

SAILING ALONE AROUND THE WORLD, Captain Joshua Slocum. First man to sail around the world, alone, in small boat. One of great feats of seamanship told in delightful manner. 67 illustrations. 294pp. 5⅜ × 8½. 20326-3 Pa. $4.95

LETTERS AND NOTES ON THE MANNERS, CUSTOMS AND CONDITIONS OF THE NORTH AMERICAN INDIANS, George Catlin. Classic account of life among Plains Indians: ceremonies, hunt, warfare, etc. 312 plates. 572pp. of text. 6⅛ × 9¼. 22118-0, 22119-9, Pa., Two-vol. set $17.90

ALASKA: The Harriman Expedition, 1899, John Burroughs, John Muir, et al. Informative, engrossing accounts of two-month, 9,000-mile expedition. Native peoples, wildlife, forests, geography, salmon industry, glaciers, more. Profusely illustrated. 240 black-and-white line drawings. 124 black-and-white photographs. 3 maps. Index. 576pp. 5⅜ × 8½. 25109-8 Pa. $11.95

THE BOOK OF BEASTS: Being a Translation from a Latin Bestiary of the Twelfth Century, T. H. White. Wonderful catalog of real and fanciful beasts: manticore, griffin, phoenix, amphivius, jaculus, many more. White's witty erudite commentary on scientific, historical aspects enhances fascinating glimpse of medieval mind. Illustrated. 296pp. 5⅜ × 8¼. (Available in U.S. only)   24609-4 Pa. $6.95

FRANK LLOYD WRIGHT: Architecture and Nature with 160 Illustrations, Donald Hoffmann. Profusely illustrated study of influence of nature—especially prairie—on Wright's designs for Fallingwater, Robie House, Guggenheim Museum, other masterpieces. 96pp. 9¼ × 10¾.   25098-9 Pa. $8.95

FRANK LLOYD WRIGHT'S FALLINGWATER, Donald Hoffmann. Wright's famous waterfall house: planning and construction of organic idea. History of site, owners, Wright's personal involvement. Photographs of various stages of building. Preface by Edgar Kaufmann, Jr. 100 illustrations. 112pp. 9¼ × 10.
23671-4 Pa. $8.95

YEARS WITH FRANK LLOYD WRIGHT: Apprentice to Genius, Edgar Tafel. Insightful memoir by a former apprentice presents a revealing portrait of Wright the man, the inspired teacher, the greatest American architect. 372 black-and-white illustrations. Preface. Index. vi + 228pp. 8¼ × 11.   24801-1 Pa. $10.95

THE STORY OF KING ARTHUR AND HIS KNIGHTS, Howard Pyle. Enchanting version of King Arthur fable has delighted generations with imaginative narratives of exciting adventures and unforgettable illustrations by the author. 41 illustrations. xviii + 313pp. 6⅛ × 9¼.   21445-1 Pa. $6.95

THE GODS OF THE EGYPTIANS, E. A. Wallis Budge. Thorough coverage of numerous gods of ancient Egypt by foremost Egyptologist. Information on evolution of cults, rites and gods; the cult of Osiris; the Book of the Dead and its rites; the sacred animals and birds; Heaven and Hell; and more. 956pp. 6⅛ × 9¼.
22055-9, 22056-7 Pa., Two-vol. set $21.90

A THEOLOGICO-POLITICAL TREATISE, Benedict Spinoza. Also contains unfinished *Political Treatise*. Great classic on religious liberty, theory of government on common consent. R. Elwes translation. Total of 421pp. 5⅜ × 8½.
20249-6 Pa. $7.95

INCIDENTS OF TRAVEL IN CENTRAL AMERICA, CHIAPAS, AND YUCATAN, John L. Stephens. Almost single-handed discovery of Maya culture; exploration of ruined cities, monuments, temples; customs of Indians. 115 drawings. 892pp. 5⅜ × 8½.   22404-X, 22405-8 Pa., Two-vol. set $17.90

LOS CAPRICHOS, Francisco Goya. 80 plates of wild, grotesque monsters and caricatures. Prado manuscript included. 183pp. 6⅜ × 9⅜.   22384-1 Pa. $5.95

AUTOBIOGRAPHY: The Story of My Experiments with Truth, Mohandas K. Gandhi. Not hagiography, but Gandhi in his own words. Boyhood, legal studies, purification, the growth of the Satyagraha (nonviolent protest) movement. Critical, inspiring work of the man who freed India. 480pp. 5⅜ × 8½. (Available in U.S. only)
24593-4 Pa. $6.95

ILLUSTRATED DICTIONARY OF HISTORIC ARCHITECTURE, edited by Cyril M. Harris. Extraordinary compendium of clear, concise definitions for over 5,000 important architectural terms complemented by over 2,000 line drawings. Covers full spectrum of architecture from ancient ruins to 20th-century Modernism. Preface. 592pp. 7½ × 9⅝. 24444-X Pa. $15.95

THE NIGHT BEFORE CHRISTMAS, Clement C. Moore. Full text, and woodcuts from original 1848 book. Also critical, historical material. 19 illustrations. 40pp. 4⅝ × 6. 22797-9 Pa. $2.50

THE LESSON OF JAPANESE ARCHITECTURE: 165 Photographs, Jiro Harada. Memorable gallery of 165 photographs taken in the 1930s of exquisite Japanese homes of the well-to-do and historic buildings. 13 line diagrams. 192pp. 8⅜ × 11¼. 24778-3 Pa. $10.95

THE AUTOBIOGRAPHY OF CHARLES DARWIN AND SELECTED LETTERS, edited by Francis Darwin. The fascinating life of eccentric genius composed of an intimate memoir by Darwin (intended for his children); commentary by his son, Francis; hundreds of fragments from notebooks, journals, papers; and letters to and from Lyell, Hooker, Huxley, Wallace and Henslow. xi + 365pp. 5⅜ × 8. 20479-0 Pa. $6.95

WONDERS OF THE SKY: Observing Rainbows, Comets, Eclipses, the Stars and Other Phenomena, Fred Schaaf. Charming, easy-to-read poetic guide to all manner of celestial events visible to the naked eye. Mock suns, glories, Belt of Venus, more. Illustrated. 299pp. 5¼ × 8¼. 24402-4 Pa. $8.95

BURNHAM'S CELESTIAL HANDBOOK, Robert Burnham, Jr. Thorough guide to the stars beyond our solar system. Exhaustive treatment. Alphabetical by constellation: Andromeda to Cetus in Vol. 1; Chamaeleon to Orion in Vol. 2; and Pavo to Vulpecula in Vol. 3. Hundreds of illustrations. Index in Vol. 3. 2,000pp. 6⅛ × 9¼. 23567-X, 23568-8, 23673-0 Pa., Three-vol. set $41.85

STAR NAMES: Their Lore and Meaning, Richard Hinckley Allen. Fascinating history of names various cultures have given to constellations and literary and folkloristic uses that have been made of stars. Indexes to subjects. Arabic and Greek names. Biblical references. Bibliography. 563pp. 5⅜ × 8½. 21079-0 Pa. $8.95

THIRTY YEARS THAT SHOOK PHYSICS: The Story of Quantum Theory, George Gamow. Lucid, accessible introduction to influential theory of energy and matter. Careful explanations of Dirac's anti-particles, Bohr's model of the atom, much more. 12 plates. Numerous drawings. 240pp. 5⅜ × 8½. 24895-X Pa. $6.95

CHINESE DOMESTIC FURNITURE IN PHOTOGRAPHS AND MEASURED DRAWINGS, Gustav Ecke. A rare volume, now affordably priced for antique collectors, furniture buffs and art historians. Detailed review of styles ranging from early Shang to late Ming. Unabridged republication. 161 black-and-white drawings, photos. Total of 224pp. 8⅜ × 11¼. (Available in U.S. only) 25171-3 Pa. $14.95

VINCENT VAN GOGH: A Biography, Julius Meier-Graefe. Dynamic, penetrating study of artist's life, relationship with brother, Theo, painting techniques, travels, more. Readable, engrossing. 160pp. 5⅜ × 8½. (Available in U.S. only) 25253-1 Pa. $4.95

HOW TO WRITE, Gertrude Stein. Gertrude Stein claimed anyone could understand her unconventional writing—here are clues to help. Fascinating improvisations, language experiments, explanations illuminate Stein's craft and the art of writing. Total of 414pp. 4⅜ × 6⅜. 23144-5 Pa. $6.95

ADVENTURES AT SEA IN THE GREAT AGE OF SAIL: Five Firsthand Narratives, edited by Elliot Snow. Rare true accounts of exploration, whaling, shipwreck, fierce natives, trade, shipboard life, more. 33 illustrations. Introduction. 353pp. 5⅜ × 8½. 25177-2 Pa. $9.95

THE HERBAL OR GENERAL HISTORY OF PLANTS, John Gerard. Classic descriptions of about 2,850 plants—with over 2,700 illustrations—includes Latin and English names, physical descriptions, varieties, time and place of growth, more. 2,706 illustrations. xlv + 1,678pp. 8½ × 12¼. 23147-X Cloth. $75.00

DOROTHY AND THE WIZARD IN OZ, L. Frank Baum. Dorothy and the Wizard visit the center of the Earth, where people are vegetables, glass houses grow and Oz characters reappear. Classic sequel to *Wizard of Oz.* 256pp. 5⅜ × 8. 24714-7 Pa. $5.95

SONGS OF EXPERIENCE: Facsimile Reproduction with 26 Plates in Full Color, William Blake. This facsimile of Blake's original "Illuminated Book" reproduces 26 full-color plates from a rare 1826 edition. Includes "The Tyger," "London," "Holy Thursday," and other immortal poems. 26 color plates. Printed text of poems. 48pp. 5¼ × 7. 24636-1 Pa. $3.95

SONGS OF INNOCENCE, William Blake. The first and most popular of Blake's famous "Illuminated Books," in a facsimile edition reproducing all 31 brightly colored plates. Additional printed text of each poem. 64pp. 5¼ × 7. 22764-2 Pa. $3.95

PRECIOUS STONES, Max Bauer. Classic, thorough study of diamonds, rubies, emeralds, garnets, etc.: physical character, occurrence, properties, use, similar topics. 20 plates, 8 in color. 94 figures. 659pp. 6⅛ × 9¼. 21910-0, 21911-9 Pa., Two-vol. set $15.90

ENCYCLOPEDIA OF VICTORIAN NEEDLEWORK, S. F. A. Caulfeild and Blanche Saward. Full, precise descriptions of stitches, techniques for dozens of needlecrafts—most exhaustive reference of its kind. Over 800 figures. Total of 679pp. 8⅛ × 11. 22800-2, 22801-0 Pa., Two-vol. set $23.90

THE MARVELOUS LAND OF OZ, L. Frank Baum. Second Oz book, the Scarecrow and Tin Woodman are back with hero named Tip, Oz magic. 136 illustrations. 287pp. 5⅜ × 8½. 20692-0 Pa. $5.95

WILD FOWL DECOYS, Joel Barber. Basic book on the subject, by foremost authority and collector. Reveals history of decoy making and rigging, place in American culture, different kinds of decoys, how to make them, and how to use them. 140 plates. 156pp. 7⅞ × 10¾. 20011-6 Pa. $8.95

HISTORY OF LACE, Mrs. Bury Palliser. Definitive, profusely illustrated chronicle of lace from earliest times to late 19th century. Laces of Italy, Greece, England, France, Belgium, etc. Landmark of needlework scholarship. 266 illustrations. 672pp. 6⅛ × 9¼. 24742-2 Pa. $16.95

ILLUSTRATED GUIDE TO SHAKER FURNITURE, Robert Meader. All furniture and appurtenances, with much on unknown local styles. 235 photos. 146pp. 9 × 12. 22819-3 Pa. $8.95

WHALE SHIPS AND WHALING: A Pictorial Survey, George Francis Dow. Over 200 vintage engravings, drawings, photographs of barks, brigs, cutters, other vessels. Also harpoons, lances, whaling guns, many other artifacts. Comprehensive text by foremost authority. 207 black-and-white illustrations. 288pp. 6 × 9. 24808-9 Pa. $9.95

THE BERTRAMS, Anthony Trollope. Powerful portrayal of blind self-will and thwarted ambition includes one of Trollope's most heartrending love stories. 497pp. 5⅜ × 8½. 25119-5 Pa. $9.95

ADVENTURES WITH A HAND LENS, Richard Headstrom. Clearly written guide to observing and studying flowers and grasses, fish scales, moth and insect wings, egg cases, buds, feathers, seeds, leaf scars, moss, molds, ferns, common crystals, etc.—all with an ordinary, inexpensive magnifying glass. 209 exact line drawings aid in your discoveries. 220pp. 5⅜ × 8½. 23330-8 Pa. $5.95

RODIN ON ART AND ARTISTS, Auguste Rodin. Great sculptor's candid, wide-ranging comments on meaning of art; great artists; relation of sculpture to poetry, painting, music; philosophy of life, more. 76 superb black-and-white illustrations of Rodin's sculpture, drawings and prints. 119pp. 8⅜ × 11¼. 24487-3 Pa. $7.95

FIFTY CLASSIC FRENCH FILMS, 1912–1982: A Pictorial Record, Anthony Slide. Memorable stills from Grand Illusion, Beauty and the Beast, Hiroshima, Mon Amour, many more. Credits, plot synopses, reviews, etc. 160pp. 8¼ × 11. 25256-6 Pa. $11.95

THE PRINCIPLES OF PSYCHOLOGY, William James. Famous long course complete, unabridged. Stream of thought, time perception, memory, experimental methods; great work decades ahead of its time. 94 figures. 1,391pp. 5⅜ × 8½. 20381-6, 20382-4 Pa., Two-vol. set $25.90

BODIES IN A BOOKSHOP, R. T. Campbell. Challenging mystery of blackmail and murder with ingenious plot and superbly drawn characters. In the best tradition of British suspense fiction. 192pp. 5⅜ × 8½. 24720-1 Pa. $4.95

CALLAS: Portrait of a Prima Donna, George Jellinek. Renowned commentator on the musical scene chronicles incredible career and life of the most controversial, fascinating, influential operatic personality of our time. 64 black-and-white photographs. 416pp. 5⅜ × 8¼. 25047-4 Pa. $8.95

GEOMETRY, RELATIVITY AND THE FOURTH DIMENSION, Rudolph Rucker. Exposition of fourth dimension, concepts of relativity as Flatland characters continue adventures. Popular, easily followed yet accurate, profound. 141 illustrations. 133pp. 5⅜ × 8½. 23400-2 Pa. $4.95

HOUSEHOLD STORIES BY THE BROTHERS GRIMM, with pictures by Walter Crane. 53 classic stories—Rumpelstiltskin, Rapunzel, Hansel and Gretel, the Fisherman and his Wife, Snow White, Tom Thumb, Sleeping Beauty, Cinderella, and so much more—lavishly illustrated with original 19th-century drawings. 114 illustrations. x + 269pp. 5⅜ × 8½. 21080-4 Pa. $4.95

SUNDIALS, Albert Waugh. Far and away the best, most thorough coverage of ideas, mathematics concerned, types, construction, adjusting anywhere. Over 100 illustrations. 230pp. 5⅜ × 8½. 22947-5 Pa. $5.95

PICTURE HISTORY OF THE NORMANDIE: With 190 Illustrations, Frank O. Braynard. Full story of legendary French ocean liner: Art Deco interiors, design innovations, furnishings, celebrities, maiden voyage, tragic fire, much more. Extensive text. 144pp. 8⅞ × 11¾. 25257-4 Pa. $10.95

THE FIRST AMERICAN COOKBOOK: A Facsimile of "American Cookery," 1796, Amelia Simmons. Facsimile of the first American-written cookbook published in the United States contains authentic recipes for colonial favorites—pumpkin pudding, winter squash pudding, spruce beer, Indian slapjacks, and more. Introductory Essay and Glossary of colonial cooking terms. 80pp. 5⅜ × 8½. 24710-4 Pa. $3.50

101 PUZZLES IN THOUGHT AND LOGIC, C. R. Wylie, Jr. Solve murders and robberies, find out which fishermen are liars, how a blind man could possibly identify a color—purely by your own reasoning! 107pp. 5⅜ × 8½. 20367-0 Pa. $2.95

ANCIENT EGYPTIAN MYTHS AND LEGENDS, Lewis Spence. Examines animism, totemism, fetishism, creation myths, deities, alchemy, art and magic, other topics. Over 50 illustrations. 432pp. 5⅜ × 8½. 26525-0 Pa. $8.95

ANTHROPOLOGY AND MODERN LIFE, Franz Boas. Great anthropologist's classic treatise on race and culture. Introduction by Ruth Bunzel. Only inexpensive paperback edition. 255pp. 5⅜ × 8½. 25245-0 Pa. $6.95

THE TALE OF PETER RABBIT, Beatrix Potter. The inimitable Peter's terrifying adventure in Mr. McGregor's garden, with all 27 wonderful, full-color Potter illustrations. 55pp. 4¼ × 5½. (Available in U.S. only) 22827-4 Pa. $1.75

THREE PROPHETIC SCIENCE FICTION NOVELS, H. G. Wells. *When the Sleeper Wakes, A Story of the Days to Come* and *The Time Machine* (full version). 335pp. 5⅜ × 8½. (Available in U.S. only) 20605-X Pa. $8.95

APICIUS COOKERY AND DINING IN IMPERIAL ROME, edited and translated by Joseph Dommers Vehling. Oldest known cookbook in existence offers readers a clear picture of what foods Romans ate, how they prepared them, etc. 49 illustrations. 301pp. 6⅛ × 9¼. 23563-7 Pa. $7.95

SHAKESPEARE LEXICON AND QUOTATION DICTIONARY, Alexander Schmidt. Full definitions, locations, shades of meaning of every word in plays and poems. More than 50,000 exact quotations. 1,485pp. 6½ × 9¼. 22726-X, 22727-8 Pa., Two-vol. set $31.90

THE WORLD'S GREAT SPEECHES, edited by Lewis Copeland and Lawrence W. Lamm. Vast collection of 278 speeches from Greeks to 1970. Powerful and effective models; unique look at history. 842pp. 5⅜ × 8½. 20468-5 Pa. $12.95

THE BLUE FAIRY BOOK, Andrew Lang. The first, most famous collection, with many familiar tales: Little Red Riding Hood, Aladdin and the Wonderful Lamp, Puss in Boots, Sleeping Beauty, Hansel and Gretel, Rumpelstiltskin; 37 in all. 138 illustrations. 390pp. 5⅜ × 8½. 21437-0 Pa. $6.95

THE STORY OF THE CHAMPIONS OF THE ROUND TABLE, Howard Pyle. Sir Launcelot, Sir Tristram and Sir Percival in spirited adventures of love and triumph retold in Pyle's inimitable style. 50 drawings, 31 full-page. xviii + 329pp. 6½ × 9¼. 21883-X Pa. $7.95

THE MYTHS OF THE NORTH AMERICAN INDIANS, Lewis Spence. Myths and legends of the Algonquins, Iroquois, Pawnees and Sioux with comprehensive historical and ethnological commentary. 36 illustrations. 5⅜ × 8½. 25967-6 Pa. $8.95

GREAT DINOSAUR HUNTERS AND THEIR DISCOVERIES, Edwin H. Colbert. Fascinating, lavishly illustrated chronicle of dinosaur research, 1820s to 1960. Achievements of Cope, Marsh, Brown, Buckland, Mantell, Huxley, many others. 384pp. 5¼ × 8¼. 24701-5 Pa. $7.95

THE TASTEMAKERS, Russell Lynes. Informal, illustrated social history of American taste 1850s-1950s. First popularized categories Highbrow, Lowbrow, Middlebrow. 129 illustrations. New (1979) afterword. 384pp. 6 × 9. 23993-4 Pa. $8.95

DOUBLE CROSS PURPOSES, Ronald A. Knox. A treasure hunt in the Scottish Highlands, an old map, unidentified corpse, surprise discoveries keep reader guessing in this cleverly intricate tale of financial skullduggery. 2 black-and-white maps. 320pp. 5⅜ × 8½. (Available in U.S. only) 25032-6 Pa. $6.95

AUTHENTIC VICTORIAN DECORATION AND ORNAMENTATION IN FULL COLOR: 46 Plates from "Studies in Design," Christopher Dresser. Superb full-color lithographs reproduced from rare original portfolio of a major Victorian designer. 48pp. 9¼ × 12¼. 25083-0 Pa. $7.95

PRIMITIVE ART, Franz Boas. Remains the best text ever prepared on subject, thoroughly discussing Indian, African, Asian, Australian, and, especially, Northern American primitive art. Over 950 illustrations show ceramics, masks, totem poles, weapons, textiles, paintings, much more. 376pp. 5⅜ × 8. 20025-6 Pa. $7.95

SIDELIGHTS ON RELATIVITY, Albert Einstein. Unabridged republication of two lectures delivered by the great physicist in 1920-21. *Ether and Relativity* and *Geometry and Experience*. Elegant ideas in nonmathematical form, accessible to intelligent layman. vi + 56pp. 5⅜ × 8½. 24511-X Pa. $3.95

THE WIT AND HUMOR OF OSCAR WILDE, edited by Alvin Redman. More than 1,000 ripostes, paradoxes, wisecracks: Work is the curse of the drinking classes, I can resist everything except temptation, etc. 258pp. 5⅜ × 8½. 20602-5 Pa. $4.95

ADVENTURES WITH A MICROSCOPE, Richard Headstrom. 59 adventures with clothing fibers, protozoa, ferns and lichens, roots and leaves, much more. 142 illustrations. 232pp. 5⅜ × 8½. 23471-1 Pa. $3.95

CATALOG OF DOVER BOOKS

PLANTS OF THE BIBLE, Harold N. Moldenke and Alma L. Moldenke. Standard reference to all 230 plants mentioned in Scriptures. Latin name, biblical reference, uses, modern identity, much more. Unsurpassed encyclopedic resource for scholars, botanists, nature lovers, students of Bible. Bibliography. Indexes. 123 black-and-white illustrations. 384pp. 6 × 9.   25069-5 Pa. $8.95

FAMOUS AMERICAN WOMEN: A Biographical Dictionary from Colonial Times to the Present, Robert McHenry, ed. From Pocahontas to Rosa Parks, 1,035 distinguished American women documented in separate biographical entries. Accurate, up-to-date data, numerous categories, spans 400 years. Indices. 493pp. 6½ × 9¼.   24523-3 Pa. $10.95

THE FABULOUS INTERIORS OF THE GREAT OCEAN LINERS IN HISTORIC PHOTOGRAPHS, William H. Miller, Jr. Some 200 superb photographs capture exquisite interiors of world's great "floating palaces"—1890s to 1980s: *Titanic, Ile de France, Queen Elizabeth, United States, Europa,* more. Approx. 200 black-and-white photographs. Captions. Text. Introduction. 160pp. 8⅜ × 11¼.
24756-2 Pa. $9.95

THE GREAT LUXURY LINERS, 1927–1954: A Photographic Record, William H. Miller, Jr. Nostalgic tribute to heyday of ocean liners. 186 photos of *Ile de France, Normandie, Leviathan, Queen Elizabeth, United States,* many others. Interior and exterior views. Introduction. Captions. 160pp. 9 × 12.
24056-8 Pa. $10.95

A NATURAL HISTORY OF THE DUCKS, John Charles Phillips. Great landmark of ornithology offers complete detailed coverage of nearly 200 species and subspecies of ducks: gadwall, sheldrake, merganser, pintail, many more. 74 full-color plates, 102 black-and-white. Bibliography. Total of 1,920pp. 8⅜ × 11¼.
25141-1, 25142-X Cloth., Two-vol. set $100.00

THE SEAWEED HANDBOOK: An Illustrated Guide to Seaweeds from North Carolina to Canada, Thomas F. Lee. Concise reference covers 78 species. Scientific and common names, habitat, distribution, more. Finding keys for easy identification. 224pp. 5⅜ × 8½.   25215-9 Pa. $6.95

THE TEN BOOKS OF ARCHITECTURE: The 1755 Leoni Edition, Leon Battista Alberti. Rare classic helped introduce the glories of ancient architecture to the Renaissance. 68 black-and-white plates. 336pp. 8⅜ × 11¼.   25239-6 Pa. $14.95

MISS MACKENZIE, Anthony Trollope. Minor masterpieces by Victorian master unmasks many truths about life in 19th-century England. First inexpensive edition in years. 392pp. 5⅜ × 8½.   25201-9 Pa. $8.95

THE RIME OF THE ANCIENT MARINER, Gustave Doré, Samuel Taylor Coleridge. Dramatic engravings considered by many to be his greatest work. The terrifying space of the open sea, the storms and whirlpools of an unknown ocean, the ice of Antarctica, more—all rendered in a powerful, chilling manner. Full text. 38 plates. 77pp. 9¼ × 12.   22305-1 Pa. $4.95

THE EXPEDITIONS OF ZEBULON MONTGOMERY PIKE, Zebulon Montgomery Pike. Fascinating firsthand accounts (1805–6) of exploration of Mississippi River, Indian wars, capture by Spanish dragoons, much more. 1,088pp. 5⅜ × 8½.
25254-X, 25255-8 Pa., Two-vol. set $25.90

A CONCISE HISTORY OF PHOTOGRAPHY: Third Revised Edition, Helmut Gernsheim. Best one-volume history—camera obscura, photochemistry, daguerreotypes, evolution of cameras, film, more. Also artistic aspects—landscape, portraits, fine art, etc. 281 black-and-white photographs. 26 in color. 176pp. 8⅜ × 11¼.
25128-4 Pa. $14.95

THE DORÉ BIBLE ILLUSTRATIONS, Gustave Doré. 241 detailed plates from the Bible: the Creation scenes, Adam and Eve, Flood, Babylon, battle sequences, life of Jesus, etc. Each plate is accompanied by the verses from the King James version of the Bible. 241pp. 9 × 12. 23004-X Pa. $9.95

WANDERINGS IN WEST AFRICA, Richard F. Burton. Great Victorian scholar/adventurer's invaluable descriptions of African tribal rituals, fetishism, culture, art, much more. Fascinating 19th-century account. 624pp. 5⅜ × 8½. 26890-X Pa. $12.95

FLATLAND, E. A. Abbott. Intriguing and enormously popular science-fiction classic explores the complexities of trying to survive as a two-dimensional being in a three-dimensional world. Amusingly illustrated by the author. 16 illustrations. 103pp. 5⅜ × 8½. 20001-9 Pa. $2.50

THE HISTORY OF THE LEWIS AND CLARK EXPEDITION, Meriwether Lewis and William Clark, edited by Elliott Coues. Classic edition of Lewis and Clark's day-by-day journals that later became the basis for U.S. claims to Oregon and the West. Accurate and invaluable geographical, botanical, biological, meteorological and anthropological material. Total of 1,508pp. 5⅜ × 8½.
21268-8, 21269-6, 21270-X Pa., Three-vol. set $29.85

LANGUAGE, TRUTH AND LOGIC, Alfred J. Ayer. Famous, clear introduction to Vienna, Cambridge schools of Logical Positivism. Role of philosophy, elimination of metaphysics, nature of analysis, etc. 160pp. 5⅜ × 8½. (Available in U.S. and Canada only) 20010-8 Pa. $3.95

MATHEMATICS FOR THE NONMATHEMATICIAN, Morris Kline. Detailed, college-level treatment of mathematics in cultural and historical context, with numerous exercises. For liberal arts students. Preface. Recommended Reading Lists. Tables. Index. Numerous black-and-white figures. xvi + 641pp. 5⅜ × 8½.
24823-2 Pa. $11.95

HANDBOOK OF PICTORIAL SYMBOLS, Rudolph Modley. 3,250 signs and symbols, many systems in full; official or heavy commercial use. Arranged by subject. Most in Pictorial Archive series. 143pp. 8⅛ × 11. 23357-X Pa. $7.95

INCIDENTS OF TRAVEL IN YUCATAN, John L. Stephens. Classic (1843) exploration of jungles of Yucatan, looking for evidences of Maya civilization. Travel adventures, Mexican and Indian culture, etc. Total of 669pp. 5⅜ × 8½.
20926-1, 20927-X Pa., Two-vol. set $11.90

DEGAS: An Intimate Portrait, Ambroise Vollard. Charming, anecdotal memoir by famous art dealer of one of the greatest 19th-century French painters. 14 black-and-white illustrations. Introduction by Harold L. Van Doren. 96pp. 5⅜ × 8½.
25131-4 Pa. $4.95

PERSONAL NARRATIVE OF A PILGRIMAGE TO AL-MADINAH AND MECCAH, Richard F. Burton. Great travel classic by remarkably colorful personality. Burton, disguised as a Moroccan, visited sacred shrines of Islam, narrowly escaping death. 47 illustrations. 959pp. 5⅜ × 8½.
21217-3, 21218-1 Pa., Two-vol. set $19.90

PHRASE AND WORD ORIGINS, A. H. Holt. Entertaining, reliable, modern study of more than 1,200 colorful words, phrases, origins and histories. Much unexpected information. 254pp. 5⅜ × 8½.
20758-7 Pa. $5.95

THE RED THUMB MARK, R. Austin Freeman. In this first Dr. Thorndyke case, the great scientific detective draws fascinating conclusions from the nature of a single fingerprint. Exciting story, authentic science. 320pp. 5⅜ × 8½. (Available in U.S. only)
25210-8 Pa. $6.95

AN EGYPTIAN HIEROGLYPHIC DICTIONARY, E. A. Wallis Budge. Monumental work containing about 25,000 words or terms that occur in texts ranging from 3000 B.C. to 600 A.D. Each entry consists of a transliteration of the word, the word in hieroglyphs, and the meaning in English. 1,314pp. 6⅜ × 10.
23615-3, 23616-1 Pa., Two-vol. set $35.90

THE COMPLEAT STRATEGYST: Being a Primer on the Theory of Games of Strategy, J. D. Williams. Highly entertaining classic describes, with many illustrated examples, how to select best strategies in conflict situations. Prefaces. Appendices. xvi + 268pp. 5⅜ × 8½.
25101-2 Pa. $6.95

THE ROAD TO OZ, L. Frank Baum. Dorothy meets the Shaggy Man, little Button-Bright and the Rainbow's beautiful daughter in this delightful trip to the magical Land of Oz. 272pp. 5⅜ × 8.
25208-6 Pa. $5.95

POINT AND LINE TO PLANE, Wassily Kandinsky. Seminal exposition of role of point, line, other elements in nonobjective painting. Essential to understanding 20th-century art. 127 illustrations. 192pp. 6½ × 9¼.
23808-3 Pa. $5.95

LADY ANNA, Anthony Trollope. Moving chronicle of Countess Lovel's bitter struggle to win for herself and daughter Anna their rightful rank and fortune—perhaps at cost of sanity itself. 384pp. 5⅜ × 8½.
24669-8 Pa. $8.95

EGYPTIAN MAGIC, E. A. Wallis Budge. Sums up all that is known about magic in Ancient Egypt: the role of magic in controlling the gods, powerful amulets that warded off evil spirits, scarabs of immortality, use of wax images, formulas and spells, the secret name, much more. 253pp. 5⅜ × 8½.
22681-6 Pa. $4.50

THE DANCE OF SIVA, Ananda Coomaraswamy. Preeminent authority unfolds the vast metaphysic of India: the revelation of her art, conception of the universe, social organization, etc. 27 reproductions of art masterpieces. 192pp. 5⅜ × 8½.
24817-8 Pa. $6.95

CHRISTMAS CUSTOMS AND TRADITIONS, Clement A. Miles. Origin, evolution, significance of religious, secular practices. Caroling, gifts, yule logs, much more. Full, scholarly yet fascinating; non-sectarian. 400pp. 5⅜ × 8½.
23354-5 Pa. $6.95

THE HUMAN FIGURE IN MOTION, Eadweard Muybridge. More than 4,500 stopped-action photos, in action series, showing undraped men, women, children jumping, lying down, throwing, sitting, wrestling, carrying, etc. 390pp. 7⅞ × 10⅝.
20204-6 Cloth. $24.95

THE MAN WHO WAS THURSDAY, Gilbert Keith Chesterton. Witty, fast-paced novel about a club of anarchists in turn-of-the-century London. Brilliant social, religious, philosophical speculations. 128pp. 5⅜ × 8½. 25121-7 Pa. $3.95

A CÉZANNE SKETCHBOOK: Figures, Portraits, Landscapes and Still Lifes, Paul Cézanne. Great artist experiments with tonal effects, light, mass, other qualities in over 100 drawings. A revealing view of developing master painter, precursor of Cubism. 102 black-and-white illustrations. 144pp. 8¾ × 6⅜. 24790-2 Pa. $6.95

AN ENCYCLOPEDIA OF BATTLES: Accounts of Over 1,560 Battles from 1479 B.C. to the Present, David Eggenberger. Presents essential details of every major battle in recorded history, from the first battle of Megiddo in 1479 B.C. to Grenada in 1984. List of Battle Maps. New Appendix covering the years 1967–1984. Index. 99 illustrations. 544pp. 6½ × 9¼. 24913-1 Pa. $14.95

AN ETYMOLOGICAL DICTIONARY OF MODERN ENGLISH, Ernest Weekley. Richest, fullest work, by foremost British lexicographer. Detailed word histories. Inexhaustible. Total of 856pp. 6½ × 9¼.
21873-2, 21874-0 Pa., Two-vol. set $19.90

WEBSTER'S AMERICAN MILITARY BIOGRAPHIES, edited by Robert McHenry. Over 1,000 figures who shaped 3 centuries of American military history. Detailed biographies of Nathan Hale, Douglas MacArthur, Mary Hallaren, others. Chronologies of engagements, more. Introduction. Addenda. 1,033 entries in alphabetical order. xi + 548pp. 6½ × 9¼. (Available in U.S. only)
24758-9 Pa. $13.95

LIFE IN ANCIENT EGYPT, Adolf Erman. Detailed older account, with much not in more recent books: domestic life, religion, magic, medicine, commerce, and whatever else needed for complete picture. Many illustrations. 597pp. 5⅜ × 8½.
22632-8 Pa. $8.95

HISTORIC COSTUME IN PICTURES, Braun & Schneider. Over 1,450 costumed figures shown, covering a wide variety of peoples: kings, emperors, nobles, priests, servants, soldiers, scholars, townsfolk, peasants, merchants, courtiers, cavaliers, and more. 256pp. 8⅜ × 11¼. 23150-X Pa. $9.95

THE NOTEBOOKS OF LEONARDO DA VINCI, edited by J. P. Richter. Extracts from manuscripts reveal great genius; on painting, sculpture, anatomy, sciences, geography, etc. Both Italian and English. 186 ms. pages reproduced, plus 500 additional drawings, including studies for *Last Supper, Sforza* monument, etc. 860pp. 7⅞ × 10¾. (Available in U.S. only) 22572-0, 22573-9 Pa., Two-vol. set $31.90

THE ART NOUVEAU STYLE BOOK OF ALPHONSE MUCHA: All 72 Plates from "Documents Decoratifs" in Original Color, Alphonse Mucha. Rare copyright-free design portfolio by high priest of Art Nouveau. Jewelry, wallpaper, stained glass, furniture, figure studies, plant and animal motifs, etc. Only complete one-volume edition. 80pp. 9⅜ × 12¼.   24044-4 Pa. $10.95

ANIMALS: 1,419 Copyright-Free Illustrations of Mammals, Birds, Fish, Insects, Etc., edited by Jim Harter. Clear wood engravings present, in extremely lifelike poses, over 1,000 species of animals. One of the most extensive pictorial sourcebooks of its kind. Captions. Index. 284pp. 9 × 12.   23766-4 Pa. $10.95

OBELISTS FLY HIGH, C. Daly King. Masterpiece of American detective fiction, long out of print, involves murder on a 1935 transcontinental flight—"a very thrilling story"—*NY Times.* Unabridged and unaltered republication of the edition published by William Collins Sons & Co. Ltd., London, 1935. 288pp. 5⅜ × 8½. (Available in U.S. only)   25036-9 Pa. $5.95

VICTORIAN AND EDWARDIAN FASHION: A Photographic Survey, Alison Gernsheim. First fashion history completely illustrated by contemporary photographs. Full text plus 235 photos, 1840-1914, in which many celebrities appear. 240pp. 6½ × 9¼.   24205-6 Pa. $8.95

THE ART OF THE FRENCH ILLUSTRATED BOOK, 1700-1914, Gordon N. Ray. Over 630 superb book illustrations by Fragonard, Delacroix, Daumier, Doré, Grandville, Manet, Mucha, Steinlen, Toulouse-Lautrec and many others. Preface. Introduction. 633 halftones. Indices of artists, authors & titles, binders and provenances. Appendices. Bibliography. 608pp. 8⅜ × 11¼.   25086-5 Pa. $24.95

THE WONDERFUL WIZARD OF OZ, L. Frank Baum. Facsimile in full color of America's finest children's classic. 143 illustrations by W. W. Denslow. 267pp. 5⅜ × 8½.   20691-2 Pa. $7.95

FOLLOWING THE EQUATOR: A Journey Around the World, Mark Twain. Great writer's 1897 account of circumnavigating the globe by steamship. Ironic humor, keen observations, vivid and fascinating descriptions of exotic places. 197 illustrations. 720pp. 5⅜ × 8½.   26113-1 Pa. $15.95

THE FRIENDLY STARS, Martha Evans Martin & Donald Howard Menzel. Classic text marshalls the stars together in an engaging, nontechnical survey, presenting them as sources of beauty in night sky. 23 illustrations. Foreword. 2 star charts. Index. 147pp. 5⅜ × 8½.   21099-5 Pa. $3.95

FADS AND FALLACIES IN THE NAME OF SCIENCE, Martin Gardner. Fair, witty appraisal of cranks, quacks, and quackeries of science and pseudoscience: hollow earth, Velikovsky, orgone energy, Dianetics, flying saucers, Bridey Murphy, food and medical fads, etc. Revised, expanded In the Name of Science. "A very able and even-tempered presentation."—*The New Yorker.* 363pp. 5⅜ × 8.
20394-8 Pa. $6.95

ANCIENT EGYPT: Its Culture and History, J. E. Manchip White. From predynastics through Ptolemies: society, history, political structure, religion, daily life, literature, cultural heritage. 48 plates. 217pp. 5⅜ × 8½.   22548-8 Pa. $5.95

CATALOG OF DOVER BOOKS

SIR HARRY HOTSPUR OF HUMBLETHWAITE, Anthony Trollope. Incisive, unconventional psychological study of a conflict between a wealthy baronet, his idealistic daughter, and their scapegrace cousin. The 1870 novel in its first inexpensive edition in years. 250pp. 5⅜ × 8½. 24953-0 Pa. $6.95

LASERS AND HOLOGRAPHY, Winston E. Kock. Sound introduction to burgeoning field, expanded (1981) for second edition. Wave patterns, coherence, lasers, diffraction, zone plates, properties of holograms, recent advances. 84 illustrations. 160pp. 5⅜ × 8¼. (Except in United Kingdom) 24041-X Pa. $3.95

INTRODUCTION TO ARTIFICIAL INTELLIGENCE: Second, Enlarged Edition, Philip C. Jackson, Jr. Comprehensive survey of artificial intelligence—the study of how machines (computers) can be made to act intelligently. Includes introductory and advanced material. Extensive notes updating the main text. 132 black-and-white illustrations. 512pp. 5⅜ × 8½. 24864-X Pa. $10.95

HISTORY OF INDIAN AND INDONESIAN ART, Ananda K. Coomaraswamy. Over 400 illustrations illuminate classic study of Indian art from earliest Harappa finds to early 20th century. Provides philosophical, religious and social insights. 304pp. 6⅝ × 9⅝. 25005-9 Pa. $11.95

THE GOLEM, Gustav Meyrink. Most famous supernatural novel in modern European literature, set in Ghetto of Old Prague around 1890. Compelling story of mystical experiences, strange transformations, profound terror. 13 black-and-white illustrations. 224pp. 5⅜ × 8½. (Available in U.S. only) 25025-3 Pa. $6.95

PICTORIAL ENCYCLOPEDIA OF HISTORIC ARCHITECTURAL PLANS, DETAILS AND ELEMENTS: With 1,880 Line Drawings of Arches, Domes, Doorways, Facades, Gables, Windows, etc., John Theodore Haneman. Sourcebook of inspiration for architects, designers, others. Bibliography. Captions. 141pp. 9 × 12. 24605-1 Pa. $7.95

BENCHLEY LOST AND FOUND, Robert Benchley. Finest humor from early 30s, about pet peeves, child psychologists, post office and others. Mostly unavailable elsewhere. 73 illustrations by Peter Arno and others. 183pp. 5⅜ × 8½. 22410-4 Pa. $4.95

ERTÉ GRAPHICS, Erté. Collection of striking color graphics: *Seasons, Alphabet, Numerals, Aces* and *Precious Stones*. 50 plates, including 4 on covers. 48pp. 9⅜ × 12¼. 23580-7 Pa. $7.95

THE JOURNAL OF HENRY D. THOREAU, edited by Bradford Torrey, F. H. Allen. Complete reprinting of 14 volumes, 1837–61, over two million words; the sourcebooks for *Walden*, etc. Definitive. All original sketches, plus 75 photographs. 1,804pp. 8½ × 12¼. 20312-3, 20313-1 Cloth., Two-vol. set $130.00

CASTLES: Their Construction and History, Sidney Toy. Traces castle development from ancient roots. Nearly 200 photographs and drawings illustrate moats, keeps, baileys, many other features. Caernarvon, Dover Castles, Hadrian's Wall, Tower of London, dozens more. 256pp. 5⅜ × 8¼. 24898-4 Pa. $6.95

CATALOG OF DOVER BOOKS

AMERICAN CLIPPER SHIPS: 1833-1858, Octavius T. Howe & Frederick C. Matthews. Fully-illustrated, encyclopedic review of 352 clipper ships from the period of America's greatest maritime supremacy. Introduction. 109 halftones. 5 black-and-white line illustrations. Index. Total of 928pp. 5⅜ × 8½.
25115-2, 25116-0 Pa., Two-vol. set $17.90

TOWARDS A NEW ARCHITECTURE, Le Corbusier. Pioneering manifesto by great architect, near legendary founder of "International School." Technical and aesthetic theories, views on industry, economics, relation of form to function, "mass-production spirit," much more. Profusely illustrated. Unabridged translation of 13th French edition. Introduction by Frederick Etchells. 320pp. 6⅛ × 9¼. (Available in U.S. only)
25023-7 Pa. $8.95

THE BOOK OF KELLS, edited by Blanche Cirker. Inexpensive collection of 32 full-color, full-page plates from the greatest illuminated manuscript of the Middle Ages, painstakingly reproduced from rare facsimile edition. Publisher's Note. Captions. 32pp. 9⅜ × 12¼.
24345-1 Pa. $5.95

BEST SCIENCE FICTION STORIES OF H. G. WELLS, H. G. Wells. Full novel *The Invisible Man*, plus 17 short stories: "The Crystal Egg," "Aepyornis Island," "The Strange Orchid," etc. 303pp. 5⅜ × 8½. (Available in U.S. only)
21531-8 Pa. $6.95

AMERICAN SAILING SHIPS: Their Plans and History, Charles G. Davis. Photos, construction details of schooners, frigates, clippers, other sailcraft of 18th to early 20th centuries—plus entertaining discourse on design, rigging, nautical lore, much more. 137 black-and-white illustrations. 240pp. 6⅛ × 9¼.
24658-2 Pa. $6.95

ENTERTAINING MATHEMATICAL PUZZLES, Martin Gardner. Selection of author's favorite conundrums involving arithmetic, money, speed, etc., with lively commentary. Complete solutions. 112pp. 5⅜ × 8½.
25211-6 Pa. $3.50

THE WILL TO BELIEVE, HUMAN IMMORTALITY, William James. Two books bound together. Effect of irrational on logical, and arguments for human immortality. 402pp. 5⅜ × 8½.
20291-7 Pa. $8.95

THE HAUNTED MONASTERY and THE CHINESE MAZE MURDERS, Robert Van Gulik. 2 full novels by Van Gulik continue adventures of Judge Dee and his companions. An evil Taoist monastery, seemingly supernatural events; overgrown topiary maze that hides strange crimes. Set in 7th-century China. 27 illustrations. 328pp. 5⅜ × 8½.
23502-5 Pa. $6.95

CELEBRATED CASES OF JUDGE DEE (DEE GOONG AN), translated by Robert Van Gulik. Authentic 18th-century Chinese detective novel; Dee and associates solve three interlocked cases. Led to Van Gulik's own stories with same characters. Extensive introduction. 9 illustrations. 237pp. 5⅜ × 8½.
23337-5 Pa. $5.95

Prices subject to change without notice.

Available at your book dealer or write for free catalog to Dept. GI, Dover Publications, Inc., 31 East 2nd St., Mineola, N.Y. 11501. Dover publishes more than 175 books each year on science, elementary and advanced mathematics, biology, music, art, literary history, social sciences and other areas.